THE EXPLANATION OF THE CHAPTERS ON
PATIENCE, GREETINGS & ADVICE ON WOMEN

First Edition: 2015

ISBN: 978-1-910015-06-3

Printed and Distributed by:

Darussalam International Publications Ltd.
Leyton Business Centre
Unit-17, Etloe Road, Leyton, London, E10 7BT
Tel: 0044 208539 4885 Fax: 00442085394889
Website: www.darussalam.com
Email: info@darussalam.com

Cover design, editing and typesetting by:
Abū Fātimah Azhar Majothī
www.ihsaandesign.com

THE EXPLANATION OF THE CHAPTERS ON
PATIENCE, GREETINGS & ADVICE ON WOMEN

From the Classical Collection of Hadith
Riyaadh As-Saaliheen by Imam An-Nawawi

Explained by the Esteemed Shaykh,
And Reviver of the Sunnah,
Shaykh Muhammad Ibn Saalih Uthaymeen ﷺ

Translated and Summarised by
Taalib Ibn Tyson Al-Britaani

DARUSSALAM
GLOBAL LEADER IN ISLAMIC BOOKS
Riyadh • Jeddah • Al-Khobar • Sharjah • Lahore • London • Houston • New York

بسم الله الرحمن الرحيم

CONTENTS

باب الصبر

THE CHAPTER ON PATIENCE

[Chapter] Regarding Patience

Allah the Exalted says:

يَـٰٓأَيُّهَا ٱلَّذِينَ ءَامَنُوا۟ ٱصْبِرُوا۟ وَصَابِرُوا۟

"O you who believe! Endure and be more patient."
(Aali Imraan, 200)

Allah ﷻ also says:

وَلَنَبْلُوَنَّكُم بِشَىْءٍ مِّنَ ٱلْخَوْفِ وَٱلْجُوعِ وَنَقْصٍ مِّنَ ٱلْأَمْوَٰلِ وَٱلْأَنفُسِ

وَٱلثَّمَرَٰتِ ۗ وَبَشِّرِ ٱلصَّـٰبِرِينَ

"And certainly, We shall test you with something of fear, hunger, loss of wealth, lives and fruit, but give glad tidings to *As-Saabiroon* (the patient)." (Al-Baqarah, 155)

Allah also says:

إِنَّمَا يُوَفَّى ٱلصَّـٰبِرُونَ أَجْرَهُم بِغَيْرِ حِسَابٍ

"Only those who are patient shall receive their reward in full, without reckoning." (Az-Zumar, 10)

Allah again says in another Verse:

وَلَمَن صَبَرَ وَغَفَرَ إِنَّ ذَٰلِكَ لَمِنْ عَزْمِ ٱلْأُمُورِ

"And verily, whosoever shows patience and forgives, that would truly be from the things recommended by Allah."
(Ash-Shura, 43)

Allah again says:

ٱسْتَعِينُوا بِٱلصَّبْرِ وَٱلصَّلَوٰةِ ۚ إِنَّ ٱللَّهَ مَعَ ٱلصَّـٰبِرِينَ

"Seek help in patience and *As-Salaat* (the prayer). Truly, Allah is with *As-Saabiroon* (the patient)." (Al-Baqarah 153)

Allah the Exalted also says:

وَلَنَبْلُوَنَّكُمْ حَتَّىٰ نَعْلَمَ ٱلْمُجَٰهِدِينَ مِنكُمْ وَٱلصَّـٰبِرِينَ وَنَبْلُوَا۟ أَخْبَارَكُمْ

"And surely, We shall try you till We test those who strive hard (for the Cause of Allah) and *As-Saabiroon* (the patient)." (Muhammad, 31)

There are numerous verses of the Noble Quran instructing patience and extolling it.

[EXPLANATION OF CHAPTER HEADING AND SUPPORTING VERSES]

Firstly, we would like to explain the meaning of the subject: patience. Linguistically, patience means: to withhold, restrain and keep. Technically, it is to confine oneself to the following three matters:

1. To confine oneself to the obedience of Allah.
2. To keep oneself away from the impermissible matters.
3. To submit to whatever decrees (for you, be it good that happens to you or be it bad).'

Regarding the first of the three matters mentioned, then it is: being patient in obeying Allah the Exalted. It is known that at times obeying and strictly submitting to Allah the Exalted entails some hardship, and this could be due to a person being in a weak and tired state, or due to some hardships one may encounter in doing certain acts of worship such as paying *Zakaat* or performing *Hajj*. In short, whatever the act of worship is, certainty one will encounter some hardship in fulfilling it, so in this case, one will have to be patient and seek Allah's assistance and help, and for this reason Allah the Exalted says in the Quran:

يَـٰٓأَيُّهَا ٱلَّذِينَ ءَامَنُوا۟ ٱصْبِرُوا۟ وَصَابِرُوا۟ وَرَابِطُوا۟

"O you who believe! Endure and be more patient (than your enemy), and guard your territory (by stationing army units permanently at the place from where the enemy can attack you)."(Aali Imraan, 200)

So, the second of the three matters is: patience in refraining from the impermissible matters, i.e. distancing oneself from what Allah the Exalted has forbidden, as the self is always inclined towards the impermissible and forbidden matters, so one has to withhold oneself from falling into them and committing them.

And from those things that one should refrain from, is lying, cheating, devouring peoples' wealth unjustly, taking interest, fornication, drinking intoxicants and stealing and in general, whatever is considered a sin. One has to distance himself from indulging in such sins and this, without a shadow of a doubt, entails abstaining, refraining, forbearing and controlling the self and one's desires.

And the last of the three matters is: being patient in the matters Allah the Exalted destined, and this is because whatever He decrees for a person, then it is suitable for that individual and compatible. One has to be grateful and thankful to Allah for whatever He the Exalted decrees for him; it is also worth mentioning that thankfulness is an act of worship which falls under the first of the three matters we have just mentioned. Therefore, it is upon the individual not to blame; but instead, submit to his fate, and this is by acknowledging that he will be tested in his health and wealth over time by their decrease, and certainly he will be tested in his family (wife, children etc.) and in his society; whatever the case maybe, one has to know that patience is the key during such testing times and one will certainly need Allah's assistance during them.

So know, patience in what one has been forbidden from is to refrain from being impatient and worrying, and that could be by committing negative words and deeds. When tested and trailed, one falls in to any one of the four following states:

1. Impatience;
2. Patience;
3. Contentment;
4. Gratefulness.

As for the first state, then it is that one shows impatience as we said through word, statement or deed. As for being impatient in one's heart, than it is by being discontent and unhappy with that which Allah has decreed, whatever matter it may be, and this is a thing we seek refuge from! It is equal to one saying, "Allah has wronged me by decreeing such a matter!"

As for words and statements that express displeasure with Allah's decree, then it is statements of dissatisfaction and crying, and words like: "Woe to me!" and the likes as well as cursing time and Allah's refuge is sought from such statements.

And as for resentment and dissatisfaction in deeds then it is by one striking his cheeks or head or nose, or by pulling out his hair or tearing his garment and matters similar to this. Such forms of impatience destroy and prevent one from obtaining reward from such testing matters and it does not aid or prevent or lessen the matter which has been decreed, rather, one only obtains sin! So now, one has two misfortunes, a misfortune in one's faith and a misfortune in one's worldly matters which Allah the Exalted is testing them with or decreed for them.

Regarding the second of the four states, then it is patience, and that is expressed by being content and grateful, and remaining patient with whatever misfortune one encounters. There is no doubt that at times a person will dislike trails and being afflicted, but he does not let his tongue get carried away by showing dislike to what Allah has decreed for him; he does not let such trails get the better of him by way of him displaying unbecoming behaviour that only brings Allah's anger upon him, and he holds not the least disliking toward Allah in his heart whatsoever. Such a person is considered the patient one, but at the same time, he dislikes such afflictions.

As for the third state, which is being content, then it is being completely content and accepting of the misfortune with a joyful heart, and by such acceptance of Allah's decree, one is completely satisfied with the trail so much so that it is as if no trail is taking place.

As for the fourth and last state, then it is displaying gratefulness or thankfulness; i.e. he is grateful to Allah for such trails. It was the habit of the Prophet (Muhammad) ﷺ to say when he was trailed in any matter *"All praise be to Allah no matter what."* And the reason he would say this was because he was certain Allah the Exalted would reward Him for having patience with the trail he was being tested with.

It is mentioned that among some of the righteous womenfolk of the past, one was once inflicted in her hand with a wound, so she glorified Allah, so it was said to her, *"How is it that you have been inflicted in your hand and you merely glorify Allah!?"* So she replied, *"My glorifying Allah is merely due to the fact that the reward will be greater that I shall receive the more patient I am."*

So, Allah the Exalted and High encourages patience and praises those who exhibit it, such as in His statement:

يَٰٓأَيُّهَا ٱلَّذِينَ ءَامَنُواْ ٱصْبِرُواْ وَصَابِرُواْ وَرَابِطُواْ

"O you who believe! Endure and be more patient (than your enemy), and guard your territory (by stationing army units permanently at the place from where the enemy can attack you)."(Aali Imraan, 200)

Here, Allah the Exalted orders the believers and addresses them with the title 'believers' to endure in these three – rather, four matters: *endurance, patience, guarding* and *fearing none but Him* (as this verse goes on to say at the end: "Fear Allah").

This refers to patience in avoiding the forbidden, patience in fulfilling Allah commandments and in safeguarding the territory and then *Taqwa* (piety) which appears last due to its abundant good and great virtue it contains among the other virtues mentioned in this verse. So patience from the forbidden matters does not merely mean one should not commit them, but it also means not coming close to them and refraining and completely avoiding them.

It must be mentioned that patience from the forbidden matters is only when one's desires invite him to commit *Haraam*, in this case one undoubtedly deserves the title of 'the patient one', but as for the case of a person who commits something *Haraam* but was not invited to it then this is different and is not from those who refrained and was patient. The one deserving the title of 'the patient one' is the obedient one. A point of benefit regarding obedience (to Allah) is that it is one of the two following types:

1. That which is made binding upon the individual or that which one has been commanded to do.

2. That which is heavy in responsibility, such as avoiding the *Haraam,* which is certainly considered an act of obedience because, as we have said, the soul is always inclining towards sin, always!

So we see that patience in obeying Allah and sticking to His Commandments is more virtuous than patience in refraining from *Haraam*; why? Allah says: **"And be more patient."** This is an encouragement to endure and be patient, and this verse is like someone prompting you to be patient. By following it, one endures just as one who endures while engaged in fighting *Jihaad* in the cause of Allah.

Ribaat (as we have mentioned) means staying on the frontier of an Islamic country for security and defence purposes and contains great virtue as the Prophet ﷺ said in a *Hadith*:

إِسْبَاغُ الْوُضُوءِ على الْمَكَارِهِ وَكَثْرَةُ الْخُطَا إِلَى الْمَسَاجِدِ وَانْتِظَارُ الصَّلَاةِ بَعْدِ الصَّلَاةِ ، فَذَلِكُمُ الرِّبَاطُ

"Should I not direct you to something by which Allah obliterates sins and elevates (your ranks)." [The companions] said: "Yes, O Messenger of Allah!" He said, "Performing Wudu properly, even in difficulty, frequently going to the Masjid and waiting eagerly for the next Salaat (prayer) after a Salaat is over; indeed, that, is Ribaat."

Allah ﷻ mentions that those who implement these four acts, are those who are deemed successful and victorious, as He says at the end of Verse after mentioning these four things: **"So that you be successful."** And this word "successful" mentioned here has two meanings:

1. Obtaining what one strives for.
2. Being saved from what one is fearful from.

As for the second verse the author Imam An-Nawawi mentioned, is Allah's statement:

وَلَنَبْلُوَنَّكُم بِشَىْءٍ مِّنَ ٱلْخَوْفِ وَٱلْجُوعِ وَنَقْصٍ مِّنَ ٱلْأَمْوَٰلِ وَٱلْأَنفُسِ وَٱلثَّمَرَٰتِ ۗ وَبَشِّرِ ٱلصَّٰبِرِينَ

"And certainly, We shall test you with something of fear, hunger, loss of wealth, lives and fruit, but give glad tidings to *As-Saabiroon* (the patient)." (Al-Baqarah, 155)

In this verse, Allah the Exalted makes an oath and swears to test His slaves in these matters, He says: **"And certainly, We shall test you"** - this means He will put you to trail with tests, **"With something of fear"** – which means with something merely from fear and not completely, because if one is tested with something that causes complete fear then it could certainly destroy a person completely, so Allah the Exalted mentions here something from fear and not completely. Regarding the word **"Fear,"** it means, loss of security, safety, and peace, and this is greater than mere hunger, and the reason that it is mentioned before it is because one can easily find sustenance be it even if one has to eat the bark of a tree,

17

but a person in a state of fear, and we seek Allah refuge from it, is in a constant state of insecurity, be it in his house or say, the market place. Yet we have to mostly be in the state of fear of falling into sin, and certainly sin brings about grief, fear and distress, and is a means for trials and calamities befalling one during his life.

"**Hunger**": This means one will be tested with hunger, and it is divided into two categories:

1. An epidemic that Allah inflicts His servants with, and that is that one eats and does not become satisfied no matter how much ones eats, and it so happened here in Saudi Arabia some time back and it was referred to by the common folk as, 'The year of hunger.' No matter what one ate, one would not become full or satisfied and Allah's refuge is sought! A person would eat a full container of dates and would still not be satisfied and this was due to this plague that had befallen the people and again Allah's refuge is sought!

2. A drought and this is a type and form of unproductiveness and is when one's produce or cultivation does not grow or harvest that year.

"**Loss of wealth**": As for this statement of Allah, then this refers to an economic crisis! And this is due to many people involving themselves with *Riba* (interest), so Allah the Exalted inflicts financial difficulties and strains upon the people due to this.

"**Lives**": This means that death will or could become prevalent, and this could be due to infections, such that it causes complete destruction and kills of a population. And this has occurred often. It has reached me that such an infection befell the people of this area, Najd (Saudi Arabia), and this year was given the name, "The year of *Rahmah* (mercy)." If this infection entered any household it left none alive and once again Allah's refuge is sought! It would completely wipe out a whole family in a matter of days leaving none of that residence! And it was the case that in this *Masjid* of ours in Unayzah there would be as many as seven or eight people being prayed over at one time, so as we keep saying, we seek Allah's refuge!

"**And fruit.**" This does not necessarily mean hunger but a mere loss or decrease, and this could be by a removal of its blessings such as in one's crops, plants and date palms and other types of tree whatever they may be; this is a means by which Allah the Exalted tests His slave to make them return back to the path of Allah (if they were heedless of Allah). Allah the Exalted says:

$$ إِنَّمَا يُوَفَّى ٱلصَّٰبِرُونَ أَجْرَهُم بِغَيْرِ حِسَابٍ $$

"**Only those who are patient shall receive their reward in full, without reckoning.**" (Az-Zumar, 10)

And the meaning of "**only those who are patient**" is the *Saabiroon* (patient ones) who will be rewarded and fully compensated for being patient. Allah says: "**Without reckoning.**" So why does Allah say this here? The reason is because righteous deeds done for Allah's sake are at times multiplied from one hundred up to seven hundred fold and if He wants He is able to reward greater than that.

So, this is a proof that Allah the Exalted is able to grant the patient ones innumerable rewards, only known to Him. We do not say that this verse is to be explained to mean that deeds are multiplied, rather Allah is indicating that the deeds have no limits in reward.

وَلَمَن صَبَرَ وَغَفَرَ إِنَّ ذَٰلِكَ لَمِنْ عَزْمِ ٱلْأُمُورِ

"And verily, whosoever shows patience and forgives, that would truly be from the things recommended by Allah." (Ash-Shura, 43)

The meaning here is, that those who are patient with the ill treatment they encounter by others without them returning such ill treatment, then such behaviour recommended by Allah; one will face and encounter many obstacles and hardships which he will have practise nothing but patience.

And in saying this, if one encounters such obstacles or harms from others, hardships or just general difficulties that one may encounter in the way of Allah or for the sake of Allah, especially if it is met while one is in *Jihaad*, or one is harmed greatly in different ways by others while one is embarking upon an act of worship for the sake of Allah such as in *Dawah* (ordering good and forbidding), then the reward one will receive is divided into two:

1. From the harm one encountered
2. Due to having patience after being inflicted with such harm.

This verse is an encouragement to have patience upon encountering harms from the people as well as forgiving them.

But know, that forgiving peoples' harms is not always recommended, rather, Allah ﷻ has restricted it in this verse to rectification being a result of it, as Allah says:

فَمَنْ عَفَا وَأَصْلَحَ فَأَجْرُهُ عَلَى ٱللَّهِ

"But whoever forgives and makes reconciliation, his reward is due from Allah." (Ash-Shura, 40)

This verse shows that if there is no forgiveness and no rectification and peace made, one does not have to forgive nor make amends. So again we say, in this case one should not forgive that person who continuously wrongs you; in this case demand your rights as a means of mending the situation and this is your right, but on the other hand if one forgives the person who has wronged him and by this the wronging is stopped then in that case it would be better generally to forgive such an individual as Allah the Exalted says: **"But whoever forgives and makes reconciliation, his reward is due from Allah."** In this case it would be better to forgive and make reconciliation rather than taking a person's good deeds. Allah says:

ٱسْتَعِينُوا بِٱلصَّبْرِ وَٱلصَّلَوٰةِ إِنَّ ٱللَّهَ مَعَ ٱلصَّٰبِرِينَ

"Seek help in patience and *As-Salaat* (the prayer). Truly, Allah is with *As-Saabiroon* (the patient)." (Al-Baqarah 153)

Here, the Exalted commands the believers to seek His help in their affairs through patience, and that is, if a person is patient in his (or her) affairs, relying upon Allah, then He certainly makes a way out of that affair for this individual.

If you are afflicted, or in a matter that entails patience then be patient as the Prophet ﷺ said:

"Know! Help comes through patience and relief after difficulty and ease after hardship."

As for prayer, then it helps one in one's worldly affairs as is stated in the *Hadith*:

"If the Prophet (Muhammad's) ﷺ affairs became difficult he would turn to prayer."

Allah ﷻ mentions in the Quran that the prayer prevents one from sin and immorality, so if a person seeks help from Allah in his affairs, Allah makes those affairs easy for that person, and that is because prayer is the best connection the slave has between him and his Lord. This is because the slave stands before Allah asking Him for His help and aid, seeking nearness to Him through such good deeds and actions.

Allah the Exalted says: **"Truly, Allah is with *As-Saabiroon* (the patient)."** And the meaning here is: because of their patience, Allah is with them, and this is something specifically for the patient and regarding Allah's Word: **"With"**, then this word is divided into two categories:

1. Generally, and that is when Allah the Exalted is with every individual and the proof is the statement of Allah in the Quran when He says:

$$وَهُوَ مَعَكُمْ أَيْنَ مَا كُنتُمْ$$

"And He is with you wheresoever you may be." (Al-Hadeed 4)

Also the Exalted says:

مَا يَكُونُ مِن نَّجْوَىٰ ثَلَاثَةٍ إِلَّا هُوَ رَابِعُهُمْ وَلَا خَمْسَةٍ إِلَّا هُوَ

سَادِسُهُمْ وَلَآ أَدْنَىٰ مِن ذَٰلِكَ وَلَآ أَكْثَرَ إِلَّا هُوَ مَعَهُمْ أَيْنَ مَا كَانُوا

"There is no secret council of three, but He is their fourth, nor of five but He is their sixth, not of less than that or more, but He is with them wherever they may be." (Al-Mujaadilah 7)

So, the word "**with**" here is from the first category which is in a general sense, and that means that He is with all His creation, and denotes an encompassment of His creation by way of knowledge, power, hearing seeing and in authority and caretaking.

2. Specifically, and this means, assisting and support and aiding the creation, and this second category is specifically for His Messengers and their followers and not everyone as Allah the Exalted says:

إِنَّ ٱللَّهَ مَعَ ٱلَّذِينَ ٱتَّقَوا وَّٱلَّذِينَ هُم مُّحْسِنُونَ

"Truly, Allah is with those who fear Him, keep their duty unto Him and those who are *Muhsinoon* (doers of good)." (An-Nahl 128)

Also He says: "And Allah is with *As-Saabiroon* (the patient)."

So, these two categories are in no way an indication or proof that Allah ﷻ is actually with His creation or present in their locations, no, rather He the Exalted is above His creation, above His Mighty Throne. But He is with you even if you are alone as Allah ﷻ encompasses His creation by way of knowledge, power, hearing, seeing and in authority.

As for Allah's statement: **"Truly, Allah is with As-Saabiroon (the patient)."** This is proof that Allah the Exalted aids as well as assists and supports those who actualize patience, and He the Exalted protects His slave and helps him to develop this rich trait, which is patience. Why? Because this slave has a deep sense of love and awe for his Lord Allah ﷻ. The author Imam An-Nawawi then mentions this last verse and it is the statement of Allah the Exalted:

وَلَنَبْلُوَنَّكُمْ حَتَّىٰ نَعْلَمَ ٱلْمُجَٰهِدِينَ مِنكُمْ وَٱلصَّٰبِرِينَ وَنَبْلُوَا۟ أَخْبَارَكُمْ

"And surely, We shall try you till We test those who strive hard (for the Cause of Allah) and As-Saabiroon (the patient)." (Muhammad 31)

These words: **"We shall try you"** means, we will surly test you, so test means: try you. Surely Allah will test His slaves in matters like making *Jihaad* to see who will be patient and who will not, as He says in the Quran:

ذَٰلِكَ وَلَوْ يَشَآءُ ٱللَّهُ لَٱنتَصَرَ مِنْهُمْ وَلَٰكِن لِّيَبْلُوَا۟ بَعْضَكُم بِبَعْضٍ

وَٱلَّذِينَ قُتِلُوا۟ فِى سَبِيلِ ٱللَّهِ فَلَن يُضِلَّ أَعْمَٰلَهُمْ • سَيَهْدِيهِمْ وَيُصْلِحُ

بَالَهُمْ • وَيُدْخِلُهُمُ ٱلْجَنَّةَ عَرَّفَهَا لَهُمْ

"But if it had been Allah's Will, He Himself could certainly have punished them (without you). But (He lets you fight), in order to test you, some with

others. But those who are killed in the way of Allah, He will never let their deeds be lost. He will guide them and set right their state. And admit them to Paradise which He has made known to them." (Muhammad 4-6)

Allah the Exalted says: **"Till We test those who strive hard (for the Cause of Allah)."** And with great regret, some of those who are short-sighted in the *Deen*, have claimed the Allah does not know things till they actually occur! And this is definately wrong, as Allah the Exalted knows all that will occur before it happens and the proof for this is His own words when He says in the Quran:

$$\text{أَلَمْ تَعْلَمْ أَنَّ ٱللَّهَ يَعْلَمُ مَا فِى ٱلسَّمَآءِ وَٱلْأَرْضِ ۗ إِنَّ ذَٰلِكَ فِى كِتَٰبٍ}$$

$$\text{إِنَّ ذَٰلِكَ عَلَى ٱللَّهِ يَسِيرٌ}$$

"Know you not that Allah knows all that is in heaven and on earth? Verily, it is (all) in the Book (*Al Lauh al-Mahfooz*). Verily that is easy for Allah." (Al-Hajj 70)

This clear Quranic verse and its likes prove the falsity of their claims, that He ﷻ does not know things till they actually occur. Rather, the meaning of this verse: **"Till We test those who strive hard (for the Cause of Allah)"** is, to see what one's reward will be, will he reap Allah's lofty reward or incur Allah's Punishment, as Allah knows all that His slaves will do before they do an action. What we mean here is that this verse means, that the slave himself does not know the outcome of a trail till he is actully tested with it, and the matter becomes clear to him what he himself will reap from such a test whether he deserves to be rewarded due to his obedience to Allah or whether he will be punished by Him. Therefore, the Exalted's intended meaning here: **"Till We test those who strive hard (for the Cause of Allah),"** according to the *Ulama*, is that He the Exalted will manifest and make clear the matter and its outcome as He the Exalted knows all things, that is, what will occur and what will be the outcome after a thing has occured.

Regarding knowing something or infomation about a thing, we will give you an example of what we are trying to say: if someone says to you "I will do such-and-such tommorow," in this case you now have knowledge of what this individual has informed you but on the other hand if this individaul did what he had said he was going to do, now you have knowledge regarding the outcome of the action that he has now done

Then Allah the Exalted says: **"Those who strive hard (for the Cause of Allah)."** This refers to those who strive their hardest to make the Word of Allah upmost and superior, and this is in two ways:

1. *Jihaad* with weapons (in times of war)
2. *Dawah* (Striving to propagate Islam)

Both of them are considered *Mujaahidoon,* so one who strives to promote *Ilm* (knowledge) through *Dawah* to the people in order that this *Ilm* spreads among the people so that Allah's Religion is known and practised, then this is a struggle and one who promotes this *Ilm* as we said is classified a *Mujaahid.* And also the one who struggles fighting physically with a weapon (in times of war) is, as we know, considered a

Mujaahid; both intend that the Word of Allah be superior and dominate.

The Exalted says: **"And *As-Saabiroon* (the patient)."** This means the patient ones are those who have been commanded to engage in *Jihaad* and they obey His Commands. Allah also says (at the end of this previously mentioned Verse):

وَلَنَبْلُوَنَّكُمْ حَتَّىٰ نَعْلَمَ ٱلْمُجَٰهِدِينَ مِنكُمْ وَٱلصَّٰبِرِينَ وَنَبْلُوَاْ أَخْبَارَكُمْ

And surely, We shall try you till We test those who strive hard (for the Cause of Allah) and *As-Saabiroon* (the patient) and We shall test your facts (i.e. the one who is a liar, and the one who is truthful)." **(Muhammad, 31)**

Allah says: **"And We shall test your facts"** which means We will certainly try your claims till it becomes apparent what is to become, and what you will reap of good or of bad. So when Allah the Exalted revealed this following verse regarding testing His slaves:

وَبَشِّرِ ٱلصَّٰبِرِينَ

"But give glad tidings to *As-Saabiroon* (the patient)." **(Al-Baqarah, 155)**

This was addressing the Prophet (Muhammad) ﷺ to inform the people and give them glad tiding, and encourage them to have patience, meaning "O Muhammad, give those who are patient glad tidings, those who have been inflicted with tribulations and are patient with them without displeasure with Allah's decree." So remember, one should face such afflictions accepting Allah's decree and that is with complete satisfaction and submission, and what is greater than this is thankfulness to Allah the Exalted. Allah says in the verse we cited earlier towards the end: **"(They) say: Verily! To Allah we belong."** Which means, when a misfortune, calamity or adversity befalls them then they acknowledge Allah owns all His creation and all thee affairs are at His disposal, He does what He wishes, when He wishes and as He pleases. This is what the Prophet ﷺ said to one of his daughters in the following *Hadith*:

"Whatever Allah takes away or gives, belongs to Him."

So know, you are His possession and He the Exalted does as He pleases with you and your affairs, and it is upon you to submit to your fate or decree that the Blessed and Exalted decreed for you. S

The Exalted says next: **"And Verily, to Him we shall return."** This means His servants acknowledge that one day they will surly return to Allah for judgement and reward, and if they are dissatisfied with Allah's decree, Allah takes them to account for that, but as for those mentioned, then they are the ones who have patience upon any misfortune, calamity or adversity encountered, so Allah rewards greatly those who actualize patience.

Allah the Exalted says: **"They are those on whom are the *Salawaat* (i.e. who are blessed and will be forgiven) from their Lord. And (they are those who) receive His Mercy."** Those mentioned here are the patient ones, and the word: **"*Salawaat*"** is the plural of: *"Salaat"* but the meaning here is that Allah ﷻ praises these individuals in the presence of the Noble Angels in a high station.

He the Exalted then says: **"It is they who are the guided-ones."** Allah ﷻ has guided them and this is due to them enduring the misfortune they encountered without showing dissatisfaction with Allah's decree. This verse is a proof that the meaning of: **"They are those on whom are the *Salawaat* from their Lord. And (they are those who) receive His Mercy,"** does not mean, as many think, that *Rahmah* is upon them, no! Rather it is more general, conclusive and virtuous, so whosoever interprets it from the *Ulema* to mean this is mistaken, and they say that it means, Allah's Mercy is upon them and that His Angels make *Dua* (supplication) for such individuals and His creation too. But as we said, such interpretation has no basis! As the word *Salaat* that is mentioned here does not mean *Rahmah*. And one of the reasons why we say this is because this verse reads: **"They are those on whom are the *Salawaat*_from their Lord. *And* (they are those who) receive His Mercy."** So the "And" here is the "*Waw Al-Mugaayihrah* (incompatible or contrary)," i.e. it indicates that they are not the same or they are not related; so it would mean that: **"*Salawaat*"** and **"Mercy"** have two different meanings as we said. The *Ulema* are in agreement that it is permissible to say to a person "Have mercy upon so-and-so," but they differ regarding the statement of sending salutations and invoking prayer upon so-and-so. There are three opinions regarding this:

1. Completely permissible.
2. Completely impermissible.
3. Allowed but if followed by another word.

Out of the three opinions, the third is most correct and the proof is the *Hadith* where the Prophet ﷺ told his Companion to say in their prayers:

"O Allah! Send prayers on Muhammad, and on the family of Muhammad."

And it can also be said: if not followed up by another word, as we have just said but, there has to be a reason and the proof is Allah's statement:

أَلَمْ يَعْلَمُوٓاْ أَنَّ ٱللَّهَ هُوَ يَقْبَلُ ٱلتَّوْبَةَ عَنْ عِبَادِهِۦ وَيَأْخُذُ ٱلصَّدَقَٰتِ

وَأَنَّ ٱللَّهَ هُوَ ٱلتَّوَّابُ ٱلرَّحِيمُ

"Take *Sadaqah* (alms) from their wealth in order to purify them and sanctify them with it, and invoke Allah for them." (At-Tawbah 104)

In summary, this is allowed but with the condition that it is not abused or taken as a slogan; so one can say "O Allah send salutations upon so-and-so"; to clarify what I am trying to say I will give an example: if someone came to you and said, "Take my *Zakaat* and distribute it among the poor," it would be permissible for you to say to this individual "O Allah send Your salutation upon so-and-so!" as this is a *Dua* (supplication) you are making for this person, and this is the same regarding Allah commanding the Prophet Muhammad ﷺ to do.

[Hadith 25]

Abu Maalik Al-Haarith bin Aasim Al-Ash'ari ﷺ reported that the Messenger of Allah ﷺ said:

« الطُّهُورُ شَطْرُ الإِيمَانِ، وَالْحَمْدُ لِلَّه تَمْلأُ الْمِيزانَ وسُبْحَانَ الله والحَمْدُ لله تَمْلآنِ أَوْ تَمْلأُ مَا بَيْنَ السَّموَات وَالأَرْضِ وَالصَّلاةِ نورٌ، وَالصَّدَقَةُ بُرْهَانٌ، وَالصَّبْرُ ضِيَاءٌ، وَالْقُرْآنُ حُجَّةٌ لَكَ أَوْ عَلَيْكَ. كُلُّ النَّاس يَغْدُو، فَبَائِعٌ نَفْسَهُ فَمُعْتِقُها، أَوْ مُوبِقُهَا»

رواه مسلم

"Wudu is half of Emaan (Faith); the utterance of Al-Hamdu lillah (all praise belongs to Allah); fills the scales; the utterance of SubhaanAllah wal Hamdu lillah (Allah is far removed from every imperfection and all praise belong to Allah) fills, (or) fills the space between the heaven and the earth, and Salaat (prayer) is light; and charity is the proof of Faith; and patience is light, and the Quran is a plea in your favour or against you. Every person departs; he either ransoms himself or puts himself into perdition." [Reported by Muslim]

[EXPLANATION OF HADITH 25]

The meaning of: *"And patience is light."* Light here means: illumination, which is a means to help and assist one undergoing trails and tribulations, so if one has patience when he is afflicted, Allah guides him with this light. And for this reason Allah the Exalted has meantiond a number of things that help and aid the slave, from them is: light in one's heart, and this light guides a person upon the right methodogy and helps them practise what they learn, and the closer one gets to Allah by way being patientce, Allah ﷻ increases their guidance, the light in their heart and their insight.

As for the Prophet's ﷺ statement: *"Wudu is half of Emaan (Faith)"*, the meaning of *Wudu* refers to the purification one performs; and as for the next part: *"Half of Emaan (Faith)"*, the it means half of one's faith, and faith is both adornment and abandoment. What we mean by abandonment is: distancing oneself from acts of *Shirk* (polythiesm) and sin and also that one frees themself from the polytheists and sinful individauls due to their wrong doing. In short, purification means that a person purifies themself spiritually as well as pysically from harm. For for this reason the Prophet ﷺ counted it half of *Emaan*.

As for the statement of the Prophet ﷺ: *"The utterance of Al-Hamdu lillah (all praise belongs to Allah); fills the scales."* Then Ibn Ayaan said in a brief commentary about this word *Al-Hamdu lillah*: *"In respect to these words, Al-Hamdu lillah, then although they are very few words, they are very virtuous and for this reason Allah the Exalted Himself chose to start His Book the Noble Quran with them."*

So, the word *Al-Hamdu lillah* means also, to optionally glorify Allah the Exalted and i   iption of Allah by way of praise and perfection in H   Actions.

"Fills the scales": Regarding   n they are literal and weigh the actions of a perso   tions can take the form of a shape or materialize   ighted, and the scales weigh a person's scrolls o   ne's deeds are written down on and these scales are li   ned by one's bad deeds and made heavier due to righteous actions.

So these words *Al-Hamdu lillah* hold marvellous great value and virtue in what they incorporate, and that is that they fill the scales even though the scales are enormous, as sincere righteous actions are from the matters that are weighty, and these words (*Al-Hamdu lillah*) contain an affirmation of Allah's completeness and they free Him from deficiencies as well as confirm Allah's high and lofty status.

As for the statement of the Prophet ﷺ: "*SubhaanAllah wal Hamdulillah (Allah is far removed from every imperfection and all praise belong to Allah)."* Both phrases are complete, and they negate Allah the Exalted having any deficiencies. The word: *"SubhaanAllah"* denotes Allah as having complete perfection, as does the word: *"Al-Hamdu lillah"*. Both these phrases comprise distancing ones from acts of *Shirk* (polythiesm) and sin and also that one frees themself from the polytheists and sinful individuals due to their errors, sins and misguidance. So praising Allah is to decribe Him in a manner that befits His Mesjesty and this is in His Names, Attributes as well as in His Actions as He is complete and never deficient in any of them, as He says the Quran:

وَلِلَّهِ ٱلْأَسْمَآءُ ٱلْحُسْنَىٰ

"And (all) the Most Beautiful Names belong to Allah." (Al-A'raaf 180)

Allah also says:

وَلِلَّهِ ٱلْمَثَلُ ٱلْأَعْلَىٰ

"And for Allah is the highest description." (An-Nahl 60)

Allah the Exalted has the most complete description in every possible way, as well as in His Actions as He says:

وَمَا خَلَقْنَا ٱلسَّمَٰوَٰتِ وَٱلْأَرْضَ وَمَا بَيْنَهُمَا لَٰعِبِينَ

"And We created not the heavens and the earth and all that is between them, for mere play." (Ad-Dukhaan 38)

This indicates that Allah never created the creation for mere play or amusement, rather it was due to a great wisdom and a lofty purpose. There is also great wisdom in Allah's legislations as He says in the Quran:

أَلَيْسَ ٱللَّهُ بِأَحْكَمِ ٱلْحَٰكِمِينَ

"Is not Allah the best of judges?" (At-Teen 8)

Also He the Exalted says:

أَفَحُكْمَ ٱلْجَٰهِلِيَّةِ يَبْغُونَ وَمَنْ أَحْسَنُ مِنَ ٱللَّهِ حُكْمًا لِقَوْمٍ يُوقِنُونَ

"Do they seek the judgement of (the Days of) Ignorance? And who is better in judgement than Allah for a people who have firm Faith!" (Al-Maa'idah 50)

So, (back to the word *Al-Hamdu lillah*), all praise be to Allah, and we say this no matter what the situation may be, and it was the habit of the Prophet ﷺ, that if something good happened to him he would say:

الحمدُ للهِ الذَي بنعمَتِهِ تتمُّ الصَّالِحَات

"All Praise be to Allah for His Blessings and has completed righteous actions."

And if something bad befell him he ﷺ would say:

الحمدُ للهِ عَلَى كُلِّ حَالٍ

"All Praise be to Allah no matter what the situation may be."

And there is a statement circulated among the people: *"All Praise be to Allah even though this thing we praise (Allah) is disliked."* What we say regarding this statement is that it deficient and lacking! Why? Because such statements indicate a lack of patience, or we say at least, the opposite of having complete patience upon Allah the Exalted; if it is the case that you dislike a thing, it is not becoming to mention such phrases or expressions. Rather, it is upon an individual to use those phrases that the Prophet ﷺ himself used which were: *"All Praise be to Allah no matter what the situation may be"* and *"All praise be to Allah no matter what the situation be, Who is praised like known other."*

35

Out of the two statements, the first is clearer and will greatly help the one who utters it in repelling what they dislike from what befalls them from Allah; I must say though, I am not saying that one can naturally like what befalls them, no! Rather one does dislike it, but we are saying that they should not their tongue get carried away with cursing and the likes at the expense of neglecting praising Allah, as was the case with Prophet ﷺ.

The Prophet ﷺ then said: *"And Salaat (prayer) is light."* So, prayer is the light of the believer in his heart, face, when he is in his grave and when he is raised on Judgement Day, and for this reason you find those who have the most light in their faces are none other than those who pray and have the most humility in their prayers.

And also from the things that this light benefits the people with is it opens the door to understanding Allah. And what we mean is that it enables one to understand Allah, His Legislations, His Actions, His Names and Attributes. And the prayer is the foundation of Islam and if something is founded on good, it will remain, but on the other hand, if one's structure and foundation is weak than the building will be weak due to the foundation being weak. The prayer will be light for an individual on the Day of Judgement as the *Hadith* of the Prophet ﷺ states:

> *"Whoever safeguards the prayers will be given light and proof (that he prayed them) and he will be successful on Judgement Day; whosoever does not safeguard them will have no light given to him or any proof, nor will he be successful on the Day of Judgement and he will be raised on it with Fir'awn, Hamaan, Qaroon and Ubay ibn Khalaf."*

So, pertaining to this light, it is light that illuminates all of one's affairs, so that which is biding upon the seeker of truth is to safeguard his illumination which helps him, as such light will increase his faith as well as help him to be able him practise righteous actions.

And regarding patience, then the Prophet ﷺ said (in the *Hadith*): *"And patience is light (illumination)."* So, this light or illumination, means light with warmth as Allah says:

هُوَ ٱلَّذِى جَعَلَ ٱلشَّمْسَ ضِيَآءً وَٱلْقَمَرَ نُورًا

"He is the One who has made the sun an illumination and the moon as a light." (Yunus 5)

This light has some warmth within it, and patience is likewise since it is difficult upon the soul as well as it entailing some hardships, but it is the reason that a person is given reward without due reckoning. And the difference between the light from prayer and the light from patience is that the light from patience is likened to a type of warmth or heat which assists the individual's heart, body and affairs in addition to supporting him.

The Prophet ﷺ then said: *"And charity is the proof of Faith."* This means, that when one gives charity as a means to gain closeness to Allah ﷻ, giving to the poor or for the general welfare of the Muslims as a benefit for them, and as such they build *Masaajid* and the likes, then this act becomes a proof for its recipient and giver. And the meaning of: *"And charity is the proof of Faith"* is also an evidence proving the *Ikhlaas* (sincerity) of the one giving the charity and that their goal (in life) is to be near to Allah the Exalted; the reason why we say this is because wealth is one of man's most treasured possessions, beloved to the soul and not forgetting that, nature of a man's soul is full of mere greed and great stinginess, it dislikes sharing, no matter what the thing being shared is!

So, remember O reader, one does nor part with something so beloved to his soul except for the sake of something he considerer's more beloved to him and this is a sure reality that is witnessed; giving charity is a clear indication and evidence of one's sound *Emaan* (faith) and strong certainty. We see those who give away a lot of charity for the sake of Allah are mostly the ones who have firm *Emaan* (faith) in Allah the Exalted.

Then the Prophet ﷺ said: "*And the Quran is a plea in your favour or against you.*" The Quran is the *Firm Rope of Allah* ﷻ and it is a clear proof upon His creation, and that is, that if an individual abides by its commandments and refrains from its prohibitions, believes in its message, respecting it as it should be respected and honouring it as it should be honoured, and that it is Allah's revealed message to mankind, then in this case, it becomes a proof for you. But, on the other hand, if one disregarded it, turned away from it - by not reciting it, practising it or living by it, carrying out its prohibitions, then in this case the Quran will be a proof against you on Judgement Day, as the *Hadith* says. And lastly a point worth mentioning, the Prophet ﷺ made it very clear here that the Quran is a proof for you or against, but the *Hadith* does not put the two together or in the middle! It is, as mentioned, for you or against you, in all your matters or affairs, so we ask Allah the Exalted to make the Quran a proof for us by which it guides us in this and the next world, indeed He is Generous and Honourable!

The Prophet ﷺ next said: *"Every person departs; he either ransoms himself or puts himself into perdition."* Every soul begins his (or her) day so he labours himself, works hard and tires himself, Allah the Exalted says:

وَهُوَ ٱلَّذِى يَتَوَفَّىٰكُم بِٱلَّيْلِ وَيَعْلَمُ مَا جَرَحْتُم بِٱلنَّهَارِ ثُمَّ يَبْعَثُكُمْ

فِيهِ

"It is He who takes your soul by night (when you are asleep), and has knowledge of all that you have done by day, then he raise (wakes) you up (again)." (Al-An'aam 60)

The night sleep mentioned here in this verse, is named the "minor death," and it is a means for the body to regain strength and recover and relax from a tireless day of work. A person awakes from this sleep as a vendor of his soul, either freeing it or ruining it, and those who run headlong towards good are the Muslims and the opposite, are those who run headlong towards sin and disobedience, such are the disbelievers and we seek Allah's refuge! The first thing a Muslim does when he wakes is *Wudu* as the Prophet ﷺ said: *"Wudu is half of Emaan (Faith)."* After this, he turns and devotes himself to Allah ﷻ, so if the believer acts in obedience to Allah and upholds His Devine Legislation, he frees his soul from the slavery to the Devil (*Shaytaan*) and his own desires.

And also one of the things one does upon waking up is he makes the prescribed invocation upon raising from sleep, which contains words of manifesting Allah's Oneness (*Tawheed*); after this, reads from *Surah Aali Imraan*:

إِنَّ ٱلَّذِينَ كَفَرُواْ بَعْدَ إِيمَـٰنِهِمْ ثُمَّ ٱزْدَادُواْ كُفْرًا لَّن تُقْبَلَ تَوْبَتُهُمْ

وَأُوْلَـٰٓئِكَ هُمُ ٱلضَّآلُّونَ

"Verily! In the creations of the heavens and the earth, and the alternation of night and day, there are indeed signs for the people of understanding." (Aali Imraan 190)

The end of the *Surah* is referring to the Muslim! As it is he who frees it (the soul) from all kinds of destructions and things that will ruin it completely from the time a person gets up in the morning, but this is not so with the disbeliever as he is the opposite to this. His actions bring about his own destruction, so the meaning here in this *Hadith* of the words: "*Every person departs; he either ransoms it or puts it into perdition (ruins)*" is, one brings downfall upon his own self and that is because of his sins. The disbelievers wake up and start their day embarking upon disobedience to Allah the Exalted, so even with what they eat and drink, Allah will judge them and punish them with an exact recompense on the Day of Judgement.   Likewise, whatsoever sinful thing they wear, He the Exalted will punish them accordingly on Judgement Day. Allah says in the Quran:

قُلْ مَنْ حَرَّمَ زِينَةَ ٱللَّهِ ٱلَّتِىٓ أَخْرَجَ لِعِبَادِهِۦ وَٱلطَّيِّبَـٰتِ مِنَ ٱلرِّزْقِ قُلْ

هِىَ لِلَّذِينَ ءَامَنُواْ فِى ٱلْحَيَوٰةِ ٱلدُّنْيَا خَالِصَةً يَوْمَ ٱلْقِيَـٰمَةِ كَذَٰلِكَ

نُفَصِّلُ ٱلْـَٔايَـٰتِ لِقَوْمٍ يَعْلَمُونَ

"Say: 'Who has forbidden the adoration with clothes given by Allah, which He has produced for His slaves, and all kinds of (lawful things) of food?' Say: 'They are, in the life of this world, for those who believe, (and) exclusively for them (believers) on the Day of Resurrection (the disbelievers will not share them).'" (Al-A'raaf 32)

In a somewhat similar verse as the one in *Surah Al-A'raaf* which was revealed in Makkah is the verse in *Al-Maa'idah*:

لَيۡسَ عَلَى ٱلَّذِينَ ءَامَنُواْ وَعَمِلُواْ ٱلصَّـٰلِحَـٰتِ جُنَاحٌ فِيمَا طَعِمُوٓاْ

"On those who believe and do righteous good deeds, there is no sin on them for what they ate (in the past)." (Al-Maa'idah 93)

This seems that it means that there is blame and sin on other than the believers for what they eat, so the disbeliever from the moment he awakes and we seek refuge, is that they are destined for nothing but total self-destruction and self-ruin, but in the case with those who submit their will to the Exalted and High, his sole purpose is to save himself (or herself) from Allah's punishment which is the Fire, and we ask Allah the Exalted to save us from it!

In conclusion, people are divided into the following categories:

1. Those whom the Quran is a proof for, as the Prophet ﷺ said: *"And the Quran is a plea in your favour."*

2. Those whom the Quran is a proof against, and this is also when the Prophet ﷺ said in this *Hadith:* *"Or against you"*.

3. Those who do their upmost best to save themselves through their righteous good deeds.

4. Those who destroy themselves due to their unrighteous bad deeds.

And Allah grants success!

[Hadith 26]

Abu Sa'id Al-Khudree ﷺ reported "that certain people of the Ansaar asked the Prophet of Allah ﷺ and he gave them; then they asked again asked him and he gave them until all what he possessed was exhausted. Then he ﷺ said:

« مَا يَكُنْ مِنْ خَيْرٍ فَلَنْ أَدَّخِرَهُ عَنْكُمْ، وَمَنْ يسْتَعْفِفْ يُعِفَّهُ الله وَمَنْ يَسْتَغْنِ يُغْنِهِ اللَّهُ، وَمَنْ يَتَصَبَّرْ يُصَبِّرْهُ اللَّهُ. وَمَا أُعْطِيَ أَحَدٌ عَطَاءً خَيْراً وَأَوْسَعَ مِنَ الصَّبْرِ » مُتَّفَقٌ عَلَيْهِ

"Whatsoever wealth I have, I will not withhold from you. Whosoever would be chaste and modest Allah will keep him chaste and modest and whosoever would seek sufficiency, Allah will make him self-sufficient, and whosoever would be patient, Allah will give him patience, and no one is granted a gift better and more comprehensive than patience." [Agreed upon]

[EXPLANATION OF HADITH 26]

It was the habit of our Noble Prophet (Muhammad) ﷺ (to give) and he was of the most generous of all people; it was known that any time he ﷺ was asked for a thing, whatsover it may be, he would not refuse ever! Rather, he would give freely like one who fears no poverty, and he would live a life in his home like that of an extremely poor individual.

And it is reported that even at times, due to the severty of hunger, the Prophet ﷺ would tie a stone over his belly due to the severity of hunger yet he was the most honorable and bravest of the people, so when he had given all that he had till there was nothing left over or it was exhausted, he ﷺ said: *"Whatsoever wealth I have, I will not withhold from you."* This statement means, the only thing preventing me from giving you more is, that I have nothing it my possession to offer you as I have given you all I have in my possession. So then the Prophet ﷺ encouraged the people to adopt the following qualities: chastity and modesty, seeking sufficiency and patience, saying: *"Whosoever would be chaste and modest Allah will keep him chaste and modest and whosoever would seek sufficiency, Allah will make him self-sufficient, and whosoever would be patient, Allah will give him patience, and no one is granted a gift better and more comprehensive than patience."*

Whosoever is chaste, Allah will keep him chaste. And whosoever keeps himself chaste from immorality such and falling into comitting *Zina* (furnication or adultry) with women, Allah will certainly keep him chaste and away from it. Whoever does not control himself and follows his evil vain desires, by not keeping chaste, his desires will lead him to sure destruction and Allah's refuge is sought! This is the case if one lets his desires get the better of him; surely, they will make him incline towards illicit affairs with women, which will only destroy this individual. Rememeber! The eyes, by looking at women, commit fornication, the ears also commit fornication, and that is by listening to immorality, as do the hands, they commit fornication, and that could be touching a woman one is forbiden to touch, the legs commit fornication, and that is by one walking to places of open immorality and lewdness, and finally the private parts (commit fornication), as we know, and we seek Allah's refuge from this! So if a person keeps himself chaste, Allah the Exalted keeps him chaste and protects him as well as his family.

"*Whosoever would seek sufficiency, Allah will make him self-sufficiency*". This means that one seeks self sufficiency only from Allah the Exalted and what is with Him, he relys only on Him to meet his needs, and on none other than Him, especially not from His creation. And that is, if one seeks the creation's help while avoiding the Creator, then one will surely remain poor and his heart will remain empty, and their needs will never be met no matter what the case may be. When we speak about self-sufficiency, which is of great importance, then it is the type pertaining to the heart, i.e. being content in the heart and free from always wanting what is in the hands of the people; if one strives for that which is with Allah the All-Rich, certainly Allah will make his heart free of want from the people and never be in any need of what they people have.

"*Whosoever would be patient, Allah will give him patience*": Know that if you withold and refain yourself by strictly avoiding what Allah the Exalted has forbidden you and you are pateient with what the Exalted has decreed for you, such as in matters like poverty, without you turning to the people for aid and support of the people, then Allah the Exalted is sure to keep you firmly patient and help you, and this is the main evidence of this *Hadith* at hand, which is a clear indication of the lofty station of patience and this chapter highlights that.

The Prophet ﷺ said: *"And no one is granted a gift better and more comprehensive than patience."* And what this means is, that if Allah the Exalted grants and bestows the gift of patience upon you, then surely you have been granted an everlasting abundant good. Why? Because, if Allah enriches you with the quality of patience, you will certainly endure many afflictions that the path to Allah contains. *Shaytaan* (the Devil) is lying in wait to distract a person and make him fall into the forbidden matters, so if a person is patient, he will be able to fight off his enemy the Devil, and that is by being patient in avoiding the *Haraam* matters; as the *Shaytaan* is always trying to mislead a person, being patient will be a combat kit against him, the open enemy.

If Allah bestows upon an individual this honorable noble trait of patience, then it is of the greatest gifts, and the reason why, as we said, is because if one so happens to encounter many harms or ills from the people, and this could by way of them harming him through what he hears from them or generally, by them just transgressing against him in any shape or form, this individual does take not revenge or becomes anger at these things being done to him no matter what they are. Rather, he endures patiently with that which Allah decree for him and so, he finds his heart in a state of constant ease and always at rest, and this is why the Prophet ﷺ said: *"And no*

one is granted a gift better and more comprehensive than
patience".

[Hadith 27]

Abu Yahya Suhaib ibn Sinan reported that the Messenger of Allah ﷺ said:

«عَجَباً لأَمْرِ الْمُؤْمِنِ إِنَّ أَمْرَهُ كُلَّهُ لَهُ خَيْرٌ، وَلَيْسَ ذَلِكَ لِأَحَدٍ إِلاَّ لِلْمُؤْمِنِ: إِنْ أَصَابَتْهُ سَرَّاءُ شَكَرَ فَكَانَ خَيْراً لَهُ، وَإِنْ أَصَابَتْهُ ضَرَّاءُ صَبَرَ فَكَانَ خَيْراً لَهُ » رواه مسلم

"How wonderful is the case of a believer; there is good for him in everything and this applies only to a believer. If prosperity attends him, he expresses gratitude to Allah and that is good for him; and if adversity befalls him, he endures it patiently and that is good for him." [Reported by Muslim]

[EXPLANATION OF HADITH 27]

The Prophet ﷺ indicates the approval for a matter to be considered strange, and that is the affair of a Muslim: *"How wonderful is the case of a believer,"* meaning: his situation or affair is always good for him no matter what the case may be and this is certainly only the case for a Muslim. So the Prophet ﷺ explains the matter as follows: *"If prosperity attends him, he expresses gratitude to Allah and that is good for him; and if adversity befalls him, he endures it patiently and that is good for him."* So, this is the case of the believer only, and every person obtains that which Allah ordains for him, as Allah decrees are between two matters, happiness and joy or misfortune and distress, and in respect to these two matters, people are divided into two categories: believers and disbelievers.

As for the case of the believer, no matter what his situation may be, surely his affairs are always good for him; if an illness befalls him he shows patience and submits and accepts his decree and knows that such tests or trials are from none other than Allah, so the believer waits and endures this calamity hoping on none but Allah for relief, expecting Allah's reward for enduring and being patient. So this slave obtains the reward for being patient with this trial Allah the Exalted has tested him with. As for if good comes to the believer, such as things like abundant blessings of beneficial knowledge, righteous actions, wealth, children and good family, then as a result of all of this the believer shows thankfulness to Allah which is certainly one of the ways of being grateful to Allah as well as by being obedient to Him and obeying His commandments. Sadly, it has become a habit of many people nowadays to think that being grateful or thankful to Allah is merely be way of the expression of the tongue, or verbally saying, "Thank you O Allah." Rather, it is in complying to the orders of Allah ﷻ. By being thankful, pleased and grateful to Allah ,one will obtain the two following blessings:

1. Blessings in one's *Deen* (Religion);
2. Blessing in one's *Dunyah* (worldly affairs).

As for the first category, then it is being pleased with Islam as a *Deen*. As for the second category then it is the virtue of lawful wealth one obtains. So this is the condition of the believer, but as for the disbeliever then his plight is nothing but sheer evil and we seek refuge! If evil befalls him, the disbeliever does not demonstrate patience and is completely taken over by despair and grief and he calls out for destruction, crying in bitter aguish, cursing time and day, and even cursing Allah the Exalted! But if good comes to the disbeliever he shows little gratitude and thanks to Allah, so him lacking gratitude will be a means of remorse for him on Judgement Day, as Allah says in the Quran:

قُلْ مَنْ حَرَّمَ زِينَةَ ٱللَّهِ ٱلَّتِىٓ أَخْرَجَ لِعِبَادِهِۦ وَٱلطَّيِّبَٰتِ مِنَ ٱلرِّزْقِ قُلْ

هِىَ لِلَّذِينَ ءَامَنُواْ فِى ٱلْحَيَوٰةِ ٱلدُّنْيَا خَالِصَةً يَوْمَ ٱلْقِيَٰمَةِ كَذَٰلِكَ

نُفَصِّلُ ٱلْأَيَٰتِ لِقَوْمٍ يَعْلَمُونَ

"Say (O Muhammad): 'Who has forbidden the adornment with clothes given by Allah, which He has produced for His slaves, and *At-Tayyibaat* (all types of *Halaal* (lawful) things) of food?' Say, 'They are, in this life of this world, for those who believe,

**(and) exclusively for them (believers) on the Day of Resurrection (the disbelievers will not share them).'"
(Al-A'raaf 32)**

This indicates that these things are especially for the believers on the Day of Judgement but as for those who do not believe, who take in nothing but the impermissible, there is nothing but Fire awaiting to punish them in the next life. So the disbeliever, no matter what his case is, it is the same, his plight is nothing but mere evil, day and night, in this life and the next, so it matters not in the least weather his situation is good or bad in this life as it will only be for a brief moment when Judgement Day comes upon him.

This *Hadith* encourages one to have firm belief (*Emaan*) and to always remember that a believer's situation is always good, no matter what his state is, and that Allah is always showering the believer with His great blessings. And is an incitement to the believer to endure patiently with any harm they encounter and surely this is the description of the true believer.

So, if you see yourself displaying patience upon affliction and hoping in Allah's reward for enduring, then know, this is a sure indication of your firmly-rooted *Emaan*; on the other hand if it is the opposite, then only blame yourself, and make the alteration to your journey and path towards Allah and turn towards Him in repentance.

Also this *Hadith* encourages thankfulness and gratitude when encountering a blessing from Allah ﷻ; know, that if the Exalted has made you grateful toward Him as well as thankful, then surely indeed this is from Allah's great bounty His has bestowed upon you, as He says the Quran:

وَإِذْ تَأَذَّنَ رَبُّكُمْ لَئِن شَكَرْتُمْ لَأَزِيدَنَّكُمْ وَلَئِن كَفَرْتُمْ إِنَّ عَذَابِي لَشَدِيدٌ

"And (remember) when your Lord proclaimed: 'If you give thanks, I will give you more (of My blessings), but if you are thankless, verily! My punishment is indeed severe.'" (Ibraheem 7)

If the slave is guided by Allah to remember to thank Him, that is, in and of itself, another reason to thank Him further, meaning, a second time. And why we say this is because few people even thank Him, which is with great regret! So if you see that Allah has helped you and bestowed upon you some virtue, be grateful towards Him beyond your normal ability, then know this without doubt is a tremendous blessing from Allah upon you and as the poet said in a poem:

"If a blessing of Allah is a blessing, then it is a must upon you to do nothing accept repay it equally to Him, by means of expressing thankfulness, so how could you have received such a blessing, except that it be by way of His great virtue (upon you), so if time passes, such habit (showing thankfulness) may be part of your daily life."

This poet spoke the truth! Allah bestowing upon you His bounties is all the reason to increase thanking Him even more than you normally thank Him. So, if He makes you remember to thank Him, thank Him once again, for allowing you to remember to thank Him. But as we said, we have become unmindful of being grateful to Him, so we ask Allah to awaken our heedless hearts and rectify our actions, indeed He is All-Generous All-Kind!

[Hadith 28]

Anas ﷺ reported:

لِما ثَقُلَ النَّبِيُّ صَلَّى اللهُ عَلَيْهِ وسَلَّم جَعَلَ يتغشَّاهُ الكَرْبُ فقَالتْ فاطِمَةُ رَضِيَ الله
عنْها: واكَرْبَ أبتَاهُ، فَقَالَ: « لَيْسَ عَلَى أبيكِ كَرْبٌ بعْدَ اليَوْمِ ». فلمَّا مَاتَ
قالَتْ: يَا أبتَاهُ أَجَابَ ربّاً دعَاهُ، يَا أبتَاهُ جنَّةُ الفِرْدَوْسِ مأوَاهُ، يَا أبتَاهُ إِلَى جبْرِيلَ
ننعَاهُ، فلمَّا دُفِنَ قالتْ فاطِمَةُ رَضِيَ الله عنها: أطَابتْ أنفسُكُمْ أَنْ تَحْثُوا عَلَى
رسُول الله صَلَّى اللهُ عَلَيْهِ وسَلَّم التُّرَابَ؟ روَاهُ البُخارِيُّ .

"When the last illness of the Messenger of Allah ﷺ made Him
unconscious, Fatimah ﷺ exclaimed: 'Ah, the distress of my
father.' He said: 'There will be no distress for your father after
today!' When he died she said: 'My father! Allah has called you
back and you have responded to His call. O father! A Garden of
Firdaus is your abode! We announce to Jibreel your death!'
When he ﷺ was buried, she said: 'Are you satisfied now that you
put earth over (the grave of) Messenger of Allah?'" [Reported by
Al-Bukhari]

[EXPLANATION OF HADITH 28]

As for the statement: "When the last illness of the Messenger of Allah made him unconscious…" This means, he fell unconscious from the severity of his illness, and that is because whenever the Prophet ﷺ was sick or ill, he would suffer the pain of two men. And the wisdom behind this was so that the Prophet ﷺ would obtain the highest level of patience.

Indeed, patience is a lofty station that only one who is severely tested can acquire, obtain or reach, and this lofty station cannot be reached except by way of trails and tests from Allah the Exalted. And how is it possible if an individual is not tested and trialled for him (or her) to obtain patience? How will he know how to practise being patient? Allah the Exalted says in the Quran:

وَلَنَبْلُوَنَّكُمْ حَتَّىٰ نَعْلَمَ ٱلْمُجَٰهِدِينَ مِنكُمْ وَٱلصَّٰبِرِينَ وَنَبْلُوَا۟ أَخْبَارَكُمْ

"And surely, We shall try you till We test those who strive hard (for the Cause of Allah) and the patient." (Muhammad 31)

As we said earlier, the Prophet ﷺ was tested with the trial of two people. And in his ﷺ last illness he would fall unconscious, so his daughter said: *"Ah, the distress of my father!"* She felt overwhelmed in distress for her father (the Prophet ﷺ), and as we know from these types of things, women find them hard to bear and they become at times impatient. So, the Prophet ﷺ said to her: *"There will be no distress for your father after today."* And after finishing his words he traversed from the abode of this life to the companionship on high as he ﷺ said in a narration:

> *"O Allah! The companionship on high, the companionship on high!"*

Then the Prophet ﷺ looked upwards to the ceiling, then passed away, so his daughter wept, and this type of light weeping is allowed, as this is not the type that is displaying dissatisfaction and annoyance at Allah's Decree and destiny; then his daughter ﷺ said: *"We announce to Jibreel your death!"* Why to Jibreel? Because as we know, Jibreel was the carrier of Allah's Revelation and He would be sent to deliver it to the Prophet ﷺ morning and evening. So, if the Prophet ﷺ dies, this would put an end to Jibreel visiting the earth to carry it to the Prophet ﷺ.

As for her saying: "Allah has called you back and you have responded to His call," it means: Allah the Exalted owns everything in the creation, and has power of authority over it, all belong to Him and everything shall return unto Him. So the Prophet ﷺ responded (to Allah's call), and the journey the Prophet ﷺ undertakes is that of any believer, as the soul journeys till it meets Allah above the seven heavens. And when Fatimah ﷺ said: "A Garden of *Firdaus*," what this means is, this is the highest residence in Paradise, as the Prophet ﷺ said in a *Hadith*:

> *"Ask for Al-Waseelah for me, because it is the highest place in Paradise, and it is only allotted to the true worshipper of Allah from the worshippers of Allah, and I hope (sincerely) that I am that individual."*

So, there is no doubt that the Prophet's ﷺ resting place is *Firdaus* and it is the highest place in Paradise, and above it is the Great Mighty Throne of Allah ﷻ.

When the Prophet ﷺ was buried, his daughter Fatimah ﷞ said: "Are you satisfied now that you put earth over (the grave of) the Messenger of Allah?" She uttered these words due to the severity of her loss and distress (of losing her father), and she knew what a great loss it was to the Prophet's Companions too, due to their deep love for him ﷺ and their willingness to sacrifice everything for him. Fatimah ﷞ was completely satisfied with Allah's decree and great wisdom and to Him all must return after dying as the Exalted says in the Quran:

إِنَّكَ مَيِّتٌ وَإِنَّهُم مَّيِّتُونَ ۞ ثُمَّ إِنَّكُمْ يَوْمَ ٱلْقِيَـٰمَةِ عِندَ رَبِّكُمْ تَخْتَصِمُونَ

"Verily, you (O Muhammad) will die and verily, they (too) will die, then, on the Day of Resurrection, you will dispute before your Lord." (Az-Zumar 30-31)

Based on this *Hadith* we say, that the Prophet ﷺ was a man like other men, he would get sick, be in pain, get thirsty, get hot in hot weather and get cold in cold weather, and afflictions befall him as they do with any other human; the Prophet ﷺ said:

"I am a man like you, I forget like you also forget."

This *Hadith* is a refutation against those who associate the Prophet ﷺ as a partner with Allah! They claim that the Prophet ﷺ helps them from his grave; moreover, some of them, and we seek Allah's refuge, do not ask Allah for their needs, but they ask the Prophet ﷺ instead! And they make out that it is the Prophet ﷺ that can answer or ignore *Dua*. And this is a great misguidance in Islam and is an indication of the short-sightedness of the doers of such misguidance! The Prophet ﷺ himself could not bring about good to himself nor did he have the power to prevent harm! If this is the case, then how could he ﷺ bring good to others and prevent harm from them!? Allah ﷻ ordered the Prophet ﷺ to say:

$$ قُل لَّآ أَقُولُ لَكُمْ عِندِى خَزَآئِنُ ٱللَّهِ وَلَآ أَعْلَمُ ٱلْغَيْبَ وَلَآ أَقُولُ لَكُمْ إِنِّى مَلَكٌ $$

"Say (O Muhammad): 'I don't tell you that with me are the treasures of Allah, nor (that) I know the unseen; nor do I tell you that I am an Angel.'" (Al-An'aam 50)

Rather the Prophet ﷺ was a slave of Allah like other slaves of Allah and this is why he said:

$$ إِنْ أَتَّبِعُ إِلَّا مَا يُوحَىٰ إِلَيَّ $$

"I but follow what is revealed to me by inspiration." (Al-An'aam 50)

Also Allah says:

قُل إِنِّى لَآ أَمْلِكُ لَكُمْ ضَرًّا وَلَا رَشَدًا ◆ قُلْ إِنِّى لَن يُجِيرَنِى مِنَ ٱللَّهِ أَحَدٌ

وَلَنْ أَجِدَ مِن دُونِهِۦ مُلْتَحَدًا ◆ إِلَّا بَلَـٰغًا مِّنَ ٱللَّهِ وَرِسَـٰلَـٰتِهِۦ وَمَن

يَعْصِ ٱللَّهَ وَرَسُولَهُۥ فَإِنَّ لَهُۥ نَارَ جَهَنَّمَ خَـٰلِدِينَ فِيهَآ أَبَدًا

"Say: 'It is not in my power to cause you harm, or to
bring you to the Right Path.' Say (O Muhammad):
'None can protect me from Allah's Punishment (if I
were to disobey Him), nor should I find refuge
except in Him, (mine is) but conveyance (of the
truth)." (Al-Jinn 21-23)

This was the Prophet ﷺ indicating his work or job (i.e. to
convey Allah's Message); he ﷺ said: **"From Allah and His
Messages (of Islamic Monotheism)."** And after this the
following verse was revealed to the Prophet ﷺ:

وَأَنذِرْ عَشِيرَتَكَ ٱلْأَقْرَبِينَ

**"And warn your tribe (O Muhammad) of near
kindred." (Ash-Shu'ara 214)**

The Prophet ﷺ called upon all the members of his family,
saying to them:

*"O Fatimah bint Muhammad! Buy yourself from Allah, for
I cannot defend you before Him!"*[1]

---

[1] Shaykh Uthaymeen mentions this *Hadith* in a short version but the
Hadith is longer than he mentions. For further reference of this *Hadith* see
Al-Bukhari 3527.

In short, if the Prophet ﷺ was unable to even help his own flesh and blood, his daughter Fatimah ﵂, then this indicates that others have a lesser chance of being helped by the Prophet ﷺ! This is a clear proof refuting those who turn to the Prophet ﷺ for any sort of help, and with great regret we see many Muslims at the grave of the Prophet ﷺ supplicating to Him for their needs, and in such a sincere way it is as though they are more sincere in their *Dua* (supplication) to the Prophet ﷺ more than they are to Allah the Exalted!

So, this *Hadith* is proof of the permissibility to mourn and cry or weep over the loss of someone but with a condition that this type of crying is not the type that is followed by displeasure of Allah's Decree or words of regret, shouting, cursing and the likes.

It is also proof that the Prophet's ﷺ daughter outlived him, and that none of his children outlived her, as all of the Prophet's ﷺ sons and daughters died during his life. Fatimah ﵂ was alone and had nothing to inherit from, as the Prophet ﷺ said in a *Hadith*:

> *"We Prophets neither inherit nor leave inheritance."*

And this serves a great purpose and indicated Allah's great wisdom. Why? If the Prophet's left inheritance, many people would have started claiming unthinkable claims. That is, they would say, that the Prophets were striving after the worldly kingdom, wealth, status and power! And that they were seeking glory and position for those who would inherit after them such as their family, children and so forth. And yes, people would have claimed this if they had a chance to. But certainly, by the Prophets not leaving inheritance, it puts a stop to this type of false claims that would have been made. But the Prophets do leave *Sadaqah* (charity), so those who are in need and deserving, are entitled to it and may make use of it, and Allah grants success!

[Hadith 29]

Usamah Ibn Zaid ﷺ narrated:

أَرْسَلَتْ بِنْتُ النَّبِيِّ صَلَّى اللهُ عَلَيْهِ وَسَلَّمَ: إِنَّ ابْنِي قَدِ احْتُضِرَ فَاشْهَدْنَا، فَأَرْسَلَ يَقْرِئُ السَّلَامَ وَيَقُولُ: «
إِنَّ للهِ مَا أَخَذَ، ولهُ مَا أَعْطَى، وَكُلُّ شَيْءٍ عِنْدَهُ بِأَجَلٍ مُسَمًّى، فَلْتَصْبِرْ ولتحتسبْ» فَأَرْسَلَتْ إِلَيْهِ تُقْسِمُ
عَلَيْهِ لِيَأْتِيَنَّها. فَقَامَ وَمَعَهُ سَعْدُ بْنُ عُبَادَةَ، وَمُعَاذُ ابْنُ جَبَلٍ، وَأُبَيُّ بْنُ كَعْبٍ، وَزَيْدُ بْنُ ثَابِتٍ، وَرِجَالٌ
رَضِيَ اللهُ عَنْهُمْ، فَرُفِعَ إِلَى رَسُولِ اللهِ صَلَّى اللهُ عَلَيْهِ وَسَلَّمَ الصِّبِيُّ، فَأَقْعَدَهُ في حِجْرِهِ ونَفْسُهُ تَقَعْقَعُ،
فَفَاضَتْ عَيْنَاهُ، فَقَالَ سَعْدٌ: يَا رَسُولَ اللهِ مَا هَذَا؟ فَقَالَ: « هَذِهِ رَحْمَةٌ جَعَلَهَا اللهُ تَعَلَى في قُلُوبِ عِبَادِهِ
» وفي رِوَايَةٍ : « في قُلُوبِ مَنْ شَاءَ مِنْ عِبَادِهِ وَإِنَّمَا يَرْحَمُ اللهُ مِنْ عِبَادِهِ الرُّحَمَاءَ » مُتَّفَقٌ عَلَيْهِ .

"The daughter of the Prophet ﷺ sent for him as her child was
dying, but the Prophet ﷺ returned the message and sent her good
wishes saying: 'Whatever Allah takes away or gives, belongs to
Him, and everything with Him has a limited fixed term (in this
world), and so she should be patient and anticipate Allah's
reward.' She again sent for the Prophet ﷺ insisting him to come
for the sake of Allah. The Messenger of Allah ﷺ, Sa'd Ibn
Ubadah, Mu'adh Ibn Jabal, Ubayy Ibn Ka'b, Zaid Ibn
Thaabit and some other men went to see her. The child was
lifted up to the Messenger of Allah ﷺ while his breath was
disturbed in his chest. On seeing that, the eyes of the Prophet ﷺ
streamed with tears and Sa'd said: 'O Messenger of Allah! What
is this?' He replied, 'It is compassion which Allah has placed in
the hearts of His slaves, Allah is Compassionate only to those
among His slaves who are compassionate (to others).'"

Another version says: "(The) Messenger of Allah ﷺ said: 'Allah
shows compassion only to those among His slaves who are
compassionate.'" [Agreed upon]

[EXPLANATION OF HADITH 29]

Regarding Usamah ibn Zaid ibn Haarith, he was the slave and servant of Khadijah ﷺ (one of the wives of the Prophet ﷺ) and she gave him as a present to the Prophet ﷺ who freed him, looked after him and was in charge of him, and Zaid was given the title *"The Beloved to the Prophet ﷺ"* and he was also titled "The son of Muhammad."

This *Hadith* states that one of the daughters of the Prophet ﷺ requested him because her child was at the point of death, so she pleaded for him to be present, so he said to her: *"Whatever Allah takes away or gives, belongs to Him, and everything with Him has a limited fixed term (in this world), and so she should be patient and anticipate Allah's reward."*

So, if it is the case that Allah the Exalted owns everything in the heavens and earth, and if He decides to take what belongs to Him - and what He gives you also belongs to Him-, how then can an individual be dissatisfied and grieved by Him taking whatsoever He is the owner of? When one encounters a misfortune, he has been directed to say:

إِنَّا لِلَّهِ وَإِنَّا إِلَيْهِ رَاجِعُونَ

"Verily! To Allah we belong, and verily, to Him we shall return."

We and all we possess belong to Allah, and He does as He pleases with us. We must remember Allah does what He does based on great wisdom; so know, that you really own nothing, rather He does, so how can you truly own anything when everything belong to Him and Him only? Whatever you have, be it wealth or other than it, you do not have complete ownership over it, rather you are limited in such ownership. If you decide to use such wealth in a way the *Deen* forbids you in using, then withhold from squandering it, and remember what we said, this wealth is actually not rightfully yours to waste, as Allah says in the Quran:

وَءَاتُوهُم مِّن مَّالِ ٱللَّهِ ٱلَّذِىٓ ءَاتَىٰكُمْ

"And give them something yourselves out of the wealth of Allah which He has bestowed upon you." (An-Noor 33)

This indicates that one is not allowed to just use such wealth in any way they desire; rather using it is in accordance to what the Law allows you to.

The Prophet ﷺ went on to say: *"Whatever Allah takes away or gives, belongs to Him."* How could it be that if Allah decides to take what belongs to Him and you become annoyed? This is neither rational nor sensible nor reasonable, and it was unheard of during the golden age of Islam.

Then the Prophet ﷺ said: *"And everything with Him has a limited fixed term (in this world)."* So, everything has its appointed prescribed term with Allah as Allah says in the Quran:

وَكُلُّ شَىْءٍ عِندَهُۥ بِمِقْدَارٍ

"Everything with Him is in due proportion." (Ar-Ra'd 7)

And what this means is that everything is decreed be it in time, place, description, and the likes; all of these things have already been decreed by Allah the Exalted. And one of the great wisdoms of us knowing this is so that one knows that only what was decreed or written for him will come to him and what was not will not come to him; also, knowing this makes a person be at complete rest, knowing that what passed him was not written for him and what he obtained from good was written for him and not going to pass him, as Allah says:

$$لِكُلِّ أُمَّةٍ أَجَلٌ ۚ إِذَا جَاءَ أَجَلُهُمْ فَلَا يَسْتَأْخِرُونَ سَاعَةً$$

"For every *Ummah* (community or nation), there is a term appointed; when their term is reached, neither can they delay it nor can they advance it an hour (or a moment)." (Yunus 49)

So, understand that everything has an appointed term that can neither be delayed nor can it be advanced a single moment, and as such there is no need or benefit in a person being impatient nor displaying dissatisfaction, as neither can change what is decreed.

When the Prophet ﷺ was requested by his daughter to attend, he and a group of his Companions went out to her and when he arrived he lifted the child who was having breathing difficulties in his chest, meaning that he (the child) became agitated and troubled, taking deep sighs, and the child passed away; upon this the Prophet ﷺ began to cry, and tears streamed down His face. So, Sa'd ibn Ubadah who was the chief of the tribe of Al-Kazooj exclaimed: *"What is this?"* Sa'd assumed that the Prophet ﷺ was crying due to dissatisfaction at the child's fate, so the Prophet ﷺ replied to him and said: *"It is compassion (mercy)."* Meaning: it was merely out of love, compassion and mercy for the child and not due to rejecting Allah's decree or being dissatisfied with the child's fate.

Then the Prophet ﷺ said: *"Allah shows compassion only to those among His slaves who are compassionate."* This is proof of the permissibility of crying for the one inflicted with a misfortune. So, if you see a person afflicted in say, his mind or body, and you wept or cried out of sheer pity for this individual, then know, this is a clear manifestation indicating Allah has placed in your heart compassion and mercy! And if Allah the Exalted installs compassion in your heart then know, you are counted from the compassionate ones, those whom Allah shows compassion to. We ask Him the Exalted to show us mercy and show you mercy also!

And in this *Hadith* is a proof that it is an obligation upon a person to have *Sabr* (patience) and it is in the statement of the Prophet ﷺ when He said: *"Order her that she should be patient and anticipate Allah's reward."* So this version we have mentioned is the more correct and better version from the other versions of this narration which is *"Order her."* And this is better than what many people say nowadays (if the person is undergoing difficulties) *"May Allah increase your reward,"* or generally to offer ones condolence, or to say *"May Allah forgive this person who has just passed away."* These condolences we have just mentioned, they have been stated by some of the *Ulema*, but that which is better is what the Prophet ﷺ himself used in this *Hadith*, and the wisdom why one should say these words is because they will certainly give the one suffering contentment and satisfaction.

As for what is done in our time by the name of "gatherings of condolence", this is not the right time for well-wishing as supposed by the command folk! This is known as a type of party where these people put chairs for people to sit around and light candles, food and have a person reciting the Quran! No, this is not condolence; rather the condolence which is encouraged is inciting the afflicted one to have *Sabr*! And at times if a person is afflicted with say, the loss of his son or the likes, if their relatives do not have these gathering of chairs and candles, they pay him no mind, solely because he does not have such open gathers as we have described.

So the confirmed guidance of the Prophet ﷺ is to console the bereaved one, not necessarily the closest relatives to the deceased. As at times, a person's close relative could pass away but this does not affect this individual or individuals emotionally, so they don't really need much consoling or comforting, but it could be the case that one of the deceased person's distant friends, colleagues or distant relatives are overtaken by this tragedy, so they would be more deserving of condolence, support and comforting.

So, nowadays with great regret many have become backwards! And condolence is offered to the relative by way of *Haraam* means such as the beating of drums and the likes and they perceive this to be an act of condolence! And it has become the case that many poor individuals have problems with their uncle's son, so if he leave millions for them to inherit, they are very pleased at his death. Why? Because they will inherit this wealth, and they say "All Praise be to Allah who has relieved us of him and now I shall enjoy my inheritance he has left me!" In this case do we say this inheritor who has inherited this wealth, is grieving at the loss of a family member? No! We say certainly he is not grieving or in any distress rather quite the opposite. And this is certainly not an act of honour or any form of expressing sympathy, and this is what we have to say regarding this and Allah grants success.

[Hadith 30]

Suhaib ؓ reported that the Messenger said ﷺ:

«كَانَ مَلِكٌ فِيمَنْ كَانَ قَبْلَكُمْ، وَكَانَ لَهُ سَاحِرٌ، فَلَمَّا كَبِرَ قَالَ لِلْمَلِكِ: إِنِّي قَدْ كَبِرْتُ فَابْعَثْ إِلَيَّ غُلَاماً أُعَلِّمْهُ السِّحْرَ، فَبَعَثَ إِلَيْهِ غُلَاماً يُعَلِّمُهُ، وَكَانَ فِي طَرِيقِهِ إِذَا سَلَكَ رَاهِبٌ، فَقَعَدَ إِلَيْهِ وَسَمِعَ كَلَامَهُ فَأَعْجَبَهُ، وَكَانَ إِذَا أَتَى السَّاحِرَ مَرَّ بِالرَّاهِبِ وَقَعَدَ إِلَيْهِ، فَإِذَا أَتَى السَّاحِرَ ضَرَبَهُ، فَشَكَا ذَلِكَ إِلَى الرَّاهِبِ فقال: إِذَا خَشِيتَ السَّاحِرَ فَقُلْ: حَبَسَنِي أَهْلِي، وَإِذَا خَشِيتَ أَهْلَكَ فَقُلْ: حَبَسَنِي السَّاحِرُ. فَبَيْنَمَا هُوَ عَلَى ذَلِكَ إِذْ أَتَى عَلَى دَابَّةٍ عَظِيمَة قَدْ حَبَسَت النَّاس فقال: الْيَوْمَ أَعْلَمُ السَّاحِرُ أَفْضَل أم الرَّاهِبُ أَفْضَلُ؟ فَأَخَذَ حَجَراً فقَالَ: اللهُمَّ إِنْ كان أَمْرُ الرَّاهِبِ أَحَبَّ إِلَيْكَ مِنْ أَمْرِ السَّاحِرِ فَاقْتُلْ هَذِهِ الدَّابَّة حَتَّى يَمْضِيَ النَّاسُ، فَرَماها فقَتلَها ومَضى النَّاسُ، فأَتَى الرَّاهِبَ فأخْبَرَهُ. فقال له الرَّاهِبُ: أَيْ بُنَيَّ أَنْتَ الْيَوْمَ أَفْضلُ مِنِّي، قَدْ بَلَغَ مِنْ أَمْرِكَ ما أَرَى، وإِنَّكَ سَتُبْتَلَى، فإِن ابْتُلِيتَ فَلَا تَدُلُّ عليَّ، وَكانَ الْغُلَامُ يُبْرِئُ الأَكْمَهَ والأبْرصَ، ويُدَاوِي النَّاس مِنْ سائِرِ الأدْواءِ. فَسَمِعَ جِلِيسٌ لِلْمَلِكِ كانَ قَدْ عَمِيَ فأَتَاهُ بِهَدايَا كَثِيرَةٍ فقال: ما ههُنَا لك أَجْمَعُ إِنْ أَنْتَ شَفَيْتَنِي، فقال إِنِّي لا أَشْفِي أَحَداً، إِنَّما يشْفِي الله تَعَالَى، فإِنْ آمَنْتَ بِاللهِ تَعَالَى دَعَوْتُ الله فشَفاكَ، فآمَنَ بِاللهِ تَعَالَى فشَفاهُ اللهُ تَعَالَى، فأَتَى الملِكَ فجَلَسَ إِلَيْهِ كما كانَ يجْلِسُ فقالَ لهُ المِلكُ: مَنْ رَدَّ عَلَيْكَ بصَرَك؟ قال: رَبِّي. قَالَ: ولكَ رَبٌّ غَيْرِي؟ قَالَ: رَبِّي ورَبُّكَ الله، فأَخَذَهُ فَلَمْ يزَلْ يُعَذِّبُهُ حَتَّى دَلَّ عَلَى الْغُلَامِ فجِئَ بِالْغُلَامِ، فقال له الملِكُ: أَيْ بُنَيَّ قَدْ بَلَغَ مِنْ سِحْرِك ما تَبْرِئُ الأَكْمَةَ والأبْرصَ وتفْعَلُ وتفْعَلُ فقالَ: إِنِّي لا أَشْفِي أَحَداً، إِنَّما يشْفِي الله تَعَالَى، فأَخَذَهُ فَلَمْ يزَلْ يعذِّبُهُ حَتَّى دَلَّ عَلَى الرَّاهِبِ، فجِئَ بِالرَّاهِبِ فقِيل

لَهُ: ارجِعْ عن دِينِكَ، فأبَى، فدَعا بالمِنْشَارِ فوُضِعَ المِنْشَارُ في مفرِقِ رأسِهِ، فشقَّهُ حتَّى وقَعَ شقَّاهُ، ثُمَّ جِئَ بجَلِيسِ المَلِكِ فقِيلَ لَهُ: ارجِعْ عن دِينِكَ فأبَى، فوُضِعَ المِنْشَارُ في مفرِقِ رأسِهِ، فشقَّهُ بِهِ حتَّى وقَعَ شقَّاهُ، ثُمَّ جِئَ بالغُلامِ فقِيلَ لَهُ: ارجِعْ عن دِينِكَ، فأبَى، فدَفَعَهُ إلَى نَفَرٍ مِن أصحابِهِ فقال: اذهَبُوا بِهِ إلَى جبَلِ كَذَا وكَذَا فاصعَدُوا بِهِ الجبَلَ، فإذَا بلغْتُمْ ذِروَتَهُ فإنْ رجَعَ عن دِينِهِ وإلاَّ فاطرَحُوهُ فذهَبُوا بِهِ فصعِدُوا بِهِ الجبَلَ فقال: اللَّهُمَّ اكفِنِيهِمْ بِمَا شِئْتَ، فرجَفَ بِهِمُ الجبَلُ فسَقَطُوا، وجَاءَ يمْشِي إلَى المَلِكِ، فقَالَ لَهُ المَلِكُ: ما فَعَلَ أصحابُكَ؟ فقالَ: كفانِيهِمُ الله تعالَى، فدَفَعَهُ إلَى نَفَرٍ مِن أصحابِهِ فقال: اذهَبُوا بِهِ فاحمِلُوهُ في قُرقُورٍ وتَوَسَّطُوا بِهِ البحرَ، فإنْ رجَعَ عن دِينِهِ وإلاَّ فاقْذِفُوهُ، فذَهبُوا بِهِ فقال: اللَّهُمَّ اكفِنِيهِمْ بِمَا شِئْتَ، فانكَفَأَت بِهِمُ السَّفِينةُ فغرِقوا، وجَاءَ يمْشِي إلَى المَلِكِ. فقالَ لَهُ المَلِكُ: ما فَعَلَ أصحابُكَ؟ فقالَ: كفانِيهِمُ الله تعالَى. فقالَ للمَلِكِ إنَّكَ لسْتَ بقَاتِلِي حتَّى تفعَلَ ما آمرُكَ بِهِ. قال: ما هُوَ؟ قال: تجْمَعُ النَّاس في صَعيدٍ واحدٍ، وتصلُبُنِي عَلَى جذْعٍ، ثُمَّ خُذ سهْماً مِن كنَانتِي، ثُمَّ ضَع السَّهْمَ في كبِدِ القَوْسِ ثُمَّ قُل: بسْمِ اللهِ رَبِّ الغُلامِ ثُمَّ ارمِنِي، فإنَّكَ إذَا فَعَلْتَ ذَلِكَ قَتَلْتِنِي. فجَمَع النَّاس في صَعيدٍ واحدٍ، وصلَبَهُ عَلَى جذْعٍ، ثُمَّ أَخَذَ سهْماً مِن كنَانتِهِ، ثُمَّ وضَعَ السَّهمَ في كبِدِ القَوْسِ، ثُمَّ قَالَ: بسْمِ اللهِ رَبِّ الغُلامِ، ثُمَّ رمَاهُ فوَقَعَ السَّهمُ في صُدْغِهِ، فوَضَعَ يدَهُ في صُدْغِهِ فمَاتَ. فقَالَ النَّاسُ: آمَنَّا بِرَبِّ الغُلامِ، فأُتِيَ المَلِكُ فقِيلَ لَهُ: أَرَأَيْت ما كُنْت تحْذَر قَدْ وَاللهِ نَزَلَ بِكَ حذَرُكَ. قَد آمنَ النَّاسُ. فأَمَرَ بالأخْدُودِ بأفْوَاهِ السِّكَكِ فخُدَّتَ وأضرِمَ فِيها النِّيرانُ وقال: مَن لَمْ يرْجِع عن دِينِهِ فأقْحِمُوهُ فِيهَا أَو قِيلَ لَهُ: اقْتحِم، ففعَلُوا حتَّى جَاءَتِ امرَأَةٌ ومعَها صَبيٌّ لَهَا، فتَقَاعَسَت أَنْ تَقعَ فِيهَا، فقال لَهَا الغُلامُ: يا أُمَّاه اصبِرِي فإنَّكِ عَلَي الحقِّ » رَوَاهُ مُسلِمٌ.

"There lived a king before you and he had a court magician. As he (the magician) grew old, he said to the king: 'I have grown old, so send me a young boy in order to teach him magic.' The king sent him a young boy to serve the purpose. And on his way (to the magician) the young boy met a monk to whom he listened to and liked. It became his habit that on his way to the magician, he would meet the monk and sit there and would come to the magician (late). The magician used to beat him because of his delay. He complained about this to the monk who said to him; 'When you feel afraid of the magician, say: "Members of my family detained me." And when you fear your family, say: "The magician detained me."' So it happened that there came a huge beast and it blocked the way of the people, and the young boy said: 'I will know today whether the magician or the monk is better.' He picked up a stone and said: 'O Allah, if the way of the monk is dearer to You than the way of the magician, bring about death to the animal so that the people be able to move about freely.' He threw that stone at it and killed it and the people began to move about freely. He then came to the monk and told him the story. The monk said: 'Son, today you are superior to me. You have come to a stage where I feel that you would be soon put to trail, and in that case do not reveal me.' That young boy began to heal those born blind and the leapers and he, in fact, began to cure people from all kinds of illnesses. When a courtier of the king who had gone blind heard about him, he came to him with numerous gifts and said: 'If you cure me, all these things will be yours.' He said, 'I myself do not cure anyone. It is Allah, the Exalted, Alone Who cures; and if you affirm faith in Allah, I shall also supplicate to Allah to cure you.' This courtier affirmed faith in Allah and Allah cured him. He came to the king and sat by his side as he used to sit before. The king said to him, 'Who restored your eyesight?' He said, 'My

Rabb (Lord).' Thereupon he said, 'Do you have another lord besides me?' He said, 'My Lord your Lord is Allah.' So the king kept torturing him until he revealed the young boy. The young boy was thus summoned and the king said to him, 'O boy, it has been conveyed to me that you have become so much proficient in your magic that you cure the blind and the leapers you do such-and-such.' Thereupon he said, 'I do not cure anyone; it is Allah Alone who cures,' and the king took hold of him and began to torture him until he revealed the monk. The monk was summoned and it was said to him: 'You should turn back from religion.' But he refused. The king sent for a saw, placed it in the middle of his head and cut him into two parts that fell down. Then the courtier of the king was brought forward and it was said to him: 'Turn back from your religion.' He too refused, and the saw was placed in the midst of his head and he was torn into two parts. Then the boy was sent for and it was said to him: 'Turn back from you religion.' He refused. The king handed him over to a group of his courtiers, and said to them: 'Take him to such-and-such mountain; make him climb up that mountain and when he reaches its peak ask him to renounce his faith. If he refuses to do so, push him to his death.' So they took him and made him climb up the mountain and he said: 'O Allah, save me from them in any way you like!' The mountain began to shake and they all fell down (dead) and that young boy came to the king. The king said to him, 'What happened to your companions?' He said, 'Allah has saved me from them.' He again handed him to some of his courtiers and said: 'Take him and carry him in a boat and when you reach the middle of the sea, ask him to renounce his religion. If he does not renounce his religion throw him (into the water).' So they took him and he said: 'O Allah, save me from them!' The boat turned upside *down and they all drowned except the young boy who came walking to the king. The king said: 'What happened to your companions?' He said, 'Allah has saved me from them.' Then he said to the king: 'You cannot kill me until you do what I command you to do.' The king asked, 'What is that.' He said, 'Gather all the people in one place and tie me up to a trunk of a tree, then take an arrow from my quiver and say: "With the Name of Allah, the Lord of the boy;" then shoot me. If you do that you will be able to kill me.' The king called the people in an open field and tied the young boy to the trunk of a tree. He took out an arrow from his quiver, fixed in the bow and said, 'With the Name of Allah, the Lord of the young boy.' He then shot the arrow and it hit the boy's temple. The boy placed his hand upon his temple where the arrow had hit him and died. The people then said: 'We believe in the Lord of this young boy.' The king was told: 'Do you see what you were afraid of, by Allah it has taken place; all the people have believed.' The king then commanded that trenches be dug and fire lit in them, and said: 'He who would not turn back from (the young boy's) religion, throw him in the fire!' Or he would be ordered to jump into it. They did so till a woman came with her child. She felt hesitant in jumping into the fire. The child said to her: 'O mother! Endure (this ordeal) for you are on the Right Path.'"* [Reported by Muslim]

[EXPLANATION OF HADITH 30]

The author (Imam An-Nawawi) mentions this wonderful amazing story in the chapter of *Sabr* (patience) about a king from the kings before us who had a magician, and this king hired this magician for mere fun, play, idleness and amusement, and it was the case that this king was a tyrant and obstinate, he order the people to worship him as we will soon explain.

So, as this magician prolonged his stay with the king he began to age, so he requested from the king to allow him to teach a young boy his magic; we briefly mention a point of benefit here why the magician specifically chose or requested someone young, one of the reasons is, that when a person is still in the prime of his youth he is more suitable to be taught. And also it is a known fact that when a person is young he tends to remember more and is less likely to forget what he knows or is taught. But in saying this, do not misunderstand me, I am not saying that an older person cannot learn or memorize as a young person does, no! Rather my point is that there is greater advantage learning when one is younger, and Firstly, when a person is young it is safe to say, that a majority of young people's memories are stronger than that of elderly people. Why? A youngster has more time on his hands and he does not have as many problems as an older person or that an older person will encounter.

Secondly, what a young person memorizes stays with him, whereas the case with someone who memorizes when he is older is that he tends to forget it rather quickly, and this is a known thing among the people, and as it is said: *"Learning while one is young, is like the engraving in a stone."*

To add to what we are saying, if a young person makes seeking *Ilm* (knowledge) part of his daily routine and most of his time is spent learning while he is young this will become part of his nature when he becomes older.

This magician became old in age and requested from the king a young individual so that he could teach him magic, so the king sent to him this young boy but Allah wished for this young boy much good. So, one day this youngster happened to pass by a monk and liked what he would say to him very much, as this monk was a devout worshiper of Allah, and it is possible a monk can be knowledgeable and at the same time, more devote in carrying out other acts of worship besides seeking knowledge, so in such a case he was given the title monastic.

The monk would speak amazing things to this boy and that would please him a great deal, so this youngster would leave his family and go to the monk and be very taken by this monk's words; whenever he would sit with him it would cause him to be delayed due to him overstaying, and that would make him late in attending the magician who would beat him due to not being on time.

The boy complained to the monk about the magician beating him for going late, so the monk advised him with that which would help him in the matter, so the monk said to him: "if you attend the magician and you are late and fear such beatings, say to the magician 'my family delayed me,' - meaning I was busy in the service of my family, and when you go to back to your family, say 'the magician delayed me!' This way, you will not encounter harms from either of the two."

So, the monk encouraged him with this advice though it was a lie, why? We say, it was because the monk saw great benefit in that and that was so as to prevent greater harm coming to this young boy, this lie the monk told the young boy to tell was to prevent greater harm being inflicted upon him. So, the boy would go to the monk, listen to his words and then go to the magician and whenever the magician wanted to punish him he would say "my family delayed me," and when he delayed from his family he would say "the monk delayed me."

Later, the boy passed by an enormous beast - but the *Hadith* does not mention what type of beast it was - and the people were unable to pass this path due to it, so this boy wanted to test the monk whether he was the good person or the magician; he picked up a stone and said "*O Allah if the monk is upon good then kill this beast with this stone!*" and so the he threw the stone and it killed the beast and people were able to pass safely.

So, the boy knew that from this incident, the monk was better than the magician, and there is no doubt the affair of the magician is clear, and that is because a magician is either a transgressor or a disbeliever, a polytheist. If a magician seeks help from the devils as a means to get close to them, as well as worshiping them and supplicating to them, then this person is a disbelieving polytheist. But if on the other hand he does not do these things but transgresses against the people with magic formulas which contain magic and the likes, then in that case he is considered a wrong doer and a transgressor.

The monk worship Allah upon clarity and guidance, which, although the monk was touched with some misguidance and general ignorance, he had very good intentions at the same time; even though some things he would say were wrong. This boy informed the monk as to what had happened to him, so the monk said to him, *"You are today better than me,"* and it was due to the fact that this boy made *Dua* (supplication) to Allah to show him who was the better of the two, the monk or magician? And Allah the Exalted answered him. So from this we see this is a great blessing from Allah upon His slave: if the slave has doubts in a matter, he can turn to Allah the Exalted to show him a sign that indicates what is correct; certainly, this is a blessing on that slave; to add to this, if a person's affairs become confusing for him then it has been legislated in the *Deen* for him (or her) to pray *Istikhaarah* (the prayer of need).

If a person sincerely turns to Allah for assistance, certainly Allah will aid him, and that could be through Him helping this person being guided to which option is correct between two matters; this could be in a number of ways: it could that Allah the Exalted makes his heart inclined towards one of the two matters he is confused about, or Allah makes him see what matter to decide in a dream or that Allah allows this person to ask assistance from someone notable with *Ilm* who will give him advice and guide him to the correct course of action.

So, it became the habit of this boy to cure many of the sick such as the blind and leapers and so forth, and what we mean is that he would make *Dua* to Allah to cure them and they would get cured and this was from the miracles of Allah on this boy. And this is not the same as the story of Eesa

(Jesus) the son of Mary who just wiped or touched a handicapped person and they were healed, but in the case of this boy he would be making *Dua* for those sick people.

The monk informed the boy that he will be put to trial, meaning: through an ordeal or a calamity, and that he should not reveal the monks name to anyone; one day, one of the kings courtiers who was blind came to the boy hoping to be healed and said to the boy, *"Cure me and such-and-such gifts you will have,"* so the boy said: *"It is Allah, the Exalted, Alone Who cures."* Look at the *Emaan* of this boy! He was not deceived nor self-deluded into thinking that it was him curing all these people, rather it was Allah!

To add to this I will mention another amazing story regarding *Shaykh ul-Islam* Ibn Taymiyyah as something similar happened to him: one day a person was brought to Ibn Taymiyyah who had been possessed by a demon (*Jinn*). So, this Man who was possessed showed many signs of possession, so Ibn Taymiyyah read over him in the hope that the *Jinn* would leave the man alone but the *Jinn* would not. So Ibn Taymiyyah began to remove the *Jinn* by beating him so severely in his neck till Ibn Taymiyyah's hand started to hurt him due to the severe beating. The *Jinn* shouted loud, *"I will leave this man's body that I am possessing, and I will do so out of respect for the Shaykh, Shaykh Ibn Taymiyyah!"* So Ibn Taymiyyah replied to the *Jinn* and said *"No! Do not come out due to me, rather come out or leave this man you have possessed in obedience to Allah and His Messenger (Muhammad)!"* Ibn Taymiyyah rejected honour in such a way, rather, he said honour and virtue belongs only to Allah the Exalted, so this *Jinn* left the possessed man's body and the man jumped to his feet and said *"Why has Ibn Taymiyyah come here, for what reason?"* Either he was in the market or in his house; the man was asked "Did you feel the Shaykh beating you?" To this he said *"No, I never felt any of his beatings, and I'm in no pain either!"* So the man was cured and the *Jinn* left his body entirely. So the *Ulema* have said that it is biding upon a person to affirm that all blessings come from Allah alone.

The boy said to the king's courtier: *"And if you affirm faith in Allah, I shall also supplicate to Allah to cure you."* So, the king's courtier believed and the boy made *Dua* to Allah to cure him and Allah did and he regained his sight after being blind; the king came to know about his courtier regaining his sight after asking him. As it was the boy's habit to sit with the king it happened that one day he sit with him and the king confronted him about where he had learnt to cure the people and who had taught him; the king began the severely punish him to disclose who was teaching him. But if we remember earlier the monk said to the boy that he would be put to great trials and to not give up his name, yet the boy was unable to bear the torture and revealed the monk's name.

This king was a known tyrant and transgressor, so he started punishing his courtier who was once blind and accepted the invitation of the boy; the king tortured him just because he affirmed that Allah alone was his Lord. The king said to him *"Do you take a lord other than me as Lord!"* And we seek Allah's refuge from this! After the boy disclosed the monk's name to the king he was brought before the king who requested him to exclaim the he (the king) was his lord and not Allah, but he refused to leave his religion.

On seeing this, the king ordered that a saw be brought and that the monk be cut in to two halves, one side falling to the left and the other falling to the right, but the monk, even though he knew he would be killed still never left his religion and preferred to be killed, *MaashaaAllah*.

Now the king's courtier was brought before the king and his fate was the same as the monk, he too refused to renounce his religion and he too was sawn into two halves, and this shows that it is a must for every *Muslim* to be patient in whatever situation he encounters. The question is, should a person be patient if someone threatens to kill him if he does not say statements of *Kufr* (disbelief) or should he accept being killed and not utter such statement of *Kufr*? This issue needs further elaboration! We say, if one is threatened with being killed and the matter is related to him, meaning that he is ordered to do something *Haraam* (forbidden), like declare a statement of *Kufr*, but at the same time he only says it out of fear but his heart contradicts this and faith is still firm in his heart, and if he does not say it he will be killed, the matter is left down to this individual to decide and the affair returns to him; meaning, he may chose, either to remain firm and not utter words of *Kufr* and be killed or he may say these words but at the same time as we said, he is firm upon *Emaan*, but says these words to prevent harm then this too is ok.

As for when the matter is related to the *Deen*, for example if an *Imam* under duress declares a clear statement of disbelief in front of the people and then it is feared that the people will do the same as this, meaning declare similar statements due to this *Imam* making such statements, then in this case it would be forbidden for him to declare such statements before the people; so being patient and being killed would be a better choice for him in that case rather than people going astray due to his statements. As this is a form of *Jihaad*, the *Mujaahid* fights even though he may be killed, as his sole intention is to make the Word of Allah superior and uppermost, so in short if a person is the people's *Imam*, it would be impermissible for him to declare statements of *Kufr* before the eyes of the people, even if this is at a time of great trial and tribulations, rather he should be patient and just be killed.

And also what comes to mind is the true story of the great Imam. Ahmad Ibn Hanbal in which he was trialled with a well-known test, and that was that he was told declare that the Quran was created and that it was not the Speech of Allah; he refused to say that it was created, so he was rebuked and tied to a mule and dragged around the market place as well as flogged severely until he fell unconscious but even when he regained consciousness he still continued to say what he said before: the Quran was not created and that it was the Speech of Allah the Exalted. This noble Imam could not bring himself round to saying such a word of disbelief even though he was being forced to utter such statement of *Kufr* (disbelief). Why? Because the people were waiting to see what Imam Ahmed would say, so had it been the case that he had said it was created the people would have become corrupt. So, he risked his own life for the sake of the *Deen*, and he endured and had much patience, and the outcome was tremendous and all the praises are for Allah. As time passed the ruler at that time passed away and so did the next one, then Allah granted that generation after that a righteous ruler who honoured *Imam* Ahmed and he gained Allah's ﷻ pleasure for being steadfast and the people attested to fact that he remained firm upon the truth, and he disappointed the people of falsehood, so this clearly shows that victory comes and is the result of patience, and Allah grants success!

The young boy refused to renounce his religion so the king ordered that he (the boy) be taken to a tremendously high mountain and if he does renounce his religion, he should be thrown off the mountain; when they reached this mountain they did as the king had ordered them, and they told the young boy to renounce his religion but the boy refused, and that was because faith was firmly engraved in his heart, so when they decided to throw him off the mountain the young boy supplicated: *"O Allah, save me from them in any way you like!"* This is the *Dua* (supplication) the distressed one should make at times of difficulty, meaning *"Help me O Allah as You please!"* The mountain shook, and all the kings companions fell to their death, and the boy came to the king and the king said to him, "Where are your companions?" so the young boy replied, "Allah the Exalted has saved me from them."

Again the king commanded his companions to take the young boy out to the middle of the sea by boat and if he does not renounce his faith, to throw him overboard into the sea. When they, as was commanded, reached the middle of the sea they requested the young boy to once again renounce his religion, to disbelieve in Allah the Exalted, but again he refused as he did the first time and supplicated yet again to Allah saying: *"O Allah, save me from them in any way you like!"* The boat turned upside down and they all drowned except the boy and Allah saved him once again, so he returned to the king as he did the first time and the king to him, "Where are your companions?" so the young explained to the king what had happen to them and he said to the king, *"You will not be able to kill me until you do as I till you."* The king asked, *"What is that?"* so the young boy said to him: *"Gather all the people in one place and gather every person of that town, then tie me to a trunk of a tree, then take an arrow from my quiver and say, 'With the Name of Allah, the Lord of the boy.'"* Then the boy said, *"If you do that you will be able to kill me."* So the king did as the boy requested; he gathered all the people in an open field and tied him up and took out an arrow from his quiver, fixed it in to the bow and said: *"With the Name of Allah, the Lord of the young boy."* He then shot the arrow and it hit the boy's temple, the young boy placed his hand upon his temple - the place where the arrow hit him and died. So all the people said: *"We believe in the Lord of this young boy!"* So these people rejected the king and disbelieved in him, and this is what the young man wanted, and that is for the people to believe in Allah and disbelieve in this king.

This part of the *Hadith* is a proof for the following things:

1. The firm *Emaan* (faith) of this young boy, and that he was firm and steadfast on his religion.

2. Clear signs from the signs of Allah - that is, Allah ﷻ honored this boy by accepting his supplication by making the mountain shake ridding him of those who tried to harm him.

3. Allah the Exalted answers the supplication of the distressed when they call upon Him. So if an individual calls upon Allah at the moment of necessity with sure faith that Allah will respond, for sure He responds and that is even it be a disbeliever who

supplicates to Him the Exalted, even though Allah knows that this disbeliever will return after His response to disbelief.

4. The permissibility of jeopardising one's life for a collective benefit for the people; this young boy directed the king to the thing that would kill him, and that was that his arrow would be the only thing that would terminate his life.

Ibn Taymiyyah said regarding this *Hadith*: "This was *Jihad* in the cause of Allah because nothing was lost, rather the people all believed as a result of this boy's actions, he never killed himself and only died, which was anticipated sooner or later."

But we must stress! As for what is done by some people such as using tools, instruments or devices such as bombs that detonate, meaning, they go amongst the disbelievers then blow themselves up along with the disbelievers (i.e. suicide-bombings), then this considered as one killing oneself and we seek refuge from this!

The one who kills himself will be put in the Hellfire to remain in it and this is what a *Hadith* says from the Prophet ﷺ. This is because the one who kills himself in the name of Islam for its benefit, in reality does benefit it in the least! This does not in any way aid or help Islam in any way whatsoever in the least! How could it? How could this benefit Islam if firstly, he kills himself or he kills tens of people or one hundred or say two hundred, in what way does this benefit the *Deen* of Islam? How will people, by seeing such acts, embrace Islam? This story of the boy is not a proof for such actions, rather the opposite! Those who do such bombings only create more hostility in non-Muslims' hearts, hatred, and ill-feelings towards the Muslims and this only makes them increase their attacks even more.

And as we know in Palestine, what the Jews are doing to the people of Palestine; if one Jew is killed by a Muslim, blowing one of them up or six or seven, then what do they do it return? In return these Jews kill say sixty Muslims or at times more! So tell me how the Muslims benefit from this, how?

So what is gained? How does this help the ranks of the Muslims? How?! In what way has a Muslim benefited himself by killing himself? What he has done is wrongly and unjustly killed himself without right, and he has gained nothing by his actions; rather, he is thrown in the Hellfire and we seek refuge in Allah!

Such a person cannot ever be considered a *Shaheed* (a martyr). A person has no excuse (to commit suicide bombings and the likes knowing what we have said), but if on the other hand a person is completely unaware that such an action was Haram and they did this not knowing the Islamic ruling pertaining to it, that it is or was forbidden, we hope and only say hope, that this person may be free from sin. But we would not say regarding such a person that he is considered a *Shaheed* (martyr). No! Why? Because he has not traversed the right path to obtain martyrdom, the prescribed way, and if he sincerely believed he was right due to not being aware of the true Islamic ruling, we say, he who strived hard in a matter hoping or thinking that thing to be correct but made a mistake will get one reward.

[Hadith 31]

Anas ﷺ reported:

مَرَّ النَّبِيُّ صَلَّى اللهُ عَلَيْهِ وسَلَّم بِامْرَأَةٍ تَبْكِي عِنْدَ قَبْرٍ فَقَال: «اتَّقِي اللهَ وَاصْبِرِي» فَقَالَتْ: إِلَيْكَ عَنِّي ،
فَإِنَّكَ لَمْ تُصَبْ بِمُصِيبَتِي، وَلَمْ تَعْرِفْهُ ، فَقِيلَ لَهَا : إِنَّهُ النَّبِيُّ صَلَّى اللهُ عَلَيْهِ وسَلَّم ، فَأَتَتْ بَابَ النَّبِيِّ صَلَّى
اللهُ عَلَيْهِ وسَلَّم ، فَلَمْ تَجِدْ عِنْدَهُ بَوَّابِينَ ، فَقَالَتْ : لَمْ أَعْرِفْكَ ، فقالَ : « إِنَّمَا الصَّبْرُ عِنْدَ الصَّدْمَةِ الأُولَى »
متفقٌ عليه.

The Prophet ﷺ passed by a woman who was crying over a grave and said: "Fear Allah and be patient." She said, "Away from me! My calamity has not befallen you and you are not aware of it." The woman was later told that it was the Prophet (who had advised her). She came to his door where she found no doorkeeper. She said, "(I am sorry) I did not know it was you." The Messenger of Allah ﷺ said: "Patience is only (becoming) at the first (stroke) of grief." [Agreed Upon]

Another narration in Muslim says: *"The woman was crying over her son."*

[EXPLANATION OF HADITH 31]

Anas ﷺ narrates that the Messenger passed by a woman who was crying by a grave over her son who had died; she dearly loved him and was unable to control herself and prevent herself from going to his grave to cry over her loss, so when the Prophet ﷺ saw her he commanded her to fear Allah and to be patient. As for her statement: *"Away from me"*, then what she meant was: go away! This indicates that she felt overwhelming pain due to the loss of her son and for this reason the Prophet ﷺ left her at the grave, but after he left it was said to her, *"That was the Prophet (ﷺ);"* on realizing this she immediately felt guilty and remorseful, and went straight away to his house, and found no one at his door, meaning, he never had anyone guarding his house, so no one was preventing access. So when she saw him she said to him, *"I did not know it was you"*, so the Prophet ﷺ then said to her: *"Patience is only (becoming) at the first (stroke) of grief."*

So, the patience that one is greatly rewarded for is patience that one has at the first instance of the affliction or calamity. As for one doing the opposite and that is not having patience when the trail first occurs, then it is of little avail to the person, rather, it benefits when the calamity first befalls the person and he endures patiently, hoping for Allah's reward for having patience; the afflicted person says:

إِنَّا لِلهِ وَ إِنَّا إِلَيْهِ رَاجِعُونَ اللَّهُمَّ أَجُرْنِي فِي مُصِيبَتِي وَاخْلُفْ لِي خَيْراً مِنْهَا

"To Allah we belong to Him we will return, O Allah compensate me in my trail and give me in return better than it."

In this *Hadith* are the following benefits:

Firstly, it shows the perfect manners of the Prophet ﷺ towards the people and his great desire to always guide the people towards the truth. When the woman said, *"Away from me"*, the Prophet ﷺ did not take revenge, nor did he hit her or shout. Why? Because he knew her situation, what had befallen her, her hurt and pain at the loss of her dear son, and that she was finding it hard to control herself in the matter. So that was the reason why she had left her house to cry at the grave.

Another benefit is that people are excused due to ignorance! Whether they are ignorant of the Islamic rulings or ignorant of how to behave. And this is taken from the *Hadith* when this woman said to the Prophet: *"Away from me!"* She said this to him when he ordered her with good and that was to fear Allah and to be patient, but she did not know that she was addressing the Prophet ﷺ, so for that reason the Prophet excused her.

And also from its benefits, is that it is not befitting that people in charge of the people's affairs have door keepers at their doors or a gate keeper which prevent or bar access to the people from them. But on the other hand, if the people or the one in charge fear that allowing free access will be a burden or a major distraction, in such a case, one may then have such door keepers to limit access or to advice people about the best times to visit. And another reason for a gate keeper is to also prevent people from entering without permission so as to stop them seeing something one might dislike people from seeing in one's house, such as one being in a state of nakedness or seeing one's family in the similar state, as the Prophet ﷺ stated in a *Hadith*; also, one might not want certain individuals to visit or enter his house.

Another benefit is the praiseworthy patience mentioned in the *Hadith*, which should be at the first instance of the calamity! So it is upon an individual to remain patient expecting Allah's reward for enduring and know, that Allah the Exalted takes or gives a person as part of His divine decree.

And also from the benefits is that crying at the grave side decreases one's patience, and for this reason the Prophet ﷺ said to this woman: *"Fear Allah and be patient."* And with regret many people, when someone close to them dies, cry and are in complete confusion at that person's grave side, and again this decreases one's patience, so if you must, then remain in your home and make *Dua* for the deceased individual. This is because it serves no purpose in going to a person's grave and weeping as this will prevent him from moving on in life and have the deceased constantly in his thoughts, and it will be harder for the person to accept his (or her) faith or decree regarding this calamity that has befallen him. So one should try to divert one's attention away from this calamity and put it to rest and do his best to try to forget the affliction, and Allah grant success.

[Hadith 32]

Abu Hurariah ﷺ reported the Messenger of Allah ﷺ said:

« يَقُولُ اللهُ تَعَالَى: مَا لِعَبْدِي المُؤْمِنِ عِنْدِي جَزَاءٌ إِذَا قَبَضْتُ صَفِيَّهُ مِنْ أَهْلِ الدُّنْيَا ثُمَّ احْتَسَبَهُ إِلاَّ الجَنَّة »

رواه البخاري

"Allah the Exalted says: 'I have no reward other than Paradise for a believing slave of Mine who remains patient for My sake when I take away his beloved one from among the inhabitants of the world.'" [Al-Bukhari]

[EXPLANATION OF HADITH 32]

The *Ulema* refer to this *Hadith* as a *Hadith Qudsi* (Sacred narration) which is something that the Prophet ﷺ relates from his Lord. The word *"beloved one"* refers to someone who one has chosen from the people as a friend from among his children, brother, uncle, father, his mother or from one of his friends, i.e. it is general, and could be anyone he chooses as a close and dear friend to him; if Allah takes this close and dear friend from him and this individual is patient expecting nothing but Allah' reward then Allah grants him Paradise.

This *Hadith* is indicates the clear virtue of patience: if a person loses one of his dear and close friends and is patient, Allah will give him Paradise to this it.

And from the benefits of the *Hadith:* it is an indication of the great bounty of Allah the Exalted and His great Generosity upon His slaves; the kingdom belongs entirely to Him, including even you, and the decree or command is at His disposal, so you and your dear close friend belong solely to Allah; if He the Exalted decides to take away this close friend of yours then the reward for being patient is immensely great indeed.

And also from the benefits of the *Hadith:* it indicates that Allah the Exalted does or acts as He pleases, and this is based on the words: *"When I take away his beloved one from among the inhabitants of the world."* So know, Allah ﷻ does as He pleases when He pleases, and one most remember all of Allah's actions befit His Majesty and are good and no evil is to be attributed to Him. For example, if Allah decrees something for a person whom he dislikes, we say that from the view point of this individual, he dislikes what he encounters but to Allah, the matter is different. We will explain: Allah is All-Wise, so He only does things that are wise; He would not do something unless there is great wisdom in that matter and for the benefit of that person or a general benefit for all His creation. So say Allah decrees an affliction upon a person, this is of great benefit to this person even though the person does not perceive this. Why? Because if this person had some shortcomings, then what befalls him may make him turn back to Allah.

It is known that when a person is in a state of luxury and peace, he tends not be in a state of thankfulness towards Allah or grateful; now if he is afflicted, his state changes dramatically, and he runs back to Allah seeking His aid and help, constantly remembering Him! Surely in this trail there was a great benefit for this person even though he perceived it not.

As for the viewpoint of others, it could be that an individual is afflicted but others also benefit greatly from this affliction. Yes this is possible! I will give you an example: an individual builds a house of mud, then it so happens that soon after, such a location is befallen with terrible rain storms; to the owner of this house, a calamity has now befallen him though the people of that locality are rejoicing. Why? They never had rain and were waiting for it, all the while their crops failed and famine took hold of them.

Therefore, something could be, from one angle, considered bad to a person and at the same time, be seen as good to another; so remember, do not always look at a matter on face value; sometimes a matter cannot truly be perceived at that moment, or the matter might seem bad by human perception but in fact this matter is of great benefit to the person as well as the people in general.

Know: our return is to Allah and there is nowhere else except to Him, so one has to always remember not just what is happening to him, but what benefits and lessons may come from this trial or test. This why the author mentions this *Hadith* in this chapter to highlight the great virtue of patience and that, if Allah the Exalted and High takes one person's close dear companion or friend – and he is patient, the reward is nothing but Paradise, and Allah grants success.

[Hadith 33]

Reported from A'ishah ﷺ:

أنَّهَا سَأَلَتْ رسولَ الله صَلَّى الله عَلَيْهِ وسَلَّم عَن الطَّاعونِ ، فَأَخبَرَهَا أنَّهُ كَانَ عَذَاباً يَبْعَثُهُ الله تعالى عَلَى مِنْ يَشَاءُ ، فَجَعَلَهُ اللهُ تعالى رحمةً للْمُؤْمِنينَ ، فَلَيْسَ مِنْ عَبْدٍ يَقَعُ في الطَّاعُون فَيَمْكُثُ في بلَدِهِ صَابِراً مُحْتَسِباً يَعْلَمُ أنَّهُ لاَ يُصِيبُهُ إلاَّ مَا كَتَبَ اللهُ لَهُ إلاَّ كَانَ لَهُ مِثْلُ أجْرِ الشَّهيدِ » رواه البخاري

She asked the Messenger of Allah ﷺ about pestilence and he said: *"It is a punishment which Allah sends upon whomsoever He wills, but Allah has made it a mercy to the believers. Anyone who remains in a town which is plagued with pestilence maintaining patience expecting the reward from Allah, and knowing nothing will befall him other than what Allah has pre-ordained for him, he will receive the reward of a martyr."* [Al-Bukhari]

[Hadith 34]

Anas ﷺ said: I heard the Messenger of Allah ﷺ saying:

« إنَّ اللهَ عَزَّ وجَلَّ قَالَ : إذَا ابْتَلَيْتُ عَبْدِي بِحبيبَتَيْهِ فَصبَرَ عَوَّضْتُهُ مِنْهُمَا الْجنَّةَ » يُرِيدُ عينيْه ، رواه البخاريُّ .

"Allah, the Glorious and Exalted, said: 'When I afflict my slave by his two dear things (i.e. his eyes), and he endures patiently, I shall compensate him for them with Jannah.'" [Al-Bukhari]

[EXPLANATION OF HADITH 33 AND 34]

A'ishah 🌸 asked the Prophet ﷺ about pestilence, and the meaning of what it is, and the reply is that it is a punishment from Allah who sends it upon who whom He wills. Some said, "*Pestilence*" refers to a specific epidemic, while others say it is a general epidemic that inflicts everything, such as the land and the people and everyone dies from it. Whether it is specific or general, like sicknesses or something else, we say it is an impure sickness. Allah the Exalted sends it down, but it is as the *Hadith* says: a mercy to the believers from Allah the Exalted.

If such pestilence befalls a town and the people remain patient hoping and expecting from Allah some reward, knowing nothing could befall them except what Allah has written for them, and then someone dies from such an epidemic, the reward they receive will be that of a *Shaheed* (martyr). And it is narrated in a *Sahih Hadith* that Abdur Rahmaan ibn Auf 🌸 said: the Messenger of Allah ﷺ said:

> "*If you hear about an outbreak of plague in a land, you should not enter it; but if it spreads in the land where you are, you should not depart from it.*"

So, if a pestilence breaks out in a land then one has been forbidden to enter it, as doing so means exposing oneself to destruction, and the same goes the other way, if you are in a land in where such a calamity has befallen, then one is not allowed to leave it in order to flee from the pestilence. Why? Because it is not possible for us to ever flee from Allah's preordained decree! How could running away from Allah's Decree avail you!?

And what comes to mind is the story Allah mentions in the Quran[2] about a pestilence that descended upon a town so its inhabitants fled out of fear, so Allah the Exalted said, *"Die,"* so all of them died, then Allah brought them back to life so as to show them that one can never run or flee from His Divine Decree.

The *Hadith* of A'ishah 🌼 is a proof of the great virtue of patience and hoping in Allah's abundant reward; if a person is in a land in where a pestilence falls and this individual remains in it bearing patiently for Allah's sake and then dies due to this pestilence, he will receive the reward of a martyr.

As for the *Hadith* of Anas - that anyone whom Allah the Blessed takes away their sight and they are patient, then Allah the Exalted will return them to him in Paradise because a man's eyes are very dear to him, so if one is afflicted with their loss, Allah will grant them back to him in Paradise, which has no comparison to this world as the Prophet ﷺ said:

"A space the size of a whip in Paradise is better than this world and all that is in it."

I.e. what is equivalent to one metre or so, and the reason why such a little space is of such great value in Paradise is because this world is debased, worthless, and nearing its end whereas the next life is forever and never comes to an end.

---

[2] Allah the Exalted says: **"Did you (O Muhammad) not think of those who went forth from their homes in thousands, fearing death? Allah said to them, 'Die'. And then He restored them to life. Truly, Allah is full of Bounty to mankind, but most men thank not."** (Surah al-Baqarah, 243)

If Allah takes one of a person's five senses, a person will still have other senses which can still be utilized. You find a blind person might not be able to see but at the same time he has other very strong senses, and as witnessed, you may have even seen someone blind able to walk even in the market places, and he knows where each point that market turns to the left or the right or he knows where every slope or high point is; he is able to converse with a taxi driver to take him from the furthest part of his own town to his home; it is even possible that as he enters his district he is able to direct the taxi man left or right till he reaches his doorstep even though this taxi man has never been to that location before, and surely Allah grants success!

[Hadith 35]

وعنْ عطاءِ بْنِ أَبِي رَباحٍ قالَ : قالَ لِي ابْنُ عبَّاسٍ رضي اللهُ عنهُمَا أَلا أُريكَ امْرَأَةً مِن أَهْلِ الجَنَّةِ؟ فَقُلت : بلَى ، قَالَ : هذهِ المرأَةُ السَّوْداءُ أَتَتِ النبيَّ صَلَّى اللهُ عَلَيْهِ وسَلَّم فقالَتْ : إِنِّي أُصْرَعُ ، وإنِّي أَتكَشَّفُ ، فَادْعُ اللهَ تعالى لِي. قَالَ : « إِن شِئْتِ صَبَرْتِ ولكِ الجَنَّةُ، وإنْ شِئْتِ دعَوْتُ اللهَ تَعَالَى أَنْ يُعافِيَكِ » فقَالَتْ : أَصْبِرُ ، فَقَالت : إِنِّي أَتكَشَّفُ ، فَادْعُ اللهَ أَنْ لا أَتكَشَّفَ ، فَدَعَا لَهَا . مُتَّفقٌ عليْهِ .

Ata' ibn Abi Rabah reported that Ibn Abbas ﷺ asked him whether he would like to be shown a woman from the people of Jannah. When he replied that he certainly would, he said, *"This black woman, who came to the Prophet ﷺ and said: 'I suffer from epilepsy and during my fits my body is exposed, so make supplication to Allah for me.' He replied: 'If you endure it patiently you will be rewarded with Jannah, or if you wish, I shall make supplication to Allah to cure you?' She said, 'I shall endure it.' Then she added, 'But my body is exposed, so pray to Allah that it may not happen.' He (the Prophet ﷺ) then supplicated for her."* [Agreed upon]

[EXPLANATION OF HADITH 35]

Regarding the People of Paradise, then they are divided into two categories: the first are those we bear witness that they are the people of Paradise by their description while the second are those we bear witness due to what has been seen (of them). And we will elaborate more clearly both categories:

As for those who we bear witness to by description, then they are those who are pious God-fearing individuals as Allah the Exalted says in the Quran:

أُعِدَّتْ لِلْمُتَّقِينَ

"Prepared for *Al-Muttaqoon* (pious)." (Aali Imraan 133)

Also He says:

إِنَّ ٱلَّذِينَ ءَامَنُوا۟ وَعَمِلُوا۟ ٱلصَّٰلِحَٰتِ أُو۟لَٰٓئِكَ هُمْ خَيْرُ ٱلْبَرِيَّةِ • جَزَآؤُهُمْ عِندَ رَبِّهِمْ جَنَّٰتُ عَدْنٍ تَجْرِى مِن تَحْتِهَا ٱلْأَنْهَٰرُ خَٰلِدِينَ فِيهَآ أَبَدًا

"Verily, those who believe and do righteous good deeds, they are the best of creatures, their reward with their Lord is Gardens of Eternity (Paradise), underneath which rivers flow, they will abide therein forever)." (Al-Baiyinah 7-8)

Every pious God-fearing person we bear witness that they are from the people of Paradise. But, in saying this, we must stress, we do not say it is so-and-so! Why? Because we do not know what a person's last actions will be, or what he will be upon just before he dies; we do not know what a person is concealing within himself (or herself) - whether what they conceal is the same as what they are manifesting in their actions. To make what we are saying clearer, we will give an example: if a person we know who was upon nothing but good dies, it is hoped - and only hoped - that he will be from the people of Paradise, and we do not say, "This person is from the people of Paradise -or - he is going to Paradise."

As for the second category, then they are those we have known about or heard about and whom the Prophet ﷺ mentioned and bore witness that they are the people going to Paradise. For example, the ten men the Prophet stated will go to Paradise and they are:

1. Abu Bakr
2. Umar
3. Uthmaan
4. Ali
5. Sa'eed ibn Zaid
6. Sa'eed ibn Abi Waqaas
7. AbdurRahman ibn Auf
8. Talha ibn Ubaydullah
9. Abu Ubaydah ibn Aamir ibn Al-Jaraah
10. Az-Zubair ibn Al-Awaam

In addition to the abovementioned companions, Thaabit ibn Qais ibn Shamaasi and Sa'eed ibn Mu'adh and Abdullah ibn Salaam, Bilaal ibn Rabaah and other than them who the Prophet ﷺ had mentioned by name. These people, we bear witness to the fact that they are in Paradise. And included among those we have mentioned is this woman mentioned in the *Hadith*.

This woman would have fits and this led to her being exposes, so she informed the Prophet 鷺 and requested from him to make supplication for her, so he said to her: *"If you to endure it patiently then you will be rewarded with Jannah, or if you wish, I shall make supplication to Allah."* So, she said: *"I shall endure it."* So, even in the case that she would be harmed and pain caused be these fits, she chose to remain patient simply due to the fact that the Prophet 鷺 told her that if she endures it or is patient then she will go the Paradise; she then said (to the Prophet 鷺): *"But my body is exposed, so pray to Allah that it may not happen."* So, the Prophet 鷺 supplicated to Allah on her behalf that she does not expose herself and it was the case that after this incident, she would continue to have these fits but she would not expose herself.

Epilepsy (possession) is of two types - and we seek Allah's refuge from it:

1. **Epilepsy Caused By Fits Of The Body Or By Physical Imbalance**

   And this is considered a sickness within the limbs, and so there is a possibility it can be treated by a doctor through remedies or medicine, either to completely stop it or just calm it if it starts.

2. **Possession caused by the Devils/Shayaateen and the Jinn**

   Jinns are able to possess man and cause him to have fits so bad it could cause him to throw himself to the ground and the effects of this can be so powerful that this person feels (at times) even the least bit of pain. And the *Shayaateen* or *Jinn* are able to possess a person and even talk on this person's tongue and those who listen to this *Shaytaan* or *Jinn* would think that this is the person himself talking. But in the case of a *Jinn*, you will find in some of their speech some differences than that of the individual they are possessing.

This is a type of possession and we seek refuge for ourselves and you from it and from other than it! The prescribed treatment from it is with the Quran and the people of knowledge and people qualified in its field. And at times these *Jinn's* are able to explain to those who are conversing with the possessed person, as to why they have possessed the person. Allah says in the Quran regarding this:

$$ ٱلَّذِينَ يَأْكُلُونَ ٱلرِّبَوٰا۟ لَا يَقُومُونَ إِلَّا كَمَا يَقُومُ ٱلَّذِى يَتَخَبَّطُهُ ٱلشَّيْطَٰنُ مِنَ ٱلْمَسِّ $$

"Those who eat *Riba* (usury) will not stand (on the Day of Resurrection) except like the standing of a person beaten by *Satan* leading him to insanity." (Al-Baqarah 275)

This is proof that the *Shaytaan* (the Devil) can beat or possess a person which could be by causing the victim to have fits; as for what the *Sunnah* mentions of it then it is the *Hadith* in the *Musnad* of Ahmed:
"The Messenger ﷺ was on one of his travels from among his many travels; he passed a woman whose son was suffering from Jinn possession, so this woman approached

*the Prophet ﷺ who spoke to the Jinn; so this Jinn left this
young boy after the Prophet ﷺ had spoken to it, so the
boy's mother gave the Prophet ﷺ a gift."*

The people of knowledge have also spoken to many
Jinn while they were in the state of possessing the
individual and from them was *Shaykh ul-Islam* Ibn
Taymiyyah.

This type of possession has a cure to prevent it and a cure from
it:

As for preventing it, then its cure is preserving the
prescribed formulas (supplications) of the morning and
evening and *Aayat ul-Kursi*, for whosoever reads it will be a
protected from *Shaytaan*, until morning. Also, reading *Surahs
al-Ikhlaas* and *Falaq* and *Naas*. As for that which is confirmed
by the *Sunnah*, then one should safeguard the morning and
evening supplications as these supplications prevent evil and
harm afflicting a person from *Jinn*.

As for removing it, then if a person is possessed, the Quran
should be read over him, in particular: verses such as those
pertaining to fear, encouraging the remembrance of Allah as
well as the person seeking refuge in abundance and this should
be done until the *Jinn* leaves the person.

The point of reference of the *Hadith* is that the Prophet ﷺ
said to this woman: *"If you to endure it patiently then you will
be rewarded with Jannah."* So, she said: *"I shall endure it."* In
this is a proof of the great virtue of patience and that it is the
reason for one to enter Paradise and Allah grants success.

[Hadith 36]

Abdulla ibn Mas'ud ﷺ reported: I can still recall as if I am seeing
the Messenger of Allah ﷺ relating the story of one of the Prophets
whose people scourged him and shed his blood, while he wiped his
face, saying:

« اللَّهُمَّ اغْفِرْ لِقَوْمِي فَإِنَّهُمْ لا يعْلمُونَ » متفقٌ عَلَيْه .

*"O Allah! Forgive my people, because they certainly do not
know." [Agreed upon]*

[EXPLANATION OF HADITH 36]

This *Hadith* mentions those matters that had happened to the former Prophets, and that is that Allah the Exalted placed upon them the responsibility of conveying His Message to mankind as they are the people most worthy of this task. Allah the Exalted says:

ٱللَّهُ أَعْلَمُ حَيْثُ يَجْعَلُ رِسَالَتَهُۥ

"Allah knows best with whom to place His Message."
(Al-An'aam 124)

The Prophets are charged with the responsibility of carrying Allah's Message, calling people to good and ordering them away from the forbidden and being patience in doing so. All the Messengers were harmed or annoyed by either speech or action and at times they were even killed. Allah the Exalted says:

وَلَقَدْ كُذِّبَتْ رُسُلٌ مِّن قَبْلِكَ فَصَبَرُواْ عَلَىٰ مَا كُذِّبُواْ وَأُوذُواْ حَتَّىٰ أَتَىٰهُمْ نَصْرُنَا وَلَا مُبَدِّلَ لِكَلِمَٰتِ ٱللَّهِ

"Verily (many) Messengers were denied before you (O Muhammad) but were patient; they bore the denial, and they were hurt, till Our help reached them, and none can alter the Words (Decision) of Allah..." (Al-An'aam 34)

The Prophet ﷺ informed the companions that there was a Prophet from the Prophets, and his people denied him and beat him and they only did so due to their total disbelief and rejection of him, such that blood streamed down his face, so he wiped the blood from it saying: *"O Allah! Forgive my people for indeed they do not know!"* This *Hadith* is to be used as a great example, and the Prophet ﷺ did not just relay it for sheer passing time. No! Rather it is a lesson and reminder for us as Allah the Exalted says in the Quran:

$$لَقَدۡ كَانَ فِى قَصَصِهِمۡ عِبۡرَةٌ لِّأُوْلِى ٱلۡأَلۡبَٰبِ$$

"Indeed in their stories, there is a lesson for men of great understanding." (Yusuf 111)

Regarding this word **"lesson"**, the lesson here is patience! Patience should be taken from the Prophets' example, how they endured, whether they were harmed in speech or in action and this was all for the sake of Allah as the Prophet ﷺ said in a line of poetry:

$$هَلْ أَنْتِ إِصْبَعٌ دَمِيتِ ۝ وَفِي سَبِيلِ اللهِ مَا لَقِيتِ$$

"You are not more than a toe which has been bathed in blood in Allah's cause."

It is upon us to be more patient and endure what we hear and encounter in the way of Allah. We must remember whatever harms that we encounter are a means for Allah to exalt our rank or elevate our status as well a means to forgive us our faults or sins. Perhaps the harm one encounters while giving *Dawah* could be one's own fault. Why? It could be due to many shortcomings in the way he (or she) is giving *Dawah*, how he is talking to people or maybe he has not yet perfected his *Dawah* techniques or has problems regarding sincerity

(*Ikhlaas*), or in something general in his *Deen*. Whatever a person has encountered from harm could be expiation for his faults due to these wrong actions he has done. We have to remember a person, no matter how good a *Muslim* he is, has to fall short from time-to-time, and this harm could been a means to help him complete and perfect these shortcomings within himself as well as to perfect his *Dawah* skills or techniques.

Encountering hardship in Allah's way should not deter one in the least, rather one should exhibit patience. As this passing world is short, so one should be patient till Allah's Command comes.

[Hadith 37]

Abu Sa'eed and Abu Hurairah ﷺ reported that the Prophet ﷺ said:

«مَا يُصِيبُ الْمُسْلِمَ مِنْ نَصَبٍ وَلاَ وَصَبٍ وَلاَ هَمٍّ وَلاَ حَزَنٍ وَلاَ أَذًى وَلاَ غَمٍّ ، حَتَّى الشَّوْكَةُ يُشَاكُها إِلاَّ كَفَّرَ اللهُ بِهَا مِنْ خَطَايَاهُ» متفقٌ عليه .

"Never a believer is stricken with a discomfort, an illness, an anxiety, a grief or mental worry or even the pricking of a thorn that but Allah will expiate his sins on account of his patience." [Agreed upon]

[Hadith 38]

Ibn Mas'ud ﷺ reported:

دَخَلْتُ عَلَى النَّبِيِّ صَلَّى اللهُ عَلَيْهِ وَسَلَّم وَهُو يُوعَكُ فَقُلْتُ يا رسُولَ اللهِ إِنَّكَ تُوعَكُ عَكّاً شَدِيداً قال :
«أَجَلْ إِنِّي أُوعَكُ كَمَا يُوعَكُ رَجُلانِ مِنْكُم» قُلْتُ : ذلكَ أَنَّ لَكَ أَجْرَيْنِ ؟ قال : «أَجَلْ ذَلَك كَذَلِك مَا مِنْ مُسْلِمٍ يُصِيبُهُ أَذًى ، شَوْكَةٌ فَمَا وِقَّهَا إِلاَّ كَفَّرَ اللهُ بِهَا سِيِّئَاتِه ، وَحُطَّتْ عنْهُ ذُنُوبُهُ كَمَا تَحُطُّ الشَّجَرَةُ وَرَقَهَا» متفقٌ عليه.

I visited the Prophet ﷺ when he was suffering from fever. I said, "You seem to be suffering greatly, O Messenger of Allah." The Messenger replied: *"Yes I suffer as much as two persons."* I said, "Is that because you will have double reward?" He ﷺ replied that that was so and then said, *"No Muslim is afflicted by a harm, be it the pricking of a thorn or something more (painful than that), but Allah thereby causes his sins to fall away just as a tree sheds its leaf."* [Agreed upon]

[EXPLANATION OF HADITH 37 AND 38]

Both *Hadiths* state that if a *Muslim* is befallen or afflicted by harm, be it the pricking of a thorn or something more painful than that, then that is great for him. Why? Because Allah is testing this individual with trials and tribulations and indeed it is a means for Him to expiate this person's sins, cover them up and decrease's his faults. So, know that a person cannot always be in a state of happiness in this world. No! Life is not like that; rather he will have days when he is sad, days when things are going well and going his way and other days, the opposite.

An individual is always experiencing trials, be it in his health, community, family, etc. whatever the case, the affairs of the believer are always good: if bad befalls him he is patient and if good befalls him he is patient and both states are good for him. Do not think that the harm, pain, and misfortune that has befallen you is to no avail, rather, it brings about much good to you, plenty in fact! And it could be the case that if this person has lost a thing, Allah will return that thing to him or even better than that it, or He may expiate many of his sins and they will fall from him like leaves from a tree and this is a great blessing from Allah the Exalted. The more a person has patience and hopes in Allah's reward, the greater the reward will be.

The afflicted are two types of people:
1. At times the afflicted person realizes the great reward for being patient and he hopes for Allah's reward for enduring this affliction and obtains the following two benefits:
    i.   Expiation for his sins.

ii.   An increase in his (or her) righteous good deeds.

2. At times the afflicted one becomes heedless of the affliction and from being patient and so he encounters some hardness in his heart; at the same time some of his sins may be forgiven or some of sins will be forgiven but he will not obtain a reward and this is because of his absentmindedness in intention.

Therefore, it is biding upon the afflicted person, even if he is been pricked by something as little as a thorn, to hope in Allah's reward for what he has suffered. And this shows Allah's immense generosity and kindness because He afflicts His servant and then from His great bounty and generosity, He forgives His servant's sins because of that. And all praise belongs to Allah!

[Hadith 39]

Abu Hurairah ﷺ reported that the Messenger of Allah ﷺ said:

« مَنْ يُرِدِ اللَّهُ بِهِ خَيْراً يُصِبْ مِنْهُ » : رواه البخاري .

"He whom Allah intends good, He make him suffer from some affliction." [Al-Bukhari]

[Hadith 40]

Anas ﷺ reported that the Messenger ﷺ said:

« لا يَتَمَنينَّ أَحدُكُمُ الْمَوْتَ لِضُرّ أَصَابَهُ ، فَإِنْ كَانَ لا بُدَّ فاعلاً فليقُل : اللَّهُمَّ أَحْيِني ما كانَت الحياةُ خَيْراً لِي وتوفَّني إذَا كَانَتِ الوفاةُ خَيْراً لِي » متفق عليه .

"Let not one of you wish for death because of a misfortune which befalls him. If he cannot help doing so, he should say, 'O Allah, keep me alive as long as you know that life is better for me, and make me die when death is better for me.'" [Agreed upon]

[EXPLANATION OF HADITHS 39 AND 40]

As for the *Hadith* of Abu Hurairah ﷺ, then the following phrase *"Suffer from some affliction"* can be read in the two following ways:

1. "يُصَب": The vowel on top of the *Saad* is *Fat`ha*. When it is read with the *Fat`ha* above the *Saad*, it means that Allah Alone the Exalted has decreed afflictions or trails upon this person to see whether he (or she) will be patient or impatient.

2. "يُصِب": It can be said with the vowel *Kasrah* below the letter *Saad*; the meaning of the word now changes to a general meaning, which is that this individual is afflicted with trails by Allah ﷻ as well as afflictions by others.

If an individual does not endure and is not patient when Allah afflicting him (or her) with many afflictions, then this is an indication that Allah the Exalted has not intended good for this person. The disbelievers are afflicted by Allah the Exalted with many afflictions but persist upon disbelief until they die, so no doubt, this is a clear indication that the Exalted has not intended good for them.

Here we must shed light on something very worthy of mentioning, which is: what is the *Hikmah* (wisdom) in Allah afflicting an individual with afflictions and how can this be said to be a good thing for an individual? The answer to this is, is it not so that afflictions befalling an individual are a means for his sins being expiated? Bearing in mind we have explained this previously, we ask is this not then a good thing for the slave? Yes certainly it is! Certainly a person's sins being forgiven are the best thing for him (or her), without a doubt!

The purpose of afflictions is expiation for wrongdoings or sins. So remember, what is better: to be punished for your sins and wrongdoings in this life or to be punished for them in the next life? Which is better? No doubt, the sane person will say, to be punished for them in this life and meet Allah with no sins. Is this not correct? Yes it is! And as we know this life is quick and passing, not so for the next life! If a person is afflicted with an affliction then how long will that last? But a passing moment, then it is as though the affliction was never there. Am I not right?

So, these afflictions lighten those which one could encounter in the next life which are, as we know, more lasting and more severe and we seek Allah's refuge! In short, Allah expiating your faults by way of afflicting you with many afflictions is of great benefit for you and is a clear indication of Allah intending good for you.

As for the second *Hadith*, then the Prophet ﷺ was forbade that a person longs or wishes for death due to a misfortune befalling him (or her), and this may be due to that individual not being able to cope with or bear such misfortune, so this person wishes for death. And what is meant is that a person says for example: "O Lord! End my life!" This may occur in two ways: either by longing for it through verbal expression or longing for it in one's heart; but only Allah knows if what is happening to this person is really a good thing happening to him, so if one is afflicted with a misfortune one should say:

اللّٰهُمَّ أَعِنِّي عَلَى الصَّبْرِ عَلَيْهِ

"O Allah, help me to be patient in what I'm enduring."

Why is it forbidden for you to long or wish for death? The reason why is because who's to say that this misfortune could not be a good thing that is happening to you! We say, maybe death could be the wrong thing to happen to you! What we mean by this is that maybe you think by you dying, it will put a stop to this misfortune or trial or affliction you have encountered. But not every death puts a stop to grieving.

A man does not know, maybe he will die and face worse punishment in his grave or greater afflictions. If he remains alive there is a higher chance that he (or she) will repent and turn back to Allah and mend that which he was upon from disobedience to Allah the Exalted and become upright again.

Therefore, wish not for death for that which has befallen you! And if the Prophet has forbidden you to merely wish for that, what if you end up actually doing it yourself? And with great regret, many unwise and foolish people are afflicted with something difficult to bear, and end up killing themselves, by hanging, poisoning or another method of suicide. These people go from a light affliction to a greater affliction, and what sense does that make!? How will that bring an end to their suffering? The Prophet ﷺ stated in a *Hadith* that the one who kills himself (of herself) will be continually punished in the blazing Hellfire for a very long time! The Prophet ﷺ said that the one who kills himself using a piece of iron, knife or a nail, or other than that, and used it to plunge it into himself, will continually do likewise in the Hellfire for a very long space or period of time! Or a person who drinks poison will continually be drinking this poison over and over again; whosoever ends his (or her) life by throwing himself off a mountain, will certainly go on and on throwing himself off a mountain in the Hellfire. So such actions are senseless, and the mere fact is one is strictly forbidden from merely wishing for death, so how then could you actually go and commit suicide, and we ask Allah the Exalted and High for good health!

It was the habit of the Prophet ﷺ that whenever He forbade something, he would always mention something to do in its place from the permissible things, as this resembles what Allah the Exalted commands the Muslim to do in the Quran, when He says:

يَـٰٓأَيُّهَا ٱلَّذِينَ ءَامَنُواْ لَا تَقُولُواْ رَٰعِنَا وَقُولُواْ ٱنظُرْنَا وَٱسْمَعُواْ وَلِلْكَـٰفِرِينَ عَذَابٌ أَلِيمٌ

"O you who believe! Say not (to the Messenger) *Raa'ina* (listen to us and we listen to you, which has a negative connotation in Hebrew), but say *Unzurnah* (make us understand) and hear." (Al-Baqarah 104)

And when someone gave the Prophet ﷺ some good dates and he disliked them for some reason, he said (to his Companions): *"Are all the dates of Khaybar like this?"* They said, *"No, but we sell one Saa[3] for two Saa or two Saa for three."* So the Prophet ﷺ said to them: *"Do not do that, rather sell them as they are (bad quality) for (a set price of) Dirhams and sell the good ones for the same price in Dirhams."*[4] Meaning: buy the

---

[3] Saa: A standard measure that equals 2172 grams.

[4] The reason why the Prophet ﷺ forbade them is because it is *Riba* - that is: to sell dry dates for fresh dates. For further reference see *Bidayat ul-Mujtahid, Baab ul-Buyu* by Ibn Rushd. Daarul Kutubul Ilmiyah.

good dates (*al-Janeeb*) which are categorized as the best quality dates; when he ﷺ forbade them he then explained to them what the right thing to do was.

Thus, when the Prophet ﷺ forbade one from wishing for death he then explained what that person should do in such a situation, because wishing for death is an indication of one's lack of patience and not accepting their fate which Allah has destined for him. The alternative supplication the Prophet ﷺ taught refers the matter back to Allah the Exalted, as He knows better about a person's affairs.

Longing for death may prevent one from making repentance and increasing in plentiful righteous deeds as the Prophet ﷺ said in a *Hadith*:

> *"None of you will die except that you will regret; if the person was a good doer he will regret he did not do more, but if he was a wrong doer he will regret that he did not turn more toward Allah in repentance."*[5]

This means, he will have wished he had turned more toward Allah in asking His forgiveness for his sins and he will blame himself for not repenting often enough to Allah. If it is asked, how can one say, *"O Allah, keep me alive as long as you know that life is better for me, and make me die when death is better for me?"* We say, indeed Allah the Exalted knows what will occur, but as for man, then he does not know as Allah says in the Quran regarding this:

$$\text{قُل لَّا يَعْلَمُ مَن فِى ٱلسَّمَـٰوَٰتِ وَٱلْأَرْضِ ٱلْغَيْبَ إِلَّا ٱللَّهُ}$$

---

[5] At-Tirmidhi.

"Say: None in the heavens and the earth knows the *Ghaib* (unseen) except Allah." (An-Naml 65)

Also He says:

وَمَا تَدْرِى نَفْسٌ مَّاذَا تَكْسِبُ غَدًا ۖ وَمَا تَدْرِى نَفْسٌ بِأَيّ أَرْضٍ تَمُوتُ

"No person knows what he will earn tomorrow, and no person knows in what land he will die." (Luqmaan 34)

You know not whether remaining alive is better or the opposite or whether death is better, as it could be the case that death is better for you in some cases. And if it be the case that you supplicate for a person then you should restrict it to saying, "O Allah prolong so-and-so's life if that life he will live is spent in submission and obedience to You!"

If it is asked, did not Maryam the daughter of Imran, long and wish for death? Did she not say in the Quran:

يَٰلَيْتَنِى مِتُّ قَبْلَ هَٰذَا وَكُنتُ نَسْيًا مَّنسِيًّا

"Would that I had died before this, and had been forgotten and out of sight" (Maryam 23)?

The response we give to this is: firstly, we must acknowledge that in respect to the previous Laws before Islam, if they conflict with Islam, then they cannot be used as a decisive definite proof for us to now follow! Why? Because Islam abrogates all the previous religions before it. Secondly, Maryam was not wishing for death, before this nor after, even

117

if she had lived one thousand longer. We do not find her after this continuing to wish for death, so her statement is similar to the statement of Yusuf in the Quran when he said:

أنتَ وَلِيِّ ۦ فِى ٱلدُّنْيَا وَٱلْأَخِرَةِ تَوَفَّنِى مُسْلِمًا وَأَلْحِقْنِى بِٱلصَّـٰلِحِينَ

"You are my *Wali* (Protector, Helper, Supporter, Guardian, etc), in this world and in the Hereafter; cause me to die as a Muslim (the one submitting to Your Will), and join me with the righteous." (Yusuf 101)

This explains what was intended, and not that Yusuf was asking Allah for death or wishing for it. No! Rather, Yusuf was asking Allah the Exalted to make him die upon complete submission to His Will! And we say, this is ok, and that is, that a person says, *"O Allah make me die upon Islam, upon Eemaan, upon Tawheed (singling out Allah Alone in worship) with complete sincerity to none but You,"* or say, *"Make me die while You are pleased with me,"* and supplications similar to this.

One must know the clear difference between the two, that is: wishing for death due to misfortune that has befallen a person and asking Allah the Exalted that He makes him die in a specific way which is pleasing to Him. And the Prophet ﷺ said regarding the believer's affair:

"How wonderful is the case of a believer; there is good for him in everything and this applies only to a believer. If prosperity attends him, he expresses gratitude to Allah and that is good for him; and if adversity befalls him, he endures it patiently and that is better for him."

118

So, we see from this that a Muslim's affair is always good, be it good or bad.

[Hadith 41]

Khabbaab ibn Al-Aratt ﷺ reported:

شَكَوْنَا إِلَى رَسُولِ اللهِ صَلَّى اللهُ عَلَيْهِ وَسَلَّمَ وَهُو مُتَوسِّدٌ بُرْدَةً لَهُ فِي ظِلِّ الْكَعْبَةِ ، فَقُلْنَا: أَلَا تَسْتَنْصِرُ لَنَا
أَلَا تَدْعُو لَنَا ؟ فَقَالَ: قَدْ كَانَ مَنْ قَبْلَكُمْ يُؤْخَذُ الرَّجُلُ فَيُحْفَرُ لَهُ فِي الأَرْضِ فِي جُعِلُ فِيهَا ، ثُمَّ يُؤْتَى
بِالْمِنْشَارِ فَيُوضَعُ عَلى رَأْسِهِ فَيُجعلُ نِصْفَيْن ، وَيُمْشَطُ بِأَمْشَاطِ الحَدِيدِ مَا دُونَ لَحْمِهِ وَعظْمِهِ ، مَا يَصُدُّهُ
ذلكَ عَنْ دِينِهِ ، وَاللهُ لَيتِمَّنَّ اللهُ هَذَا الأَمْرَ حتَّى يَسِيرَ الرَّاكِبُ مِنْ صنعاءَ إِلَى حَضْرَمْوتَ لا يخافُ إِلَّا اللهَ
والذِّئْبَ عَلَى غنَمِهِ ، ولكِنَّكُمْ تَسْتَعْجِلُونَ » رواه البخاري.

We complained to the Messenger of Allah regarding the persecution inflicted upon us by the disbelievers while He was lying in the shade of the Ka'bah, having made a pillow from his cloak. We submitted: "Why do you not supplicate for our prevalence (over our opponents)?" He replied: "Among those people before you, a man would be seized and held in a pit dug for him in the ground and he would be sawed into two halves from his head, and his flesh torn away from his bones with an iron comb; but, in spite of this, he would not wean away from his Faith. By Allah, Allah will bring this matter to its consummation until a rider will travel from San'a to Hadramout fearing none except Allah, and except the wolf for his sheep, but you are in too much of a hurry!" [Al-Bukhari]

وفي رواية : « وهُوَ مُتَوسِّدٌ بُرْدةً وقَدْ لقِينَا مِنَ الْمُشْرِكِين شِدَّةً » .

Another narration states: *"He had placed his cloak under his head and we had been tortured by the polytheists."*

[EXPLANATION OF HADITH 41]

This narration explains that some of the Companions went to the Prophet ﷺ complaining to him that they were suffering from the ill treatment of the Quraish of Makkah, while he was lying in the shade of the Ka'bah, having made a pillow of his cloak. So the Prophet ﷺ explained to them that those who came before them were tested with even harder afflictions then the Companions were encountering, such that a pit would be dug for believer wherein he would be held, then he would be sawed into two halves from his head, and his flesh torn away from his bones with an iron comb and there is no doubt that these are the severest types of torture. Then the Prophet ﷺ made an oath, an oath that Allah will complete this affair, i.e. his message, an invitation to Islam.

This *Hadith* indicates the following:

A proof from Allah's clear proofs confirming the reality of what was to occur from what the Prophet ﷺ foretold. It also indicates a sign from the signs of the Prophet ﷺ, affirming his truthfulness and reliability.

Also, this *Hadith* is a proof that one must endure with patience whatsoever he encounters from misfortunes, trials or tests from the enemies of Islam as success lies in being patient. It is compulsory upon the Muslim to face his affliction with nothing but patience and hoping in Allah's great reward for enduring such afflictions, and wait patiently for Allah's aid and help, and one should not always expect his affairs to always be over in a flash or for the affair to always be easy. No! Rather this was the way Allah the Exalted decreed He would test the true believers, and that is by testing them by way of the disbelievers.

Muslims have certainly been harmed greatly and some of Allah's Prophets were even killed by members of the Children of Israel; undoubtedly, the Prophets have a greater standing with Allah then the caller to Islam and general Muslim, so if it be the case that they were patient, hoping only in victory from Allah, never losing hope or becoming faint hearted as well as being unshakable like solid rocks, then certainly the God-fearing and patient are victorious in the end.

If a patient person is assiduously firm upon the right path, surely there is no doubt he will obtain his intended goals. And this has to be done without confusion and agitation while being alert and sticking and traversing to the correct path as well as being well organized against the enemies of Islam. Then victory is certain, as the enemies of the *Deen*, who are the hypocrites and disbelievers, are upon nothing, nothing whatsoever, and in short, the more organized and arranged we are, the more likely we will overcome their feeble weak plots.

Our enemies exert their efforts, but all their efforts are in vain and to no avail and certainly all their striving against the Muslims will, sooner or later, be to no avail; in fact, they are wasting their time as they will slip sooner or later and that which they strove in building will become a disaster for them - that is to say, if what they have built would count as something worth being built by the Muslims.

Muslims should endure and be patient and stand firm and devise a decisive plan so as to regain the upper hand as we know that our enemies are waiting for a chance to make us fall and they want to push us with their futile plots to make us lose grip of things or make us lose our temper so that we will not be in control of what we are doing. Hence the Prophet ﷺ as well as his Companions endured great tribulation indeed, as well as those before them, and there is no doubt that you yourself must exhibit patience in your life also.

So know, the previous generation practiced patience beyond what is known, and we must not forget that we are the nation and followers of Prophet Muhammad ﷺ, a nation of righteousness and patience, so endure and be patient upon what befalls you until Allah's Command come sand surely the righteous have a good ending.

The Muslim should not remain silent to evils around him, rather, he should have a plan and wait for Allah's victory to prevail. Stay steadfast upon the path as we know our enemies will try to increase the trails we face so as to try to stop us gaining the upper hand, but beware and observant of such futile weak plots and do not be easily deceived! Rather be on guard, as they may plot and plan but certainly Allah the Exalted Is the best at plotting and the best at planning, and Allah grants success.

[Hadith 42]

Ibn Mas'ud ﷺ reported:

لما كانَ يَوْمُ حُنَيْنٍ آثر رسولَ اللهِ صَلَّى اللهُ عَلَيْهِ وسَلَّمَ ناساً في الْقِسْمَةِ : فأَعْطَى الأَقْرَعَ بْنَ حابِسٍ مائةً
مِنَ الإِبِلِ وأَعْطَى عُيَيْنَةَ بْنَ حِصْنٍ مِثْلَ ذلِكَ ، وأَعطى ناساً مِنْ أشرافِ الْعربِ وآثرهُمْ يومئذٍ في الْقِسْمَةِ
. فقالَ رجُلٌ : واللهِ إِنَّ هَذِهِ قِسْمةٌ ما عُدِلَ فِيها ، وما أُريد فِيها وَجهُ اللهِ ، فَقُلْتُ: واللهِ لأُخْبِرَنَّ رَسُولَ
اللهِ صَلَّى اللهُ عَلَيْهِ وسَلَّم ، فأَتيتُهُ فأَخبرتُه بِما قال ، فتغَيَّر وَجْهُهُ حَتَّى كَانَ كَالصِّرْفِ . ثُمَّ قال : « فَمَنْ
يَعْدِلُ إِذَا لَمْ يعدِلِ اللهُ ورسُولُهُ ؟ ثم قال : يرحَمُ اللهُ موسى قَدْ أُوذِيَ بِأَكْثَرَ مِنْ هَذَا فَصبرَ » فَقُلْتُ: لا
جرمَ لا أَرْفعُ إِلَيْهِ بَعْدها حديثاً. متفقٌ عليه .

After the battle of Hunain, the Messenger of Allah ﷺ favored some people during the distribution of spoils (for consolation). He gave Al-Aqra ibn Haabis and Uyainah ibn Hisn a hundred camels each and showed favour also to some more honorable persons among the Arabs. Someone said: "This division is not based on justice and it was not intended to win the pleasure of Allah!" I said to myself: "By Allah! I will inform Messenger of Allah of this." I went to him and informed him; his face became red and he ﷺ said: "Who will do justice if Allah and His Messenger do not?" Then He said: "May Allah have mercy upon on (Prophet) Musa; he was caused more distress than this but he remained patient." Having heard this I said to myself: "I shall never convey anything of this kind to him in the future." [Agreed upon]

[EXPLANATION OF HADITH 42]

Regarding Ibn Mas'ud's ﷺ statement: *"After the battle of Hunain;"* this battle was an expedition in Ta'if and it took place after the conquest of Makkah, and in it the Prophet ﷺ obtained abundant war booty, including a great number of camels, sheep and large amounts of money; then the Prophet ﷺ went to Al-Jahraanah and this is a place at the farthest point from Makkah in the direction of Ta'if. When he ﷺ arrived at this location, he divided and distributed the booty, and gave to certain people in order to win them over and make them incline more toward Islam as well as for their satisfaction and encouragement, and this was given to the influential and respectable notables of the great tribes; one of the men present said: *"This division is not based on justice and it was not intended to win the pleasure of Allah!"* And we seek refuge from such statements! This individual said this regarding the Prophet's ﷺ division of the war booty, and it was because that man overly loved this world and as we know, *Shaytaan* is always compelling man into throwing himself into destruction. So this statement this man made is without a doubt a statement of *Kufr* (disbelief)!

This is saying, that Allah and his Messenger are not just, is based upon this man's opinion that the Prophet ﷺ was not acting justly. And there is no doubt that indeed the Prophet ﷺ intended to win the pleasure of Allah, and he also wanted to win the hearts of some notables from the great clans that were about at that time. And one of the reasons for him ﷺ doing this was to strengthen their Islam. But why? The reason is that if these chief tribe-leaders become strong due to Islam and

Emaan became firm in their hearts, their followers would certainly follow them, which in turn would honour Islam. But ignorance gets the better of some people and we seek refuge, and this ignorance can lead one to his demise!

Abdullah ibn Mas'ud ؓ heard this man's statement and went and told the Prophet ﷺ what this man had said, and the Prophet's ﷺ face immediately changed, and it was like his face changed colour; then the Prophet ﷺ said: *"Who will do justice if Allah and His Messenger do not?"* And the Prophet ﷺ spoke the truth, for who can be more just than Allah and His Messenger? The Prophet ﷺ then said: *"May Allah mercy upon on (Prophet) Musa; he was caused more distress than this but he remained patient!"*

We now come to the point in the *Hadith* where patience is mentioned. The indication of this *Hadith* is that the Prophets were greatly harmed and they too were very patient. So we would like to say, that when this event occurred, it was eight years after the *Hijrah* (migration) and not in the early days of Islam; it happened after Allah the Exalted had made the Prophet ﷺ firmly established, his truthfulness become well known and his prophethood manifested, but even so, this man persisted on making false accusations that the Prophet's ﷺ distribution was distributed unfairly, not intending the pleasure of Allah!

Do not be astonished when you see the likes of this man finding fault with the Prophet ﷺ that the scholars too are defamed without just cause! You find people saying such-and-such about this Shaykh, such-and-such about that Shaykh, describing them in an unbecoming way or manner; the *Shaytaan* always finds a way to encourage man to commit sin and this is also another way he incites these people to slander the *Ulema*. The reason why undermining the status of the *Ulema* and backbiting them is so great a sin and worse than backbiting a general Muslim, is because backbiting the general person (Muslim) only harms the person who is backbitten but on the other hand, backbiting the *Ulema* greatly harms the religion (Islam). Why and how could this be? Because the *Ulema* are the carriers of the *Deen*, protecting it, conveying it, and calling to it, as well as being known to be the most truthful; if their truthfulness is lost in the eyes of the people, being that they are carriers of the *Deen*, then certainly this will distance the masses from Islam. This is how slandering and backbiting harms Islam. As is known, back-biting a layman is a major sin as is likened to eating his (or her) flesh, so if that is the case, then we say the *Ulema's* flesh would be like poison. And that is because of the great harm that occurs when they are backbitten.

So do not be astonished then when you hear the *Ulema* being spoken of badly, because we have just read the *Hadith* and seen how this individual spoke to the Prophet of God ﷺ! So, know that if this is your case, then be patient and hope for certain reward for enduring with Allah's decree for you and remember, the best ending is for the God-fearing.

As long as a person walks upon light and fearing Allah, he does not have to worry about things like this as they will lead to a good ending. With regret you find a person has a friend or someone close to him and this friend makes one mistake or falls short once or he commits one sin and instantly this person is described in the worse way possible or even cursed or backbitten over one mistake he has made.

So, it is upon if you have been spoken badly about, or say backbitten or harmed by way of someone's words to be patient and know that even the Prophets had this done to them and they were harmed greatly, annoyed and belied as well as being called mad, possessed, as well as poets, and those who do witchcraft on people, as Allah the Exalted say in the Quran:

وَلَقَدْ كُذِّبَتْ رُسُلٌ مِّن قَبْلِكَ فَصَبَرُواْ عَلَىٰ مَا كُذِّبُواْ وَأُوذُواْ حَتَّىٰ أَتَىٰهُمْ نَصْرُنَا

"Verily, (many) Messengers were denied before you (O Muhammad) but with patience they bore the denial, and they were hurt, till Our Help reached them." (Al-An'aam 34)

This is what Allah the Exalted says in the Quran. So in this *Hadith* is a proof that it is allowed for the Imam to give away that which is for a beneficial purpose even if he gives more to some over others, as well as this being a benefit for Islam. But in saying this, he should not give to a person based upon person preference at that of the expense of others, rather he, when he sees a greater benefit for Islam, may give others extra and remember that he will be questioned by Allah as to what he does and not forget not to do injustice to himself.

And also from the benefits is that the Prophet would inform about the Messengers before Him and what trails and harms they encountered. This is because the Exalted says in this light:

لَقَدْ كَانَ فِى قَصَصِهِمْ عِبْرَةٌ لِّأُوْلِى ٱلْأَلْبَبِ

"Indeed in their story, there is a lesson for men of understanding." (Yusuf 111)

Also He says:

أُوْلَـٰٓئِكَ ٱلَّذِينَ هَدَى ٱللَّهُ فَبِهُدَىٰهُمُ ٱقْتَدِهْ

"They are those whom Allah had guided, so follow their guidance." (Al-An'aam 90)

So, from this we see that it is upon us also to follow the footsteps of the Prophets pertaining to patience, and endure with patience any harms we encounter and also have hope to receive from Allah the Exalted a great reward for being patient, elevation in degree in both this life and the next, and forgiveness for our sins, and Allah grants success!

[Hadith 43]

Anas ☙ reported that the Messenger of Allah ﷺ said:

« إِذَا أَرَادَ اللهُ بِعَبْدِهِ خَيْرًا عَجَّلَ لَهُ الْعُقُوبَةَ فِي الدُّنْيَا ، وَإِذَا أَرَادَ اللهُ بِعَبْدِهِ الشَّرَّ أَمْسَكَ عَنْهُ بِذَنْبِهِ حَتَّى
يُوَافِيَ بِهِ يَوْمَ الْقِيَامَةِ » .

"When Allah intends good for His slave, He punishes him in this world, but when He intends an evil for His slave, He does not hasten to take him to task but calls him to account on the Day of Resurrection." [At-Tirmidhi]

The Prophet ﷺ also said:

« إِنَّ عِظَمَ الْجَزَاءِ مَعَ عِظَمِ الْبَلَاءِ ، وَإِنَّ اللهَ تَعَالى إِذَا أَحَبَّ قَوْمًا ابْتَلَاهُمْ ، فَمَنْ رَضِيَ فَلَهُ الرِّضَا ، وَمَنْ
سَخِطَ فَلَهُ السُّخْطُ » رواه الترمذي وقَالَ: حديثٌ حسنٌ .

"Indeed the greatness of the reward, depends on the greatness of the trial, and verily if Allah loves a people He trails (or test) them, so whosoever is pleased (with these trails), Allah is pleased with him and whosoever is unhappy (with these trails) Allah is displeased with him." [At-Tirmidhi]

[EXPLANATION OF HADITH 43]

These narrations indicate that all affairs are in the Hands of Allah and He does as He pleases as He Himself says in the Quran:

$$إِنَّ رَبَّكَ فَعَّالٌ لِّمَا يُرِيدُ$$

"Your Lord is the doer of what He will." (Hood 107)

Also the Exalted says:

$$إِنَّ ٱللَّهَ يَفْعَلُ مَا يَشَآءُ$$

"Verily! Allah does what He wills." (Al-Hajj 18)

All affairs are in the Hands of Allah. If the slave falls into error or sin or fails to implement that which he has been commanded, then if Allah wants good for such an individual, He the Exalted hastens this person's punishment in this world and this could be in his wealth, family, directly or through someone not related to him.

No matter what the error this person commits, Allah ﷻ hastens his punishment. Why? As you know, punishments are a means of expiation, so in actual fact, this is a great thing for the punished one; after being punished, the person meets Allah having been forgiven for these sins he had committed, and this person will have been purified completely due to those calamities and tests he had been afflicted with.

The Exalted is preparing his servant to meet Him and in doing so, He honours him, and this is by cleansing him totally from sin, as surely Allah has favored this slave by lessening His

131

punishment upon him; what we mean by this is that, as the punishment of the next life is severer and longer lasting, the punishment of this world is lesser in degree of severity by far. So, from this we see, Allah is decreasing His slave's wrongdoings and lightening the punishment in this world in comparison to the next.

On the other hand, the *Hadith* states that if Allah intends evil for His slave, He grants him respite, ease comfort and a relaxing life free from misfortune and prevents afflictions and harm befalling the slave and by this the slave thinks he has been granted abundant good but in actual fact it is quite the opposite. So the slave meets his Lord carrying abundant masses of reprehensible sins, which he will be punished for and we ask Allah for good health!

Know, if you see a person sinning and falling very short and at the same time you do not notice Allah the Exalted hastening his punishment for these sins he is committing, then Allah has intended nothing but evil for this person. This is because Allah will take him to account for theses sins in the next life as well as punish him for them.

Then the Prophet ﷺ said: *"Indeed the greatness of the reward depends on the greatness of the trial."* This means, depending on how hard the trial is, the more reward one will obtain, and easy trials bring little rewards and great trails bring greater reward and surely Allah is always bestowing abundant blessings upon mankind.

As for the Prophet's ﷺ statement: *"And verily if Allah loves a people He trails (or test) them, so whosoever is pleased (with these trails), Allah is pleased with him and whosoever is unhappy (with these trails) Allah is displeased with him."* This is a glad tiding from Allah to the believers that they will face many trails and afflictions! So think not by such trails that Allah dislikes or even hates you. No! Rather it is the opposite! This is an indication of His love for you; if a person shows displeasure upon encountering such trails then indeed, Allah will become displeased and angry with him and if the individual is content and accepts it and is pleased with Allah's decree and what He has destined for him, surely Allah ﷻ is pleased with him.

And also in this *Hadith* is an incitement towards being patient upon being afflicted with trails, so by this, an individual obtains Allah's great pleasure and truly Allah grants success.

[Hadith 44]

Anas ﷺ reported:

كَانَ ابْنٌ لِأَبِي طَلْحَةَ رضي الله عنه يَشْتَكِي ، فَخَرَجَ أَبُو طَلْحَةَ ، فَقُبِضَ الصَّبِيُّ ، فَلَمَّا رَجَعَ أَبُو طَلْحَةَ قَالَ : مَا فَعَلَ ابْنِي ؟ قَالَتْ أُمُّ سُلَيْمٍ وَهِيَ أُمُّ الصَّبِيِّ : هُوَ أَسْكَنُ مَا كَانَ ، فَقَرَّبَتْ إِلَيْهِ الْعَشَاءَ فَتَعَشَّى ، ثُمَّ أَصَابَ مِنْهَا، فَلَمَّا فَرَغَ قَالَتْ : وَارُوا الصَّبِيَّ ، فَلَمَّا أَصْبَحَ أَبُو طَلْحَةَ أَتَى رَسُولَ اللهِ صَلَّى اللهُ عَلَيْهِ وَسَلَّمَ فَأَخْبَرَهُ، فَقَالَ: « أَعَرَّسْتُمُ اللَّيْلَةَ ؟ قَالَ : نَعَمْ ، قَالَ : « اللَّهُمَّ بَارِكْ لَهُمَا » فَوَلَدَتْ غُلَاماً فَقَالَ لِي أَبُو طَلْحَةَ : احْمِلْهُ حَتَّى تَأْتِي بِهِ النَّبِيَّ صَلَّى اللهُ عَلَيْهِ وَسَلَّمَ ، وَبَعَثَ مَعَهُ بِتَمَرَاتٍ ، فَقَالَ: «أَمَعَهُ شَيْءٌ ؟» قَالَ : نَعَمْ ، تَمَرَاتٌ فَأَخَذَهَا النَّبِيُّ صَلَّى اللهُ عَلَيْهِ وَسَلَّمَ فَمَضَغَهَا ، ثُمَّ أَخَذَهَا مِنْ فِيهِ فَجَعَلَهَا فِي الصَّبِيِّ ثُمَّ حَنَّكَهُ وَسَمَّاهُ عَبْدَ اللهِ متفق عليه .

وَفِي رِوَايَةٍ لِلْبُخَارِيِّ : قَالَ ابْنُ عُيَيْنَةَ : فَقَالَ رَجُلٌ مِنَ الْأَنْصَارِ : فَرَأَيْتُ تِسْعَةَ أَوْلَادٍ كُلُّهُمْ قَدْ قَرَؤُوا الْقُرْآنَ ، يَعْنِي مِنْ أَوْلَادِ عَبْدِ اللهِ الْمَوْلُودِ .

وَفِي رِوَايَةٍ لِمُسْلِمٍ : مَاتَ ابْنٌ لِأَبِي طَلْحَةَ مِنْ أُمِّ سُلَيْمٍ ، فَقَالَتْ لِأَهْلِهَا : لَا تُحَدِّثُوا أَبَا طَلْحَةَ بِابْنِهِ حَتَّى أَكُونَ أَنَا أُحَدِّثُهُ ، فَجَاءَ فَقَرَّبَتْ إِلَيْهِ عَشَاءً فَأَكَلَ وَشَرِبَ ، ثُمَّ تَصَنَّعَتْ لَهُ أَحْسَنَ مَا كَانَتْ تَصَنَّعُ قَبْلَ ذَلِكَ ، فَوَقَعَ بِهَا ، فَلَمَّا أَنْ رَأَتْ أَنَّهُ قَدْ شَبِعَ وَأَصَابَ مِنْهَا قَالَتْ: يَا أَبَا طَلْحَةَ ، أَرَأَيْتَ لَوْ أَنَّ قَوْماً أَعَارُوا عَارِيَتَهُمْ أَهْلَ بَيْتٍ فَطَلَبُوا عَارِيَتَهُمْ ، أَلَهُمْ أَنْ يَمْنَعُوهَا؟ قَالَ : لَا ، فَقَالَتْ : فَاحْتَسِبْ ابْنَكَ . قَالَ : فَغَضِبَ ، ثُمَّ قَالَ : تَرَكْتِنِي حَتَّى إِذَا تَلَطَّخْتُ ثُمَّ أَخْبَرْتِنِي بِابْنِي ، فَانْطَلَقَ حَتَّى أَتَى رَسُولَ اللهِ صَلَّى اللهُ عَلَيْهِ وَسَلَّمَ فَأَخْبَرَهُ بِمَا كَانَ ، فَقَالَ رَسُولُ اللهِ صَلَّى اللهُ عَلَيْهِ وَسَلَّمَ : « بَارَكَ اللهُ لَكُمَا فِي لَيْلَتِكُمَا ». قَالَ : فَحَمَلَتْ ، قَالَ : وَكَانَ رَسُولُ اللهِ صَلَّى اللهُ عَلَيْهِ وَسَلَّمَ فِي سَفَرٍ وَهِيَ مَعَهُ وَكَانَ رَسُولُ اللهِ صَلَّى اللهُ عَلَيْهِ وَسَلَّمَ إِذَا أَتَى الْمَدِينَةَ مِنْ سَفَرٍ لَا يَطْرُقُهَا طُرُوقاً فَدَنَوْا مِنَ الْمَدِينَةِ ، فَضَرَبَهَا الْمَخَاضُ ، فَاحْتَبَسَ عَلَيْهَا أَبُو طَلْحَةَ ، وَانْطَلَقَ رَسُولُ اللهِ صَلَّى اللهُ عَلَيْهِ وَسَلَّمَ . قَالَ : يَقُولُ أَبُو طَلْحَةَ إِنَّكَ لَتَعْلَمُ يَا رَبِّ أَنَّهُ يُعْجِبُنِي أَنْ أَخْرُجَ مَعَ رَسُولِ اللهِ صَلَّى اللهُ عَلَيْهِ وَسَلَّمَ إِذَا خَرَجَ ، وَأَدْخُلَ مَعَهُ إِذَا دَخَلَ ، وَقَدِ احْتَبَسْتُ بِمَا تَرَى . تَقُولُ أُمُّ سُلَيْمٍ : يَا أَبَا طَلْحَةَ مَا أَجِدُ الَّذِي كُنْتُ أَجِدُ ، انْطَلِقْ ، فَانْطَلَقْنَا ، وَضَرَبَهَا الْمَخَاضُ حِينَ قَدِمَا فَوَلَدَتْ غُلَاماً . فَقَالَتْ لِي أُمِّي : يَا أَنَسُ لَا يُرْضِعُهُ أَحَدٌ تَغْدُو بِهِ عَلَى رَسُولِ اللهِ صَلَّى اللهُ عَلَيْهِ وَسَلَّمَ ، فَلَمَّا أَصْبَحَ احْتَمَلْتُ بِهِ إِلَى رَسُولِ اللهِ صَلَّى اللهُ عَلَيْهِ وَسَلَّمَ . وَذَكَرَ تَمَامَ الْحَدِيثِ .

"One of the sons of Abu Talhah was ailing. Abu Talhah went out and the boy died in his absence. When he came back, he inquired, 'How is the boy?' Umm Sulaim, the mother of the boy, replied, 'Better than before.' Then she placed his evening meal before him and he ate it; and thereafter she slept with him. At last, she said to him: 'Arrange for the burial of the boy.' In the morning Talhah went to Messenger of Allah ﷺ and informed of the event. He enquired: 'Did you sleep together last night?' Abu Talhah replied in the affirmative, on which the Prophet ﷺ supplicated: 'O Allah bless them!' Thereafter, she gave birth to a boy. Abu Talhah said to me: 'Take up the boy and carry him to the Prophet ﷺ' and he sent some dates with him. The Prophet ﷺ enquired: 'Is there anything with him?' He said; 'Yes, some dates.' The Prophet ﷺ took a date, chewed it and put it in the mouth of the baby and rubbed the chewed date around the baby's gum and named him 'Abdullah.'" [Agreed upon]

The narration in Al-Bukhari adds: *Ibn Uyainah relates that a man from the Ansar told him that he had seen nine sons of this Abdullah, every one of whom had committed the Noble Quran to memory.*

The narration of Muslim says: *The son of Abu Talhah who was born of Umm Sulaim died. She (Umm Sulaim) said to the members of the family: 'Do not tell Abu Talhah about his son until I mention it to him myself.' Abu Talhah came (home) and she gave him supper. He ate and drank. She then beautified herself in the best way she ever did and he slept with her. When she saw he was satisfied after sexual intercourse with her, she said: 'O Abu Talhah! If some people borrow something from another family and then (the members of the family) ask for its return, would they refuse to give it back to them?' He said, 'No.' She said, 'Then hope reward for your son.' Abu Talhah got angry, and said; 'You left me uniformed until I stained myself (with sexual intercourse) and then you told me about my son!' He went to the Messenger of Allah ﷺ and informed him about the matter. Thereupon the Messenger ﷺ said: "May Allah bless your night you spent together!"*

He (the narrator) said: She conceived. (One day) the Messenger of Allah ﷺ was in the course of a journey and she was along with him. When the Messenger of Allah ﷺ used to come back to Al-Madinah from a journey, he would not enter it (during the night). When the people came near Al-Madinah, she felt labour pains. He (Abu Talhah) remained with her and Messenger of Allah ﷺ proceeded on. Abu Talhah said: 'O Lord! You know that I love to go along with the Messenger of Allah when he goes out and enter along with him when he enters, and I have been detained as You see.' Umm Salaim then said: 'O Abu Talhah, I do not feel (so much pain) as I was feeling earlier, so we better proceed on.' So they proceeded and she felt the labour of delivery as they reached (Al-Madinah) and she gave birth to a male child. My mother said to me: 'O Anas, none should suckle him until you go to Messenger of Allah tomorrow morning.' The next morning I carried the baby with me to the Messenger of Allah ﷺ, and narrated the rest of the story.

[EXPLANATION OF HADITH 44]

This is the *Hadith* of Anas that states Abu Talhah had a son who was very sick - and Abu Talhah was the husband of Anas Ibn Malik's mother (Umm Sulaim) - so while the child was sick, Abu Talhah went out the house for some reason, and the child passed away. So when he (Abu Talhah) returned home he asked his wife how the boy was and she said: *"He is better than before."* And her statement was certainly the truth! What she said was correct because certainly nothing is greater than death (i.e., the suffering came to an end for the child). And Abu Talhah understood from her words, that the boy was recovering from that sickness, so she presented his supper to him and he ate, thinking his son was recovering and then he slept with her, so when he finished she said to him: *"Arrange for the burial of the boy."* Meaning: bury your son as he has passed away.

So when Abu Talhah awoke the next day, he buried his son and informed the Prophet ﷺ of what had happened, so the Prophet ﷺ said to him: *"Did you sleep together last night?"* So, he replied in the affirmative, so the Prophet ﷺ prayed that Allah bless them. Umm Sulaim later gave birth after that to a boy who they named Abdullah who had nine sons, all of whom had committed the entire Quran to memory and this was because of the blessings of the *Dua* (supplication) the Prophet ﷺ had made for them.

This *Hadith* contains the following benefits:

It indicates Umm Sulaim's strength of patience over the death of her son, and this is clear to see in the fact that she concealed that from her husband. And her concealing this fact is known as a type of hinting or concealing a fact. And so, she presented his supper to him, then soon after informed him that he should bury their son.

Also in this *Hadith* is an indication of the permissibility of hinting, hiding, concealing a fact or insinuating something without being direct. What is meant by this is that when an individual speaks, he contradicts what he is intending by his words. So the person who is listening to the statement, thinks something other than what this individual's truly intended. And this is permissible, but with the condition that he (or she) only resorts to this due to a great necessity, or when compelled due to a great pressing need, such as, preventing harm. But as for this not being the case, then one should avoid doing so, as this would be telling a lie, by going against the reality and truth. If for example, someone leaves some of their money with you as a deposit for a period of time out of fear that such-and-such individual (a wrongdoer) will seize it; let's say this wrongdoer comes to you and says, "Do you have so-and-so's money?" so you reply, "No, I swear I do not have so-and-so's money," then this wrongdoer will assume that what you mean is you do not have this person's money. But your intention by saying *"No"* is, *"I do not have this person's money with me right now but in actual fact, maybe this money was deposited somewhere and is not with me at that moment."* So, you are affirming something and not negating it, which is considered hinting or let's say, concealing a fact.

And also from the benefits is the blessings of the Prophet's ﷺ saliva, as indicated in the *Hadith* that Anas ﷺ carried his bother to the Prophet ﷺ with dates for him to chew and give to the baby boy to suck or eat; as the Prophet's ﷺ saliva was absolutely blessed, it was a great blessing for whoever brought their child to the Prophet ﷺ as the first thing to reach the child's belly would be his ﷺ saliva; and this was the practice of many of the Companions whenever one of their children was born. Or the Prophet ﷺ would do this act for the simple fact that the date in and of itself also contains many benefits, so he would want the date to be the first thing to reach the child's stomach.

And also from this *Hadith*, we understand a sign from the signs of Allah, and this is seen from the Prophet's ﷺ supplication for this child who later had nine sons, all whom memorized the entire Quran by heart.

And also from the benefits of this *Hadith*, is the recommendation to name one's child Abdullah as well as AbdurRahman, so if one is able to (name their child either of these two), then this is highly preferred as the Prophet ﷺ said:

> "*Indeed, the best and most beloved of your names to Allah are Abdullah and AbdurRahman.*"

As for what some say is narrated from the Prophet ﷺ:

> "*The most beloved names to Allah are those containing praise or servitude.*"

This narration is baseless and fabricated and cannot be attributed to the Prophet ﷺ. What is confirmed from the Prophet ﷺ is:

> "*Indeed, the best and most beloved names to Allah are Abdullah and AbdurRahman and the most truthful names are al-Haarith (cultivator) and Hammaam (planner).*"

These names reflect the true purpose of a person's existence. And that is: every son of Adam is a cultivator and the same goes that every son of Adam is a planner, he intends to do things and plans his matters. Allah the Exalted says in the Quran:

يَٰٓأَيُّهَا ٱلْإِنسَٰنُ إِنَّكَ كَادِحٌ إِلَىٰ رَبِّكَ كَدْحًا فَمُلَٰقِيهِ

"O Man! Verily, you are returning towards your Lord with your deeds and actions (good or bad) a sure returning." (Al-Inshiqaaq 6)

So, from this we see one is obliged to name his or her child by a good name; by this one can obtain reward, and this is an act of being good to one's child. As for naming one's child a strange name, this could be a risk that could cause him or her to feel restricted in the future. The reason why is because in the future, this child will have children and they too will have to take this odd, unknown foreign name and this too could have an impact on them like it did with their parent! So choose for your offspring good names! And do not forget that it is impermissible for one to name one's children by any of the names of the disbelievers, such as "George," etc. This is *Haraam* and is an act which is equal to imitating them and is not allowed as the Prophet ﷺ said:

"Whoever imitates a people is of them."

We are required to dislike the disbelievers and not to forget they are our sure enemies as well as the enemies of Allah and His Prophet and the righteous, and we must beware of their efforts to make us believe they are our close devoted friends!

Rather, they are Allah's greatest enemies and it does not matter whether the disbeliever is famous and well known or otherwise; it is the same, as a *Kaafir* is a *Kaafir*! And this could even occur when hiring a non-Muslim maid, so we should try to avoid hiring disbelieving men and woman which would only allow them to come into Muslim countries which goes against the follow statement of the Prophet ﷺ:

> *"Remove (all) Jews and Christians from the Arabian Peninsula."*

The Prophet ﷺ also said:

> *"I will shortly expel Jews and Christian's from the Arabian Peninsula."*

The Prophet ﷺ also said during his final illness, while he was saying his farewell to the people:

> *"Expel the Polytheist from the Arabian Peninsula."*

And with great regret many people if they have a choice between a *Muslim* servant of disbeliever they choice the disbeliever over the *Muslim* and we ask Allah for good health. It seems our hearts have greatly deviated and have no inclination towards the *Haqq* (the truth). It seems we have been greatly deceived by the Devil and He has made us believe that the *Kufaar* work harder or longer or even better than a *Muslim* and we seek refuge with Allah thinking like this!

It is said, one of the reasons we say this is only because it is known that the *Kufaar* do not pray, they do not have to go to *Hajj* nor *Umrah* where as we do, and the fast, they do not have to fast in the month of Ramadan, they are constantly hard working throughout the year, which is not the case with us! This does not make them any more important as the Creator of the heavens and earth said in the Quran regarding them:

وَلَأَمَةٌ مُّؤْمِنَةٌ خَيْرٌ مِّن مُّشْرِكَةٍ وَلَوْ أَعْجَبَتْكُمْ ۗ وَلَا تُنكِحُوا ٱلْمُشْرِكِينَ

حَتَّىٰ يُؤْمِنُوا ۚ وَلَعَبْدٌ مُّؤْمِنٌ خَيْرٌ مِّن مُّشْرِكٍ وَلَوْ أَعْجَبَكُمْ ۗ أُوْلَـٰٓئِكَ

يَدْعُونَ إِلَى ٱلنَّارِ ۖ وَٱللَّهُ يَدْعُوٓا إِلَى ٱلْجَنَّةِ وَٱلْمَغْفِرَةِ بِإِذْنِهِۦ

"And a believing female slave is better than a (free) *Muskrik* (idolater), even though she pleases you. They (the idolaters) invite you to the Fire, but Allah invites (you) to Paradise and Forgiveness by His Leave." (Al-Baqarah 221)

So know, it is upon you to advice those who bring these *Kufaar* to the Muslim countries! Surely they have been deceived by *Shaytaan* (the Devil), and what has happened is the *Kufaar* are given presidency over the Muslims and they are helped more by giving them these jobs while the Muslim is forsaken and jobless. Remember, the *Kufaar*, their wealth returns to their own country which no doubt is a *Kaafir* country, so this wealth helps, strengthens, and aids them in countless ways beyond mention! Not to mention it is used to strengthen their strategies against the Muslims! We must not forget that we have to always avoid the *Kufaar* as much as we are able to, in naming ourselves by other than their names, shunning their clubs and gathering places, and we do not show them respect or honour, we avoid preceding them in greeting, and we do not open the pathway to them as the Prophet ﷺ said in a *Hadith*:

142

"Do not greet the Jews and the Christians before they greet you; and when you meet any one of them on the road, force him to go the narrowest part of it."

So, where do we stand regarding the likes of such narrations. Where? Where are we regarding what the Prophet ﷺ has encouraged us to put into practice as he, as we know, did not speak from his desires? The Prophet ﷺ warned us about many vices and evils and many things that lead to one's destruction. One night the Prophet ﷺ awoke and was very alarmed, then said:

"La illaha illallah (There is no true God but Allah)! Woe to the Arabs because of an evil which has drawn near."

This was a warning as well as a rebuke of the Arabs, of coming trials due to vice becoming common; then the Prophet ﷺ said:

"Today an opening of this size has been made in the barrier restraining Ya'jooj and Mu'jooj (Gog and Magog people)."

And he made a circle with thumb and index. Zainab ﷺ said: *"O Messenger of Allah! Shall we perish while still there will be righteous people among us?"* He replied:

"Yes when wickedness prevails."

This word *"Al-Khabath"* (wickedness) here in the *Hadith* means wicked actions and wicked people. When many wicked actions become manifest among the people, then this will lead us to destruction or expose us to it. And if many wicked nasty people populate our land or our country we will be exposed to sheer destruction, and this something witnessed now in our times so we ask Allah to protect our countries from our enemies' plots and plans, whether these plot are from within them or outside, and may He overthrow the hypocrites and disbelievers from such plots and plan. Indeed You are All-Generous and All-Kind!

Umm Salaim ﷺ said in the remaining part of the *Hadith* at hand that we are explaining: *"If some people borrow something from another family and then (the members of that family) ask for its return, would they refuse to give it back to them."* Abu Talhah said, *"No."* She said, *"Then hope for reward for your son."* This means: your children are like something borrowed to us and they are Allah' possessions, He does with them as He pleases and He is able to take them away when He desires. Umm Salaim gave him this similitude as a means to make him be at rest regarding what had happened to their son, so if this is your situation be patient and hope in Allah's reward.

So this *Hadith* contains a strong indication of how wise Umm Salaim was and how much she only wanted Allah's reward. This is the reason why she was very patient, and remember a mother is in the same position as the father, meaning that she will also suffer in life like that of a man and it may be that due to the woman's nature being weaker and lacking more in patience, she might be grieved even more.

And also from that which can be taken from this *Hadith* is the miracle that happened to Abu Talhah and that was when he went out with the Prophet ﷺ on one of his travels and his wife was with him, so when the Prophet ﷺ was returning from that journey Abu Talhah's wife fell into labour and that was just before they reached Al-Madinah, so Abu Talhah made

Dua (supplication) to Allah saying: *"O Lord! You know that I love to go along with the Messenger of Allah when He goes out and enter along with him when he enters, and I have been detained as You see."* So, the Exalted answered his *Dua* and his wife said to him: *"I do not feel (so much pain) as I was feeling earlier."* Meaning: she no longer felt the pains of her labour and they just stopped all of a sudden. So they proceeded till they all reached Al-Madinah and entered it with the Prophet ﷺ. As soon as they arrived she gave birth. So in this is a great miracle for Abu Talhah ﷺ.

When the child was born, Umm Salaim ﷺ said to Anas ﷺ who was the child's older brother, that he should take the child to her mother (Umm Sulaim's mother); Umm Salaim's mother said when the child reached her that Anas should take him to the Prophet ﷺ that moment, so that the child could be given the date from the Prophet ﷺ. And it was also the Companions' habit after morning prayer to bring vessels with water in them to ask the Prophet ﷺ to put his hands in them, and the children would carry these vessels to their families so as to receive the blessings from that water. And some of the Companions used to almost fight over the water whenever the Prophet ﷺ would be making *Wudu* and some of the water would fall, the Companions would race to collect the water so as to obtain blessings from it, and this was also the same with his hair and sweat.

Umm Salamah one of the wives who a had container of water containing some of the Prophet's hair in it, and she would use this water for healing purposes, whereby she would receive blessings from this water, but in saying this, it was a specialty that was specific for the Prophet ﷺ and no one else.

Tahneek, like we said is to chew the date and has many benefits, and one of them is that if the date was the first thing to enter the stomach, then it has many benefits and one them is that it helps strengthen the stomach and make it stronger. So the Prophet ﷺ would do this *Tahneek* as well make *Dua* for the child for Allah to bless him.

The main benefit of the *Hadith* is that Umm Sulaim's statement to her husband Abu Talhah: "Then hope for reward for your son." And what she meant was: be patient with what has befallen you and hope in Allah's great reward. And Allah grants success.

[Hadith 45]

Abu Hurairah ﷺ reported that the Messenger of Allah ﷺ said:

« لَيْسَ الشَّديدُ بالصُّرَعةِ إنَّمَا الشَّديدُ الَّذي يَمْلِكُ نَفْسَهُ عِنْدَ الْغَضَبِ » متفقٌ عليه .

"The strong man is not the one who is good at wrestling, but the strong man is the one who controls himself in a fit of rage." [Agreed upon]

[Hadith 46]

Sulaiman ibn Surad ﷺ reported:

كُنْتُ جالِساً مع النَّبِي صَلَّى اللهُ عَلَيْهِ وسَلَّم، ورجُلان يَسْتَبَّانِ وأحدُهُمَا قَدِ احْمَرَّ وَجْهُهُ . وانْتَفَخَتْ أوْداجُهُ . فقال رسولُ الله صَلَّى اللهُ عَلَيْهِ وسَلَّم « إِنِّي لأعْلَمُ كَلِمَةً لَوْ قَالَهَا لَذَهَبَ عنْهُ ما يجِدُ ، لوْ قَالَ : أعوذُ بِاللهِ مِنَ الشَّيْطَانِ الرَّجيمِ ذَهَبَ عنْهُ ما يجِدُ . فقالُوا لَهُ : إنَّ النَّبِيَّ صَلَّى اللهُ عَلَيْهِ وسَلَّم قَالَ : «تعوَّذْ بِاللهِ مِن الشَّيْطان الرَّجيم ». متفقٌ عليه

"I was sitting with the Prophet ﷺ when two men began to quarrel and curse each other and the face of one of them turned red and the veins of his neck were swollen (from rage). The Messenger of Allah ﷺ said: 'I know a word which, if he were to utter it, then his rage would vanish and that is: "A'udhu billahi min ash-Shaytaan nir-rajeem (I seek refuge with Allah from Satan, the accursed)."' So they (Companions) said to him: 'The Prophet ﷺ tells you to seek refuge with Allah from Satan, the accursed)!'" [Agreed upon]

[EXPLANATION OF HADITHS 45 AND 46]

The author, *Imam* An-Nawawi, mentions these two *Hadith* pertaining to anger. Anger is like a live coal that *Shaytaan* (the Devil) places in the heart of the son of Adam and he does this to increase and incite it even more. As a result, one becomes inflamed in rage, his face and eyes become red and his jugular veins swell. A person will say when angry, that which he is unaware of due to his anger and he will let his anger get the better of him, or he will do an action that again, he is completely unable to control; for this reason the Prophet ﷺ made it *the* advice he gave a person who came to him asking for advice as the Prophet ﷺ knew the dangers of getting angry and not controlling it, and what it could lead a person to do; this man came to the Prophet ﷺ and said to him: *"Advise me."* So, the Prophet ﷺ advised this man and said: *"Do not become angry!"* Again this man said to the Prophet ﷺ: *"Advise me."* So, the Prophet ﷺ repeated his words: *"Do not become angry!"* So, this man for a third time said to the Prophet ﷺ: *"Advise me?"* And yet again the Prophet ﷺ gave him, for a third time, the same advice, saying to him: *"Do not become angry!"*

Regarding the *Hadith* where the Prophet ﷺ said: *"The strong man is not the one who is good at wrestling...",* what this means is, one who is strong physically, strong in strength and is able to overcome people and that could be by wrestling the people and winning, and again that is by throwing people to the ground. So this is what the people generally consider as a powerful strong person, but the Prophet said that actually this is not in reality a definition of a strong person, rather he ﷺ said: *"But the strong man is the one who controls himself in a fit of rage."* Meaning: the strong person is the one who can wrestle against his (or her) self, by controlling the self in the fit of rage or anger. So, this is the strong one, the one who is able to subdue his own outbursts of anger or rage, and control this live hot coal *Shaytaan* throws in the heart to enrage a person, as well as repelling it for *Shaytaan* is forever prompting a person using this live coal to make one lose control of their anger.

And from the benefits of this *Hadith*:

It urges a person to reign over their anger, dominate it as well as control it. Why? Because if he (or she) does not, they will only regret what they do after their anger has subsided. For example, say a man became angry and then divorced his wife, maybe this could be the last divorce. And many people, when their anger burns, throw away or even lose their money due to not being able to control their anger. And not controlling one's anger could even lead one to beating their child to death, if the son angers him, this is possible, even beating one's wife brutally, or other then what we have mentioned; any one of these things could happen merely due to a person not controlling himself when he gets angry.

As such, the Prophet ﷺ forbid an Islamic judge to judge between two people when he is angry, and this is because he will not be in the right frame of mind and unable to implement the Law of the Religion regarding their matter and he may give the wrong ruling, and by that ruling, ruin or destroy himself completely.

As for the narration of Sulaiman ibn Surad ,when two men began to quarrel and curse each other in the presence of the Prophet ﷺ and the face of one of them became red and the veins of his neck were swollen from rage, the Prophet ﷺ said: *"I know a word, that if he were to utter that, his rage would vanish, say, "I seek refuge with Allah from Satan, the accursed."* The phrase, *"I seek refuge with Allah"* means seeking Allah's protection. As for the meaning: *"I seek refuge with Allah from Satan, the accursed,"* then this means, turning to Allah for help from what the *Shaytaan* can afflict him with. Based upon this, it is upon the Muslim to, whenever he becomes angry, to brace himself, be patient and seek refuge with Allah the Exalted from the accursed Devil and to perform *Wudu*, because *Wudu* certainly decreases rage and anger. And if a person gets angry and is standing, he should sit and if he is sitting then he should lay down, and lastly, if he gets angry in a particular place he should leave that place, and Allah grants success.

[Hadith 47]

Mu'adh ibn Anas ⬥ reported that the Prophet ﷺ said:

« مَنْ كَظَمَ غَيْظاً ، وهُو قَادِرٌ عَلَى أَنْ يُنْفِذَهُ ، دَعَاهُ اللهُ سُبْحانَهُ وتَعَالَى عَلَى رُؤُوسِ الْخَلَائِقِ يَوْمَ الْقِيَامَةِ
حَتَّى يُخَيِّرَهُ مِنَ الْحُورِ الْعِينِ مَا شَاءَ » رواه أَبُو داوُدَ ، والتِّرْمِذيُّ وقال : حديثٌ حسنٌ .

"The one who suppresses anger and has the power to give effect to it, will be called out by Allah, the Exalted, to the forefront of the creation on the Day of Resurrection and he will be asked to choose any of the virgins (Hur) of his liking." [At-Tirmidhi]

[Hadith 48]

Abu Hurairah ⬥ reported:

أَنَّ رَجُلاً قَالَ لِلنَّبِيِّ صَلَّى اللهُ عَلَيْهِ وسَلَّمَ : أَوْصِنِي ، قَالَ : « لَا تَغْضَبْ » فَرَدَّدَ مِراراً قَالَ ، « لَا تَغْضَبْ »
» رواه البخاريُّ.

A man asked the Prophet ﷺ for advice and he said (to him): "Do not get angry." The man repeated that several times and He (the Prophet ﷺ) replied: "Do not get angry." [Al-Bukhari]

[Hadith 49]

Abu Hurairah ⬥ reported that the Messenger of Allah ﷺ said:

« مَا يَزَالُ الْبَلَاءُ بِالْمُؤْمِنِ وَالْمُؤْمِنَةِ في نَفْسِهِ وَوَلَدِهِ ومَالِهِ حَتَّى يَلْقَى اللهَ تعالى وَمَا عَلَيْهِ خَطِيئَةٌ» رواه
التِّرْمِذيُّ وقال : حديثٌ حسنٌ صحيحٌ .

"A Muslim, male or female, continues to remain under trial in respect to his life, property and offspring until he faces Allah the Exalted, without sin." [At-Tirmidhi]

[EXPLANATION OF HADITHS 47, 48 AND 49]

"Anger" here refers to severe raging anger. Without doubt, someone who is extremely angry, has the ability to give in to this raging outburst of anger, but there will be moments he will be unable to, due to whatever reason, so the most he is able to do is feel saddened or distressed. For this reason, Allah does not mention one feeling sorry, distress or sadness, as these three things are merely human weakness of deficiencies and anger in its right time and place, if it is controlled, is not looked down upon. If one has the ability to let go of this severe anger and rage when someone angers him, and he suppresses it seeking Allah's Face and being patient in what he is undergoing, he will certainly obtain the great reward mentioned in the *Hadith*, i.e. he will be called to the forefront of the creation on the Day of Resurrection and he will be asked to choose any of the virgins (*Hur*) of his liking.

As for the *Hadith* of Abu Hurairah ﷺ, then we have already explained it.

And as for the third *Hadith*: "A *Muslim, male or female, continues to remain under trial in respect to his life, property and offspring until he faces Allah the Exalted, without sin.*" This is proof that if a person remains patient and hoping only for Allah's reward, the Exalted forgives his sins; if a person is tested or trialed with respect to his life, offspring and property a redeeming feature of these trials is that a person's sins are pardoned, so Allah the Exalted continually tests a Muslim until he has no sins recorded against him.

And in this is a strong proof indicating that these trials in one's life, offspring and property are a major reason for the expiation and atonement for that person's wrong doings, until this person walks the earth and not a sin remains with him (or her) but, this has a condition, and that is if that person is patient. On the other hand, if this person is impatient and displeased, then certainly Allah is displeased with those who are displeased at what He has ordained for them and Allah grants success.

[Hadith 50]

Ibn Abbas ﷺ reported:

قَدِمَ عُيَيْنَة بْنُ حِصْنٍ فَنَزَلَ عَلَى ابْنِ أَخِيهِ الْحُرِّ بْنِ قَيْسٍ ، وَكَانَ مِنَ النَّفَرِ الَّذِينَ يُدْنِيهِمْ عُمَرُ رضِيَ اللَّهُ عنهُ ، وَكَانَ الْقُرَّاءُ أَصْحَابَ مَجْلِسِ عُمَرَ رضِيَ اللَّهُ عنه وَمُشَاوَرَتِهِ كُهُولاً كَانُوا أَوْ شُبَّاناً ، فَقَالَ عُيَيْنَةُ لابْنِ أَخِيهِ : يَا ابْنَ أَخِي لَكَ وَجْهٌ عِنْدَ هَذَا الأَمِيرِ فَاسْتَأْذِنْ لِي عَلَيْهِ ، فاسْتَأْذَنَ فَأَذِنَ لَهُ عُمَرُ . فَلَمَّا دَخَلَ قَالَ : هِيْ يَا ابْنَ الْخَطَّابِ ، فَوَاللَّهِ مَا تُعْطِينَا الْجَزْلَ وَلا تَحْكُمُ فِينَا بِالْعَدْلِ ، فَغَضِبَ عُمَرُ رضِيَ اللَّهُ عنه حَتَّى هَمَّ أَنْ يُوقِعَ بِهِ فَقَالَ لَهُ الْحُرُّ : يَا أَمِيرَ الْمُؤْمِنِينَ إِنَّ اللَّهَ تَعَالَى قَالَ لِنَبِيِّهِ صَلَّى اللَّهُ عَلَيْهِ وسَلَّم : ﴿ خُذِ الْعَفْوَ وَأْمُرْ بِالْعُرْفِ وَأَعْرِضْ عَنِ الجاهلين ﴾ [سورة الأعراف: ١٩٨] وإِنَّ هَذَا مِنَ الجاهلينَ، وَاللَّهِ مَا جَاوَزَهَا عُمَرُ حِينَ تلاها ، وَكَانَ وَقَّافاً عِنْدَ كِتَابِ اللَّهِ تعالى. رواه البخاري .

"Uyainah Ibn Hisn came to Al-Madinah and stayed with his nephew Hurr ibn Qais who was among those who Umar showed favour to. The knowledgeable people (Qurra), whether they were old or young had the privilege of joining Umar's council and he used to consult them. Uyainah said to Hurr: 'My nephew, the Leader of the Believers shows favour to you. Will you obtain permission for me to sit with him?' Hurr asked Umar and he accorded permission. When Uyainah came into the presence of Umar he addressed him thus: 'O son of Khattaab, you neither bestow much on us nor deal with us justly.' Umar got angry and was about to beat him up when Hurr said: 'O Leader of the Believers, Allah said to His Prophet: "Show forgiveness, enjoin what is good and turn away from the foolish (i.e. do not punish them)." (Al-A'raaf 199) This one is from the ignorant.' When Hurr recited this (Verse), Umar became motionless in his seat. He always adhered strictly to the Book of Allah." [Al-Bukhari]

[EXPLANATION OF HADITH 50]

The author (Imam An-Nawawi) mentions in the sequence of *Hadiths* pertaining to patience this narration, regarding Umar ibn Khattaab who was the Leader of the Believers and the second successor (to the Prophet 🕮 in leadership), after Abu Bakr, who was the first. And it was well known that Umar was just, pious and very humble and this was even to the point that if a woman would remind him of a Verse from the Quran, he would instantly stop in his tracks and strictly adhere to whatever was been recited to him.

Uyainah Ibn Hisn, who was a noble senior among his tribe, said to Umar: *"O son of Khattaab, you neither bestow much on us nor deal with us justly!"* Look at how this man addressed this well-known successor who was well known for being fair and just!

Ibn Abbas said: *"The knowledgeable people (Qurraa), whether they were old or young, had the privilege of joining Umar's council and he used to consult them."* The meaning of *"Qurraa"* here, is the Companions of the Prophet 🕮, who would sit with Umar, and were considered a class of scholars, that consisted of the young and old, and Umar would seek advice from them in religious matters. This shows that it is upon the ruler or leader to sit with the righteous, because if it is not done, then certainly it could be a cause of his downfall or his destruction as well as the same for the rest of the *Ummah* in general. So, if the ruler or leader is able to sit with the righteous, certainly Allah will make him greatly benefit from such sittings and of course this will certainly bring immense benefit by Allah to the Muslim nation as a whole.

The Companions who used to sit with Umar were well versed (in the Quran) on its meanings, implications as well as the lawful and unlawful, and they would memorize ten verses, learn their interpretations and how to understand them as well as how to apply and practice them and they would not move on to the next ten until this had been done.

When this man said to Umar ﷺ these words, Umar was about to beat him or strike him. So, Hurr Ibn Qais said to Umar: *"O Leader of the Believers! Allah said to His Prophet: 'Show forgiveness, enjoin what is good and turn away from the foolish (i.e. do not punish them).' (Al-A'raaf 199) This one is from the ignorant."* Umar instantly stopped in his tracks and refrained from beating this man, as he would strictly adhere to Book of Allah and accept it as well as be pleased with it. So it was only the Book of Allah that prevented Umar striking this man due to the fact that it was recited to him. And look here at how the Companions behaved and were with regards to the Book of Allah! They would not go any farther in what they were going to do once something was pointed out to them from the Quran. If it was said to them, "This is the Words of Allah!" they would instantly stop in their tracks no matter where they were.

As for Allah's statement: **"Show forgiveness,"** this means: show forgiveness to the people and demand not your full rights as this is something you all not obtain from the people. As for Allah's next statement: **"Enjoin what is good,"** this also means: enjoin what good Islam orders as well as what the people consider as righteous and refrain from enjoining evil and that which is considered bad. Regarding this we say: all affairs are divided into three categories:

1. A wrong doing one is enjoined to prohibit.
2. Something good which one is enjoined to command.
3. Something which has not been enjoined nor been forbidden; rather nothing has been said regarding it.

I advise you that you do not say a word accept it be a good one, as the Prophet ﷺ said in a *Hadith*:

> *"Whoever believers in Allah and the last Day, should either speck good or remain silent."*

As for Allah's words: **"And turn away from the foolish,"** this means: shun the foolish who behave towards you ignorantly, insolently or impudently, and this is not considered as one dishonoring or degrading himself by turning away from such people. Umar ﷺ was not looked down upon when he turned away from this insulting man though he was well capable of punishing this man by beating him. Instead, Umar's actions were in compliance with the command to turn away from the foolish. And Ignorance is of two types:

1. The absence of knowing something.
2. Foolishness and impudence, just as the poet said in *Jaahiliyyah* times (before the advent of *Islam*): "*That if someone behaves towards us in an ignorant way we behave even worse towards him in return.*" This line of poetry means: if an individual acts ignorantly or insolently against you, then in turn you act even more impudent towards him.

As for what Islam says regarding Islamic manners, then it is found in the statement of Allah the Exalted in the Quran:

وَلَا تَسْتَوِى ٱلْحَسَنَةُ وَلَا ٱلسَّيِّئَةُ ٱدْفَعْ بِٱلَّتِى هِىَ أَحْسَنُ فَإِذَا ٱلَّذِى

بَيْنَكَ وَبَيْنَهُۥ عَدَٰوَةٌ كَأَنَّهُۥ وَلِىٌّ حَمِيمٌ

"The good deed and the evil deed cannot be equal, repel (the evil) with one that is better, then verily he between whom and you there was enmity, (will become) as though he was a close friend." (Al-Fussilat 34)

Glory be to Allah! If someone wrongs you, you should repel this evil with nothing but good, and if you do so, you see the results to be as Allah the Exalted says in this verse: **"a close friend."** Meaning: he becomes a close companion and dear friend to you. Who is saying this? It is Allah the Exalted! He, who is the turner of the hearts, and there is no heart belonging to one of the children of Adam, except that it is between the fingers of the All-Merciful and He turns them as He pleases.

In short know, if we become angry or enraged over a matter, whatever it may be, remember to ponder over the Book of Allah and the example of the Prophet ﷺ so as to live by his example and follow his guidance and not go astray. Allah says:

فَإِمَّا يَأْتِيَنَّكُم مِّنِّى هُدًى فَمَنِ ٱتَّبَعَ هُدَاىَ فَلَا يَضِلُّ وَلَا يَشْقَىٰ

"Then if there comes to you guidance from Me, then whoever follows My Guidance shall neither go astray, nor fall into distress and misery." (Taha 123)

[Hadith 51]

Ibn Mas'ud ☼ reported that Messenger of Allah ﷺ said:

« إِنَّهَا سَتَكُونُ بَعْدِي أَثَرَةٌ وَأُمُورٌ تُنْكِرُونَهَا ، قَالُوا : يا رسُولَ اللهِ فَما تَأمُرُنا ؟ قالَ :تُؤَدُّونَ الْحَقَّ الَّذي عَلَيْكُمْ وتَسْألُونَ اللهَ الذي لكُمْ » متفقٌ عليه .

"You will see after me favouritism and things which you will disapprove of." The (Companions) submitted: "What do you order us to do (under such circumstances)?" He replied: "Discharge your obligations and ask your rights from Allah." [Agreed upon]

[Hadith 52]

Usaid ibn Hudhair reported:

يا رسُولَ اللهِ أَلَا تَسْتَعْمِلُني كَمَا اسْتَعْمَلتَ فُلَاناً وفلاناً فَقَالَ :« إنَّكُمْ سَتَلْقَوْنَ أَثَرَةً بَعْدي فاصْبِرُوا حَتَّى تلقَوْني عَلَى الْحَوْضِ » متفقٌ عليه .

"A person from among the Ansar said: 'O Messenger of Allah! You appointed such-and-such person so why do you not appoint me?' The Messenger of Allah ﷺ said: 'After me you will see others given preference to you, but you should remain patient till you meet me at the Haud (Al-Kauthar in Paradise).'" [Agreed upon]

[EXPLANATION OF HADITHS 51 AND 52]

Again the author, Imam An-Nawawi, mentions these *Hadiths* pertaining to patience; as for the first *Hadith*, Ibn Mas'ud reported that the Prophet ﷺ said: *"You will see after me favouritism."* *"Favouritism"* here means to seize or take hold of something others have an entitlement to. And what is intended by this is that there will be rulers who deny the Muslims their rights and give themselves preference over them when the Muslims are entitled to certain rights. This is also a form of wrongdoing and injustice.

The Companions said to the Prophet: *"What do you order us to do?"* So the Prophet ﷺ replied: *"Discharge your obligations."* This means, do not let the withholding of your rights from you cause you in turn to withhold their rights; rather, fulfill your rights towards them, especially, listening and obeying them and not making things difficult and confusing for them. Rather, be patient, listen and obey and do not differ in what Allah has given them from authority.

Then the Prophet ﷺ said: *"And ask your rights from Allah."* Meaning: ask Allah for your rights from them. For example, ask Allah the Exalted to guide them until they fulfill and give you your rights. This *Hadith* shows the wisdom of the Prophet ﷺ, and that he was fully aware of the approaching self and how it can be at times, stingy and miserly, so he encouraged being patient upon favouring oneself over others and giving those who deserve rights what they are owed.

Also, this *Hadith* contains the following benefits:

A proof verifying the truthfulness of the Prophet ﷺ as his information was totally correct in his prophecies, including that some leaders or rulers would take to favoritism with wealth, and of their traits they would be wasteful in their food, drink, clothes and in their riding beasts (transport). As we have said, if it be the case that we witness this ever happening, it is not right for us to repay an evil with an evil.

Another benefit is that this *Hadith* indicates how the Prophet ﷺ applied wisdom in matters of great concern. We know for certain that if these rulers or leaders do not give their subjects their rights and take to favoritism, this will cause the subjects to demand such rights; for this reason, the Prophet ﷺ told them how best to go about requesting such rights, and that is through patience and enduring, giving what is upon us and asking Allah to give us our rights.

The next *Hadith* is from Usaid ibn Hudhair who said that the Prophet ﷺ said: *"You should remain patient till you meet me at the Haud (a pond)."* The meaning is: if you are patient, Allah will reward you for this patience by giving you from the pond of the Prophet ﷺ to drink. O Allah please allow us to be of those who drink from this pond!

Regarding this pond, it which will be seen on the plain of Resurrection and this makes perfect sense on that Day, as the people will yearn for water due to the severity of heat, compulsive sweating, distress as well as over-worrying. The pond's length and breadth can be covered in a month's journey. Its water is whiter than milk and sweeter than honey and smells better than any perfume ever made. It also has as many cups as the stars in the sky. Whosoever drinks from it once will never feel thirsty again. In this *Hadith,* the Prophet ﷺ encourages the Muslims to be patient until they come to the pond and drink from it.

These two *Hadith* contain the following benefits:

A strong encouragement to be patient from what one may witness from favouritism as we said from the rulers and leaders; if the rulers fall short in what is between them and between Allah, Allah makes it clear that He will disgrace them as He say in the Quran:

وَكَذَٰلِكَ نُوَلِّى بَعْضَ ٱلظَّٰلِمِينَ بَعْضًا بِمَا كَانُوا۟ يَكْسِبُونَ

"And thus We make the *Zaalimoon* (polytheist and wrong-doers, etc) supporters and helpers one to another (in committing crimes etc) because of what they used to earn." (Al-An'aam 129)

If the subjects are righteous, Allah the Exalted appoints for them a righteous ruler or leader but if it is the opposite then those in authority over them will like them (unrighteous).

A man from the *Khawaarij* once came to Ali ibn Abi Taalib ﷺ and said, *"Why do the people criticize you and they did not criticize neither Abu Bakr nor Umar?"* Ali ﷺ replied to and said, *"The reason why is because the likes of those people around Abu Bakr and Umar were the likes of me! As for the men around me then they are like you!"* What Ali meant was, as long as the likes of you (the man who questioned Ali) are around and in the midst of the people, you and your likes will cause many people to be divided, making people go against Ali, even to the point that they would kill him (which they did eventually).

It is also said that one of the kings of the Bani Umaymah heard the people were talking about him, so he gathered the most notable of people around him, and if I'm right this king was Abdul Maalik ibn Marwaan; when these nobles had gathered he addressed them saying, "Do you wish I be like Abu Bakr and Umar? So they responded to him and said, *"Yes!"* So he said to them, *"If you want me to be like Abu Bakr and like Umar, then be like those men who used to be around them at that time."* And Allah is the grantor of success.

[Hadith 53]

Abdullah ibn Abu Aufi ⚬ reported that the Messenger of Allah ﷺ during one occasion when he confronted the enemy, and was waiting for the sun to set, stood and said:

وَعَنْ أَبِي إِبْرَاهِيمَ عَبْدِ اللهِ بْنِ أَبِي أَوْفَى رضي اللهُ عنهما أَنَّ رسولَ اللهِ صَلَّى اللهُ عَلَيْهِ وسَلَّم في بَعْضِ أَيَّامِهِ التي لَقِيَ فِيها العَدُوَّ ، انْتَظَرَ حَتَّى إِذَا مَالَتِ الشَّمْسُ قَامَ فِيهِمْ فَقَالَ: « يَا أَيُّهَا النَّاسُ لا تَتَمَنَّوْا لِقَاءَ العَدُوِّ ، وَاسْأَلُوا اللهَ العَافِيَةَ ، فَإِذَا لَقِيتُموهم فاصْبِرُوا ، وَاعْلَمُوا أَنَّ الجَنَّةَ تَحْتَ ظِلالِ السُّيُوفِ » ثُمَّ قَالَ النَّبِيُّ صَلَّى اللهُ عَلَيْهِ وسَلَّم : « اللَّهُمَّ مُنْزِلَ الكِتَابِ وَمُجْرِيَ السَّحَابِ ، وَهازِمَ الأَحْزَابِ ، اهْزِمْهُمْ وَانْصُرْنا عَلَيْهِمْ ». متفقٌ عليه

"O people! Do not long to encounter the enemy and supplicate to Allah to grant you security. But when you face the enemy show patience and steadfastness; and keep in mind that Paradise lies under the shade of swords." Then he invoked Allah saying: *"O Allah, Revealer of the Book, Disperser of the clouds, Defeater of the Confederates, put our enemy to rout and help us in overpowering them!"* [Agreed upon]

[EXPLANATION OF HADITH 53]

This *Hadith* explains that the Prophet ﷺ was out on one of his many expeditions and that he waited till the sun had set. For what reason did he wait until the sun had set? The reason is simple, he did this because it is known that the weather is much cooler when the sun has set, and in doing so there would be more shade as well, making it easier for the Companions to endure; this would surely increase their urge and eagerness to fight, as fighting when the sun is at its highest point entails some hardship and difficulty.

During this time, while waiting for the sun to set, the Prophet ﷺ got up and addressed the Companions, and it was his habit to always address and admonish them just as he would on Fridays at *Jumu'ah,* and at times he would admonish them with or without reason. When there was a reason, or many, and there was a pressing need, he would stand and then address them or admonish them.

On this occasion he stood and said: *"Do not long to encountering the enemy!"* What he meant here is: do not say, "O Allah please let me meet the enemy!" As it is not becoming for a person to wish such a thing; he said instead: *"Supplicate to Allah to grant you security!"* Meaning: ask Allah the Exalted by saying, "O Allah grant me safety and security!"

Then the Prophet ﷺ said: *"But when you face the enemy"* – i.e. if you are tested by meeting them – *"show patience and steadfastness..."* And this is the evidence: that one should endure and be patient when entering into battle and this is to seek the aid and help from Allah ﷻ and strive so that the Word of Allah is most High.

Then the Prophet said: *"And keep in mind that Paradise lies under the shade of swords."* What is meant here is, that Paradise lies under the shade of the sword, i.e. the sword of the *Mujaahid* who fights for the sake of Allah, and the reason why, is because if a *Mujaahid* is killed (during battle) he becomes one of the People of Paradise, as Allah says in the Quran:

وَلَا تَحْسَبَنَّ ٱلَّذِينَ قُتِلُواْ فِى سَبِيلِ ٱللَّهِ أَمْوَٰتًا ۚ بَلْ أَحْيَآءٌ عِندَ رَبِّهِمْ

يُرْزَقُونَ • فَرِحِينَ بِمَآ ءَاتَىٰهُمُ ٱللَّهُ مِن فَضْلِهِۦ وَيَسْتَبْشِرُونَ بِٱلَّذِينَ لَمْ

يَلْحَقُواْ بِهِم مِّنْ خَلْفِهِمْ أَلَّا خَوْفٌ عَلَيْهِمْ وَلَا هُمْ يَحْزَنُونَ ۞

يَسْتَبْشِرُونَ بِنِعْمَةٍ مِّنَ ٱللَّهِ وَفَضْلٍ وَأَنَّ ٱللَّهَ لَا يُضِيعُ أَجْرَ ٱلْمُؤْمِنِينَ

"Think not of those who are killed in the Way of Allah as dead. Nay, they are alive, with their Lord, and they have provision. They rejoice in what Allah has bestowed upon them of His Bounty, rejoicing for those who have not yet joined them, but are left behind (not yet martyred) on them no fear shall come, nor shall they grieve. They rejoice in a Grace and a Bounty from Allah, and that Allah will not waste the reward of the believers." (Aali Imraan 169-171)

The *Shaheed,* when he dies, he does not feel any pain, nor a stab or any hit, and this is due to the fact his soul is taken out and taken to a blissful everlasting place of abundant joys.

One of the Companions of the Prophet ﷺ, Anasi Nadr ؓ said in a narration: *"I can smell the fragrance of Paradise from a place closer than Uhud mount!"* Look at this! Allah allowed this man's senses to open up to smell the fragrance of Paradise! He was killed at the same battle in which he smelt the smell of Paradise, so for this reason the Prophet ﷺ said: *"And keep in mind that Paradise lies under the shade of swords"*

Then the Prophet ﷺ said: *"O Allah, Revealer of the Book, Disperser of the clouds, Defeater of the Confederates, put our enemy to rout and help us in over-powering them."* It is upon the *Mujaahid* to say this *Dua* (supplication) when he meets the enemy just as the Prophet ﷺ would beseech and implore Allah indicating Allah's Lordship, His Attributes and also by way of universal signs.

"Disperser of the clouds" This is one of Allah's universal signs, indicating Allah's ability; the clouds are between the heavens and the earth and none but Allah has control over them. And if all of mankind gathered together to control them (the clouds) they would fail to do so, as Allah alone has this ability to; if intends to disperse them He but says "Be!" and it is.

Then the Prophet ﷺ said. *"Defeater of the Confederates."* Again, Allah Alone has this capability and power to defeat the enemies, and Allah utterly crushed the disbelievers at the battle of *Al-Ahzaab*, even though the disbelievers numbered over ten thousand and the Prophet ﷺ (and Companions) killed them all around *Al-Madinah*. The disbelievers were defeated and their plots were laid in vein and they obtained nothing but disgrace and humiliation, and Allah the Exalted sent upon them severe winds and armies of Angels which made the ground shake beneath them; their tents were blown away and they were unable to stand firmly, and the wind was so strong they could only disperse and flee in rage. Allah says regarding this in the Quran:

$$وَرَدَّ ٱللَّهُ ٱلَّذِينَ كَفَرُواْ بِغَيْظِهِمْ لَمْ يَنَالُواْ خَيْرًا ۚ وَكَفَى ٱللَّهُ ٱلْمُؤْمِنِينَ ٱلْقِتَالَ ۚ وَكَانَ ٱللَّهُ قَوِيًّا عَزِيزًا$$

"And Allah drove back those who disbelieved in their rage, they gained no advantage (booty). Allah sufficed for the believers in the fighting." (Al-Ahzaab 25)

Allah the Exalted defeated the confederates and it is not to be said that this was due to man's efforts; strength can be of use but at the same time it also can be of no avail. So we are still encouraged to take our precautions, but ultimately, and without doubt, Allah is the cause and reason for victory.

From the benefits of this *Hadith*:

The fact that one has been discouraged from longing to meet the enemy does not mean one cannot wish and long for martyrdom. No! Rather wishing for martyrdom is allowed and there is nothing prohibiting it, and at times it is recommended.

A person should ask Allah for safety and security, as nothing is equal to it, so implore and beseech Allah for His aid, victory and help, but when one encounters the enemy, he should endure and remain patient.

If a person encounters the enemy it is *Waajib* upon him to be a patient as Allah says:

يَـٰٓأَيُّهَا ٱلَّذِينَ ءَامَنُوٓاْ إِذَا لَقِيتُمْ فِئَةً فَٱثْبُتُواْ وَٱذْكُرُواْ ٱللَّهَ كَثِيرًا

لَّعَلَّكُمْ تُفْلِحُونَ • وَأَطِيعُواْ ٱللَّهَ وَرَسُولَهُۥ وَلَا تَنَـٰزَعُواْ فَتَفْشَلُواْ

وَتَذْهَبَ رِيحُكُمْ وَٱصْبِرُوٓاْ إِنَّ ٱللَّهَ مَعَ ٱلصَّـٰبِرِينَ

"O you who believe! When you meet (an enemy) force, take a firm stand against them and remember the Name of Allah much (both with tongue and mind), so that you may succeed. And obey Allah and His Messenger, and do not dispute (with one another) lest you lose courage and your strength depart, and be patient. Surely, Allah is with those who are patient." (Al-Anfaal 45-46)

From the benefits of this *Hadith*:

It is upon the commander of an army to be lenient and considerate towards his soldiers and not to start fighting until it is considered a suitable time. He should choose the most practical time, be it the latter time during the day or early part of the day, especially when it is summer and very ho; during such times when it is very hot, it is better to postpone fighting till the weather has cooled down otherwise it would cause some difficulty and hardship upon the fighters. And the same goes when it is very cold, again this could cause some hardship, so it is better that in the winter, to weigh up the pros and cons and neither lean towards being too lax in the matter nor going overboard.

This *Hadith* also shows that this *Dua* is highly recommended: *"O Allah, Revealer of the Book, Disperser of the clouds, Defeater of the Confederates, put our enemy to rout and help us in over-powering them."*

Another benefit is the permissibility to make *Dua* against the disbelievers that Allah defeats them and this is because the disbeliever is an enemy to you, your Lord, the Prophet, the Angels and the Messengers and the Muslims general. And Allah grants success.

باب السلام

THE CHAPTER ON GREETINGS

[Chapter] The Excellence Of Promoting Greetings

Allah, the Exalted says:

يَـٰٓأَيُّهَا ٱلَّذِينَ ءَامَنُواْ لَا تَدْخُلُواْ بُيُوتًا غَيْرَ بُيُوتِكُمْ حَتَّىٰ تَسْتَأْنِسُواْ وَتُسَلِّمُواْ عَلَىٰٓ أَهْلِهَا

"O you who believe! Enter not houses other than your own, until you have asked permission and greeted those in them." (An-Noor 27)

Allah ﷻ also says:

فَإِذَا دَخَلْتُم بُيُوتًا فَسَلِّمُواْ عَلَىٰٓ أَنفُسِكُمْ تَحِيَّةً مِّنْ عِندِ ٱللَّهِ مُبَـٰرَكَةً طَيِّبَةً

"But when you enter the houses, greet one another with a greeting from Allah (i.e. say *As-Salaamu Alaykum* [peace be upon you], blessed and good)." (An-Noor 61)

Also Allah says:

وَإِذَا حُيِّيتُم بِتَحِيَّةٍ فَحَيُّواْ بِأَحْسَنَ مِنْهَآ أَوْ رُدُّوهَآ ۗ إِنَّ ٱللَّهَ كَانَ عَلَىٰ كُلِّ شَىْءٍ حَسِيبًا

"When you are greeted with a greeting, greet in return with what is better than it, or at least return it equally." (An-Nisaa' 86)

Also He says:

هَلْ أَتَىٰكَ حَدِيثُ ضَيْفِ إِبْرَٰهِيمَ ٱلْمُكْرَمِينَ • إِذْ دَخَلُواْ عَلَيْهِ فَقَالُواْ سَلَـٰمًا ۖ قَالَ سَلَـٰمٌ قَوْمٌ مُّنكَرُونَ

"Has the story reached you, of the honourable guest [three angels; Jibreel (Gabriel) along with another two] of (Ibraheem)? When they came in to him, and said, 'Salaaman (peace be upon you)!' He answered: 'Salaamun (peace be upon you), you are a people unknown to me.'" (Az-Zariyaat 24-25)

[EXPLANATION OF THE CHAPTER HEADING AND SUPPORTING VERSES]

Firstly, the meaning of *"Salaam"* or *"Assalaamu Alaykum"*: it is a form of *Dua* (supplication) one is making for the person he is giving this greeting to. What we mean, for example, is: if you meet an individual and greet him, this greeting is a form of supplication for him that Allah the Exalted protects him from all forms of harm such as all forms of illnesses, sicknesses, insanity, as well as afflictions, from falling into sin as well as all forms of sickness of the heart, from him entering the Hell-Fire, etc. It is general, from every possible harm one can encounter.

The Companions of the Prophet used to say in their prayers: *"Peace be upon Allah from His servants, peace be upon (Angel) Jibraeel and upon so-and-so."* Upon realizing this, the Prophet ﷺ forbade them and said: *"(Do not say this;) Indeed Allah is Salaam (the source of peace)."* Meaning: Allah is free from all forms of deficiencies and shortcomings, so there is no point in making supplication for Him, as He Himself is in no need of such supplications as He without need and free of all wants. Then, the Prophet ﷺ taught them what they should say, which was: *"(Say:) Peace be upon us and on the righteous slaves of Allah..."* So let everyone look to himself, whether he is heedful that he is actually supplicating for himself and others. Be mindful of this, for when you are supplicating for peace upon Allah's righteous slaves, it is upon Allah's Prophets and their Companions, such as Eesa (Jesus) and his followers, the Companions of Prophet Muhammad ﷺ, their followers, Musa and his followers - who were seventy in number, and

174

other than them. It is also upon Allah's angels, like Jibraeel, Mikaeel, Israfeel, Maalik - the gate keeper of the Hell-Fire, and upon all the Angels in general. So, take heed and do your best to be aware what you intend and what you say.

Regarding the greeting, Islam legislates the greetings among the Muslims, and has instructed its followers to propagate it. The Prophet ﷺ said:

> *"You will not enter Paradise till you believe, and you will not believe till you love another, shall I tell you something that if you do it, it will cause you to love one another? Promote the greetings among one another."*

And what the Prophet ﷺ meant is greet everyone you meet or make your greetings be known when you meet your fellow Muslim. And the Prophet ﷺ spoke the truth! It is a great cause for love and harmony to be spread. Why? Because we have come to know, that if you meet, say along the path, another Muslim and he avoids greeting you, you instantly have aversion for him. But, on the other hand, if you meet him and he greets you, such a greeting causes you to instantly like and love him, even if he was a stranger. And those with perfect Islam are those who greet those they know and those they don't.

Firstly, regarding the verses pertaining to promoting the greetings, then we say, the greeting is something known among Allah's Prophets and Angels. As we see when the Angels come to Ibraheem ﷺ they said: "*Salaamun* (peace be upon you)!" He answered: "*Salaaman* (peace be upon you)." So from this we see that the greeting *"peace be upon you"* was

175

something known among the Prophets of old as well as Allah's Noble Angels.

The second thing regarding the next verse (An-Noor 27), is that it makes clear that it is forbidden for an individual to enter other than his own home without first seeking permission. This is because if you entered someone else's house without their permission this could scare them, and is considered impolite in the very least. Allah the Exalted goes on to say: **"Greeted those in them."** Meaning: greet (say *"Assalamu Alaykum"*) those in that location, and ask *"may I enter?"* But this is not the same if it is your own house, which one does not have to first seek permission, because it is your house, but one does have to greet those who are in it. And it is the *Sunnah* and practice of the Prophet ﷺ, before giving greetings, to use the *Siwaaq* (tooth stick i.e. brush ones teeth).

Regarding the next verse (Az-Zariyaat 24-25), the words **"Has reached you"** is used to draw the reader's attention; so Allah starts the sentence in the format of a question, which would no doubt make the reader say to himself "No, I have not heard such a story." By this, the reader will give full ear. Regarding Ibraheem's ﷺ statement: "You are a people unknown to me," then the meaning here is that Ibraheem ﷺ did not know them prior to meeting them on that occasion.

In the fourth verse (An-Noor 61), the Exalted says: **"Greet one another."** This means: you should greet those in residences yourselves. And the meaning of "أَنفُسِكُمۡ" (yourselves) here, is that Allah is saying you are part of them, (i.e.) you are all one and together, as the believers are one, strengthing one another and this is simlar to Allah's Words when He says:

لَقَدْ جَآءَكُمْ رَسُولٌ مِّنْ أَنفُسِكُمْ عَزِيزٌ عَلَيْهِ مَا عَنِتُّمْ

"Verily, there has come unto you a Messenger (Muhammad) from among <u>yourselves</u>. It grieves him that you should receive any injury or difficulty." (At-Tawbah 128)

What is intended here is that when you greet those in the dwellings, remember you are all one body, together. And sometimes when the word "yourselves" is used, it could also mean not you, as is the statement of Allah:

وَلَا تَلْمِزُوٓاْ أَنفُسَكُمْ

"Nor defame one another." (Al-Hujaraat 11)

Meaning, do not defame one another and it does not mean do not defame yourself.

And those you greet in these dwellings (be it in yours or in other than yours), it is *Waajib* (obligation) upon them who hear your greeting to respond back (i.e. by saying *"wa alaykumus Salaam"*).

As for the third verse which the author mentioned: **"When you are greeted with a greeting, greet in return with what is better than it, or at least return it equally."** This is an order from Allah the Exalted to return the greeting with that which is better or with that which is equal. So if someone greets you saying: *"Assalamu Alaykum,"* you reply on an equal footing which is by saying *"Wa Alaykumus Salaam,"* and one is not allowed to reply with less than this. And if someone greeted you saying: *"Assalamu Alaykum wa Rahmatullahi,"* you reply equally by responding: *"Wa Alaykumus Salaam wa*

Rahmatullah." And if the person greets you by saying "*Assalamu Alaykum wa Rahmatullahi wa Barakaatuhu,*" you respond: "*Wa Alaykumus Salaam wa Rahmatullahi wa Barkaatuhu.*" This is the way because the Exalted has said: **"Or at least return it equally."** If someone said to you: "*Assalamu Alaykum,*" and you replied: "*Wa Alaykumus Salaam wa Rahmatullah,*" then this is better than his greeting to you but, it is not an obligation.

Allah also says: **"With what is better than it."** And this has many meanings in terms of *type, amount* and *way.*

For example, if someone greets you saying "*Assalamu alaykum*" and you reply by saying: "*Welcome, Hello, Greetings, Hi...*" and the likes, such un-Islamic greetings are unacceptable and will never suffice or be sufficient as a reply. You would be a sinner if you replied in such a manner, and this is because you have not replied equally, and neither have you replied with something better! Why is such a reply a sin? Because this person has given you the Islamic greeting and as we said, it is a form of *Dua* for you and by replying with "*Welcome*" and the likes, which is not a form of supplication, it means you have fallen very short regarding your brother (or sister) and not replied with something equal or better. So this is not a better *type.*

As for *amount*, then it is, if one says to you: "*Assalamalykum wal Rahmatullah,*" you respond by merely saying "*Wa alaykus Salaam*" only! This is not allowed! Why? Because, you have not responded with that which is better or that which is equal.

As for the *way*, if someone greets you in a clear tone or clear voice, you respond in a very low unclear tone or using one side of your mouth, or he greets you face to face but you respond to him facing away from him, this too is also falling short regarding the way he greeted you and is not considered better nor equal to his greeting to you.

And what seems to be apparent from this verse is that if a *Kaafir* greets you, saying in a clear voice: "*Assalamu alaykum*" (peace be upon you), there is no problem if you respond to him by saying: "*Wa alaykumus Salaam* (and to you be peace)!" Why? Because this would be responding equally to his greeting. As for the statement of the Prophet ﷺ:

> "*If the People of the Book (Jews and Christians) greet you, then respond by saying: 'Wa Alaykum (and upon you).'*"

Here, it seems that the Prophet ﷺ was forbidding us to say "*Wa alaykumus Salaam*" if they say: "*As-Saamu Alaykum (May death be upon you)*" i.e. to wish death upon you! But it is ok to respond to their greetings if it is the clear Islamic greeting.

[Hadith 845]

Abdullah ibn Amr reported:

عن عبد الله بن عمرو بن العاص رضي الله عنهما أن رجلا سأل رسول الله صَلَّى اللهُ عَلَيْهِ وسَلَّم أيُّ
الإسلام خَيْرٌ ؟ قال « تُطْعِم الطَّعَامَ ، وَتَقْرَأُ السَّلام عَلَى مَنْ عَرِفْتَ وَمَنْ لَمْ تَعْرِفْ » متفق عليه

A man asked the Messenger of Allah ﷺ: *"Which act in Islam is best?"* He replied: *"To give food, and greet everyone, whether you know (them) or not."* [Agreed upon]

[Explanation of Hadith 845]

Whenever the Prophet's ﷺ Companions asked him a question, it was not merely for the reason of inquiring knowledge. Rather they asked him for none other than to put that knowledge into practice. When they received the knowledge they would race to implement it, and they would never seek knowledge and ask questions to merely test a scholar, as to what he knew from Islamic knowledge.

The Prophet ﷺ said: "*To give food.*" This means, to give food to those who are in need of it, and without doubt, those who are in a greater need of sustenance are first, your family. This is because feeding one's family is a great charity and blessing. Those closest to you have more right and deserve this food more than those who are farther away for it is an obligation upon one to feed one's family, but on the other hand, it is only highly encouraged to feed those who are not family; and the obligatory deed is more beloved to Allah than the encouraged deed. And the proof for this is what is narrated in the *Hadith Al-Qudsi*:

> "*My servant does not draw near to me with anything more beloved to Me than what I have obligated upon him.*"

With regret, some people spend upon their families but forget to make the intention that they are doing it to get close to Allah, but on the other hand if some poor person came to this individual asking him for help and he gives him charity he would make his intention, by this act of charity, to get closer to Allah! With his own family, he is heedless of this but there is no doubt that feeding one's family has a greater and lofty reward, and this is what is considered the best in Islam.

The Prophet ﷺ then said: *"Greet everyone, whether you know (them) or not."* And this is the point of the *Hadith*… the meaning here is, one greets those he knows as well as those he does not; if a person limited his greetings to only those whom he knows, much reward or good would escape him! However, if it is know that the person is a *Kaafir* (disbeliever) then the Muslim is prohibited from initiating the greeting, as the Prophet ﷺ said:

"Do not salute Jews and Christians before they greet you."

This is not just restricted to Jews and Christians; it includes the *Mushrikoon* (polytheists) and *Shia's* and the likes; we do not precede them in greetings and the same goes to the open sinner, one should not greet him, but in this issue, one has to weigh up the pros and cons. What we mean is that, if it serves a great purpose in not saluting him and due to this, the individual repents and refrains from such sin, then this serves a great benefit and avoiding greeting him is better; on the other hand, if not greeting him does not have this effect, and he remains upon the sin and only increases his dislike for you after you have advised him then it would be better for you to greet him. Regarding this the people are divided into the following three groups:

1. Open sinners, manifesting their sin, so we only avoid greeting them if it serves a purpose, if not, then we greet him.

2. The *Kufaar*, who we do not salute first; but, if they salute you first, you may respond to his greetings.

3. The general Muslims not known for openly sinning, in which case, one should strive to be the first to propagate the greeting as this was the habit of the Prophet ﷺ, he would always precede the people in the greetings, and as is known, he was the best the people. Regarding this it is narrated that the Prophet said: *"It is unlawful for a Muslim to forsake his brother for more than three days, turning their heads away from each other. The best of them is the one who greets the other first."*

[Hadith 846]

Abu Hurairah ﷺ reported that the Prophet ﷺ said:

« لَمَّا خَلَقَ اللهُ آدَمَ صَلَّى اللهُ عَلَيْهِ وسَلَّم قال : اذْهَبْ فَسَلِّمْ عَلَى أُولَئِكَ نَفَرٍ مِنَ الْمَلَائِكة جُلُوسٌ فاسْتَمِعْ تَحِيَّتُونَكَ فَإِنَّها تَحِيَّتُكَ وَتَحِيَّةُ ذُرِّيَّتِكَ. فقال : السَّلام عَلَيْكُمْ، فقالوا : السَّلام عَلَيْكَ وَرَحْمَةُ الله ، فَزَادُوهُ : وَرَحْمَةُ الله » متفق عليه

"When Allah created Adam, He said to him: 'Go and greet that company of Angels who are sitting there and then listen to what they are going to say in reply to your greeting because that will be your greeting and that of your off-spring.' Adam said to the Angels, 'Assalamu Alaykum.' They replied: 'Assalamu Alayka wa Rahmatullah' - adding 'wa Rahmatullah' to the greeting." [Agreed upon]

[EXPLANATION OF HADITH 846]

The following benefits can be derived from this *Hadith*:

The first benefit we would like to shed light on and explain is, man was created and there was a period when he was not in existence or worth any mention, as Allah says:

هَلْ أَتَىٰ عَلَى ٱلْإِنسَٰنِ حِينٌ مِّنَ ٱلدَّهْرِ لَمْ يَكُن شَيْئًا مَّذْكُورًا

"Has there not been over man a period of time, when he was nothing to be mentioned." (Al-Insaan 1)

So Allah created mankind for a great lofty purpose, and due to this the Angels said, when Allah was going to create man generations after generations on the earth:

قَالُوٓا۟ أَتَجْعَلُ فِيهَا مَن يُفْسِدُ فِيهَا وَيَسْفِكُ ٱلدِّمَآءَ وَنَحْنُ نُسَبِّحُ بِحَمْدِكَ

وَنُقَدِّسُ لَكَ ۖ قَالَ إِنِّىٓ أَعْلَمُ مَا لَا تَعْلَمُونَ

"[They said:] 'Will You place therein those who will make mischief therein and shed blood - while we glorify You with praise and thanks and sanctify You?' He (Allah) said: 'I know that which you do not know.'" (Al-Baqarah 30)

So Allah ﷻ created man and from them He appointed Messengers, Prophets, the truthful, the martyrs and the righteous.

The second benefit is regarding the Angels, that Allah the Exalted created them with physical bodies or real distinct existences and not merely having souls, they sat which indicates that they have are a physical entity. Prophet Muhammad ﷺ saw Jibraeel in his natural state or how he was originally created, with six hundred wings filling the horizon, as Allah the Exalted says in the Quran:

$$جَاعِلِ ٱلْمَلَٰٓئِكَةِ رُسُلًا أُو۟لِىٓ أَجْنِحَةٍ$$

"Who made the Angels messengers with wings." (Al-Faatir 1)

So the Exalted made them have physical bodies with real distinct existences but at the same time, He has made them unseen to us, and the same goes with the *Jinn*, He has also made them unseen to us. However at times, Allah has made the Angels visible to mankind as in the case of the narration where Jibraeel came to Prophet Muhammad ﷺ in the form of a dog and another time, Jibraeel came to the Prophet ﷺ in the form of a human with no signs of travel with extremely black hair and extremely white clothes, and he sit next to Prophet ﷺ asking him about Islam, *Emaan*, *Ihsaan*, and about the Hour (i.e. Judgement Day) and its signs.

The third benefit from the *Hadith* is, if a person greets a single individual, he greets him with the singular pronoun as was used by the Angels in replying to Adam; they said to him: *"Assalamu Alayka."* If one greets a group of people he uses the plural pronoun: *"Assalamu Alaykum."* And the reason for this is that it conforms to the Arabic language, whereby the single pronoun is used when addressing a single person and the plural pronoun when addressing a group of people.

The forth benefit is, the Angels reply to Adam was a command from Allah as to how Adam's off-spring should reply to each other, because Allah says in this *Hadith*: *"Listen to what they are going to say in reply to your greetings because that will be your greeting and that of your off-spring."* But dear reader, there seems to be a little problem here in this *Hadith*! And the problem is that these Angels replied to his greeting saying: *"Assalamu Alayka wa Rahmatullah."* i.e. it is known that the predicate (*Al-Khabr*) comes first when replying to someone's greeting: *"Alaykas Salaam."* But in this case the Angels did not do this, rather they said to Him: *"Assalamu Alayka."* What we say regarding this is, this seems to have been how the greeting was then at that time or that with the coming of Islam or Law of Muhammad, it changed and become how it is now.

The fifth benefit is, that when someone responds to a person's greeting, it is better to add: *"Wa Rahmatullah."* And in the *Hadith,* this is what we see the Angels responded to Adam's greeting with, because Allah says: **"Greet in return with what is better than it."** The Exalted states in this verse, that one should respond with better first, then He says: **"Or at least return it equally."** This shows it is better to reply to someone's greeting first with that which is better.

[Hadith 847]

Al-Baraa ibn Aazib ﷺ reported:

أمرنا رسولُ الله صَلَّى الله عَلَيْهِ وسَلَّم بِسَبعٍ : «بِعَيادَةِ الَمريضِ . وَاتِّباع الجَنائز ، وَتشْميت العَاطس ، ونصرِ الضَّعيف ، وَعَوْن المظلوم، وإفْشاءِ السَّلام ، وإبرارِ المَقسم » متفق عليه ، هذا لفظ إحدى روايات البخاري

*"The Messenger ﷺ commanded us to do seven things:
'To visit the sick, to follow the funeral (of a dead believer), to invoke the Mercy of Allah upon one who sneezes (i.e., by saying to him Yarhamuk-Allah), to support the weak, to help the oppressed, to promote the greeting of "Assalamu Alaykum", and to help those who swear to do something to keep their oaths.'"
[Agreed upon, the wording is according to one version in Al-Bukhari]*

[Hadith 848]

Abu Hurairah ﷺ reported the Messenger ﷺ said:

« لا تَدْخُلُوا الجَنَّةَ حَتَّى تُؤْمِنُوا وَلا تُؤمِنوا حَتى تَحَابُوا ، أَوَلا أَدُلُّكُمْ عَلَى شيءٍ إذا فَعَلْتُمُوهُ تَحَابَبْتُم ؟ أفْشُوا السَّلام بَيْنَكُم » رواه مسلم

"You will not enter Paradise till you believe, and you will not believe till you love another, shall I tell you something that if you do it, it will cause you to love one another? Promote the greetings among one another." [Muslim]

[Hadith 849]

Abdullah ibn Salaam ❀ reported: I heard the Messenger of Allah ﷺ saying:

« يَا أَيُّهَا النَّاسُ أَفْشُوا السَّلَامَ ، وَأَطْعِمُوا الطَّعَامَ، وَصِلُوا الْأَرْحَامَ ، وَصَلُّوا وَالنَّاسُ نِيَامٌ ، تَدْخُلُوا الْجَنَّةَ بِسَلَامٍ » رواه الترمذي وقال : حديث حسن صحيح

"O people, exchange the greetings of peace (i.e., say 'Assalamu Alaykum' to one another), feed people, strengthen the ties of kinship, and be in prayer when others are asleep, you will enter Paradise in peace." [At-Tirmidhi]

[Hadith 850]

At-Tufail ibn Ubayd ibn Ka'b ❀ reported:

أنه كان يأتي عبد الله بن عمر فيغدو مَعَهُ إلى صاحب بيعة وَلا مسكين وَلا أ حد إلا سَلَّم عَلَيه ، قال الطُّفَيل : فَجِئْتُ عبد الله بنَ عُمرَ يَوْماً فاستَتْبَعَني إلى السُّوقِ فقُلْتُ لَه : ماتَصْنعُ بالسوقِ وأنْتَ لا تَقِفُ على البَيع وَلا تَسْأَلُ عَن السلعِ وَلا تَسُومُ بها وَلا تَجْلِسُ في مجالسِ السّوق ؟ وأقولُ اجْلِسْ بنا ههُنا نَتَحدَّثُ ، فقال يا أبا بَطْن. وَكانَ الطُّفَيلُ ذَا بَطْنٍ إنَّما نَغدو مِنْ أَجْلِ السَّلام نُسَلِّم عَلَى مَنْ لَقِيناهُ ، رواه مالك في المُوطَّأِ بإسناد صحيح

"I used to visit Abdullah ibn Umar in the morning and accompany him to the market. Abdullah offered greetings of peace to everyone he met on the way, be they sellers of petty goods, traders or poor people. One day when I came to him, he asked me to accompany him to the market. I said to him: 'What is the point of you going to the market when you do not sell, or ask about articles, or offer a price for them, or sit down with any company of people? Let us sit down and talk!' He replied: 'O Abu Batn (father of the belly)! (Tufail had a large belly), we go to the market to greet everyone we meet!'" [Al-Muwatta]

[EXPLANTION OF HADITHS 847 TO 850]

We have previously explained the virtues of the greeting so we see no need to repeat the commentary on the *Hadiths* of Al-Baraa ibn Azib, Abu Hurairah and Abdullah ibn Salaam; as for this last *Hadith,* At-Tufail mentions a story of him accompanying Ibn Umar one day to the market, and it was Ibn Umar's habit to greet those in their places of work, those he knew and those he did not. One day Ibn Umar said to At-Tufail: "Come with me to the market." So At-Tufail enquired why when he did not buy anything. Ibn Umar explained he would simply go to these markets for the sole purpose of giving the greetings.

If we hear of a person in the habit of spreading the greetings to the people, then it will be as the Prophet ﷺ said, a cause for him to enter Paradise, as in the *Hadith* of Abu Hurairah, that the Messenger ﷺ said:

> *"You will not enter Paradise till you believe, and you will not believe till you love another; shall I till you something that if you do it, it will cause you to love one another? Promote the greetings among one another."*

The reason for this is: if one person greets someone, he gets ten good deeds and if he greets ten people, he gets one hundred good deeds. There is no doubt that this better than buying and selling in the market, so the reason why Ibn Umar chose the market in particular, was because there were many Muslims there and not many people came to his house, and even if they did, it would amount to the number of people he would see in the market place.

This is proof that a person should not be lax in greeting people but rather he should spread as much greetings as he is able to. If you passed a hundred people on the way to the *Masjid*, greet them all, by this you will obtain one thousand good deeds, and there is no doubt that this is a great blessing from Allah bestowed upon us!

And also another benefit from this is that we see the Companions' great zeal for obtaining rewards for their deeds, as it was Ibn Umar's habit to supersede many other Companions in righteous good deeds. And this brings to mind the narration of Abu Hurairah ﷺ that the Messenger ﷺ said:

> *"Whoever accompanies the funeral procession till it is prayed over will have a reward equal to Qiraat and whoever accompanies it till burial, will get a reward equal to two Qiraat."* It was asked, "What are two Qiraat?" He replied, *"Like two huge mountains, the smallest is like mount Uhud."*

So when Ibn Umar ﷺ was told of this he said: *"Indeed we have lost numerous Qiraat!"* After he was told this, he would always follow the funeral processions. This was the way of the Companions, if they came to know of the great reward of doing righteous deeds, they hastened in doing them and from this, we see that it is upon every Muslim to safeguard and put into practice any deed he comes to know about and be quick in doing so. We ask Allah the Exalted to make us be the swiftest of those who put into practice that which we come to know!

As for Ibn Umar nicknaming At-Tufail, we say one can call a person his epithetic name by way of jest or joking and this is not considered insulting but for mere sport and play, just as in the case of the Prophet ﷺ calling Abu Hurairah *"Abaa Hir"* (father of the cat).

[Chapter] Words to be Used for Offering Greetings

It is recommended for the one offering greetings to say: *"Assalamu Alaykum wa Rahmatullahi wa Barakaatuhu."* The reply is *"Wa Alaykumus Salaamu wa Rahmatullahi wa Barakaatuhu."*

[Hadith 851]

Imraan ibn Husain ﷺ reported:

عن عِمران بن حصين رضي الله عنهما قال : جاءَ رجُل إلى النبي صَلَّى اللهُ عَلَيْهِ وسَلَّم فقال : السَّلامُ
عَلَيكُم ، فَرَدَّ عَلَيْهِ ثم جَلَسَ ، فقال النبي صَلَّى اللهُ عَلَيْهِ وسَلَّم : «عَشْرٌ» ثم جَاءَ آخَرُ فَقَالَ : السَّلامُ
عَلَيكُم وَرَحْمَةُ الله ، فَرَدَّ عليهِ فَجَلَسَ ، فقال : «عِشْرون» ، ثم جَاءَ آخَرُ فَقَالَ : السَّلامُ عَلَيكُم وَرَحْمَةُ
الله وَبَرَكَاتُهُ ، فَرَدَّ عليهِ فَجَلَسَ ، فقال : « ثَلاثُونَ » . رواه أبو داود والترمذي وقال . حديث حسن .

"A man came to the Prophet and said: 'Assalamu Alaykum.' The Messenger of Allah responded to his greetings and the man sat down. The Prophet ﷺ said: 'Ten (meaning the man had earned the merits of ten good acts).' Another one came and said: 'Assalamu Alaykum wa Rahmatullah.' The Messenger of Allah ﷺ responded to his greeting and the man sat down. The Messenger said: 'Twenty.' A third man one came and said: 'Assalamu Alaykum wa Rahmatullahi wa Barakaatuhu.' The Messenger of Allah ﷺ responded to his greeting and the man sat down. The Messenger said: 'Thirty.' [Abu Dawood and At-Tirmidhi]

[Hadith 852]

A'ishah ﷺ reported:

عن عائشة رضي الله عنها قالت : قال لي رسولُ الله صلى الله عليه وسلم :((هذا جبريلُ يَقْرَأُ عَلَيْكِ السَّلَامَ)) قالَتْ : قُلْتُ : ((وَعَلَيْهِ السَّلامُ ورحْمَةُ الله وَبَرَكَاتُهُ)) متفقٌ عليه.

"The Messenger said to me: 'This is Jibraeel (Gabriel) who is conveying you greetings of peace.' I responded: 'Wa Alayhis Salaamu wa Rahmatullahi wa Barakaatuhu.'" [Agreed upon]

[Hadith 853]

Anas ﷺ reported:

أن النبي صَلَّى اللهُ عَلَيْهِ وسَلَّم كان إذا تكلم بِكَلمة أعَادهَا ثَلاثاً حتَّى تُفْهَم عنه، وإذا أتى على قوْم فَسَلَّم عَلَيهم سَلَّم عَلَيهم ثَلاثاً ، رواه البخاري . وهذا محمُولٌ عَلَى ما إذا كان الجَمْعُ كثيراً

"The Prophet used to repeat his words thrice so that the meaning thereof would be fully understood, and whenever he came upon a gathering of people, he would greet them. He would repeat the Salaam thrice." [Al-Bukhari]

[EXPLANATION OF HADITHS 851 TO 853]

The author presents these three *Hadiths* to explain the manner of spreading the Islamic greetings and what greetings one is to say when meeting someone, and what reply one has to make.

So firstly we will comment on the *Hadith* of Imraan ibn Husain. The first person received ten rewards, the second twenty rewards and the third thirty rewards.

Briefly we will go back to the issue on whether one greets a single person saying: *"Assalamu Alayka"* (Peace be upon you) or *"Assalamu Alaykum"* (Peace be upon you all). The *Ulema*, may Allah have mercy upon them, differ regarding this issue! The correct stance regarding this issue is that you should greet the single person using a single pronoun: *"Assalamu Alayka."* And the proof for this is the narration of the man who prayed badly and he greeted the Prophet ﷺ saying: *"Assalamu Alayka."*

As for the *Hadith* of Imraan ibn Husain, then it cannot be used to say that you should say to one person *"Assalamu Alaykum."* Why? Because, the Prophet ﷺ was with a group of the Companions and the Companions joining the gathering were greeting the Prophet ﷺ and those with him. If person adds to his greetings to someone, *"Wa Rahmatullah,"* this is better, and *"Wa Rahmatullahi wa Barakaatuhu"* is even better, because the first addition is ten extra good deeds whereas the second is a further ten (30 in total). If one just greets normally saying *"Assalamu Alayka"* or *"Assalamu Alaykum,"* this would be enough.

The one replying to someone's greetings should reply starting with the *"Wa"* or one could just say: *"Alaykum (us-*

Salaam)." Both ways are ok, and this is what Ibraheem ﷺ replied to the Angels who greeted him:

إِذْ دَخَلُواْ عَلَيْهِ فَقَالُواْ سَلَـٰمًا قَالَ سَلَـٰمٌ قَوْمٌ مُّنكَرُونَ

"(They) said, '*Salaaman* (peace be upon you)!' He answered: '*Salaamun* (peace be upon you).'" (Az-Zariyaat 25)

Here we see Prophet Ibraheem ﷺ not using the "*Waw*"; in short, if one uses the "*Wa*" then that is better, if not, it is still ok without it.

Regarding the *Hadith* of A'ishah ﷻ, if someone informs you that so-and-so conveys his (or her) greeting to you, that which is upon you to reply is: "*Alayka wa Alayhis Salaam*" (Upon you and upon him be peace) or one may say: "*Alayhi wa Alaykas Salaam*" (Upon him and upon you be peace). The reason for you saying "And upon you be peace" is for the one who says to you so-and-so greets you, you are repaying him for carrying so-and-so's greetings to you. But, if one for example said: "So-and-so told me to give you greetings." And you replied: "*Wa Alayhis Salaam*" (And upon him be peace) then this way would also be okay, as indicated in the *Hadith* we are explaining when A'ishah ﷻ said: "*Wa Alayhis Salaamu wa Rahmatullahi wa Barakaatuhu.*" In summary, this shows the matter is one of ease.

If someone says to you, "O so-and-so, if you meet so-and-so, give him my greetings." Is this something upon you to do, i.e. carry his greetings to the person as requested! The *Ulema*, may Allah have mercy upon them, have explained this matter by saying, if the person says to you, "O so-and-so, you must and its upon you to give so-and-so my greetings and do not forget!" Then in this case he has made it a condition upon you that you have to fulfil the request and it becomes a must upon you; the proof they (the *Ulema*) use is Allah's statement in the Quran when He says:

إِنَّ ٱللَّهَ يَأْمُرُكُمْ أَن تُؤَدُّواْ ٱلْأَمَـٰنَـٰتِ إِلَىٰٓ أَهْلِهَا

"Verily! Allah commands that you should render back the trust to those, to whom they are due." (An-Nisaa' 58)

We will conclude by saying, if someone says to you: "Give my greetings to so-and-so" and he makes it a must upon you, "if you meet so-and-so," or "if you remember" and the likes, in this case it is not a must upon you, but if you remember you should convey the greetings.

But dear brothers (and sisters), it is better not to oblige anyone by using terms like "you must!" or "it is upon you!" The reason why we say this is, it could become difficult upon one person to remember to convey that greeting you have asked him to convey, but rather one should use terms such as, "If anyone asks about me, then give them my greetings." So this is better, because you might forget to convey his greetings to so-and-so and say, "I will convey your greetings to so-and-so" out of mere shyness.

As for the *Hadith* of Anas ibn Maalik, then the Prophet ﷺ would only repeat his words if they were not understood. On the other hand, if his words were understood, he would not repeat them. If he was addressing someone and they never caught on to what he was saying and he explained it to them three times and still after that they still never understood, he would leave that matter completely. And the same goes when you greet someone and they do not reply to your greetings, greet them for a second time, and if they still do not reply, it maybe because of some noise around them, or whatever it may be, greet them for a third time, and then if they do not reply leave greeting them completely. If you greet someone and they reply, "*Ahlan wa Marhaban* (welcome)," then in this case you repeat the greetings "*Assalamu Alayka*;" If they still say "*Ahlan*" to you again for the third time, greet them and if they still say "*Ahlan*," you should advise them that what they are doing is wrong and is not allowed and that they must reply saying "*Wa Alaykas Salaam.*"

[Hadith 854]

Al-Miqdaad 🕮 reported in the course of a long *Hadith*:

كُنَّا نَرْفَعُ للنبي صَلَّى الله عَلَيْهِ وسَلَّم نَصِيبهُ مِنَ الَّلبَن فَيَجيءُ مِنَ اللَّيلِ فَيُسَلِّمُ تسليماً لايوقظُ نَائِماً
وَيُسمِعُ الَيَقظان فَجَاء النبي صَلَّى الله عَلَيْهِ وسَلَّم فَسَلَّمَ كما كان يُسَلِم ، رواه مسلم

"We used to reserve for the Prophet 🕮 his share of the milk, and he would come at night and offer greetings in such a manner so as not to disturb those asleep and was heard only by those who were awake...." [Muslim]

[Hadith 855]

Asmaa' bint Yazeed 🕮 reported:

عن أسماء بنتِ يزيد رضي الله عنها أن رسول الله صَلَّى الله عَلَيْهِ وسَلَّم مَرَّ في المَسْجِد يوْماً وَعصْبةٌ مِنَ
النِّساء قُعوُدٌ فألْوَى بِيده بالتسليم. رواه الترمذي وقال : حديث حسن

"The Messenger 🕮 passed through the Masjid one day and there was a group of women sitting in the Masjid. He raised his hand to offer greetings." [At-Tirmidhi]

[Hadith 856]

Abu Juraiy Al-Hajaimi 🕮 reported:

عن أبي جُرَيّ الهجُيْمِيّ رضي الله عنه قال : أتيت رسول الله صَلَّى الله عَلَيْهِ وسَلَّم فقلُت : عَلَيْك
السَّلام يا رَسول الله . فقال : لاتَقُلْ عَلَيْكَ السَّلام، فإن عَلَيْكَ السَّلام تَحِيَّةُ الموتى » رواه أبو داود ،
والترمذي وقال : حديث حسن صحيح

"I saw the Messenger of Allah 🕮 and said: 'Alaykas Salaamu ya Rasoolallah!" (Upon you be peace, O Messenger of Allah)!' He said: 'Do not say: "Alaykas Salaamu." This is the Salaam to the dead.'" [Abu Dawood and At-Tirmidhi]

[EXPLANATION OF HADITHS 854 TO 856]

Imam An-Nawawi mentions these *Hadiths* to present the etiquettes of greetings. The first *Hadith*, from Al-Miqdaad ibn Al-Aswad ﷺ, describes the habit of the Prophet ﷺ whenever he entered his house at night; he would greet with a soft tone so as to avoid waking those who were asleep and just enough for those awake to hear. This shows that whenever one enters his dwellings or room, he should greet those who are present in the lowest tone possible, just enough for those awake to hear and avoid waking those in deep asleep. And the reason behind this is, that those sleeping dislike been awoke from their deep sleep, especially when such individuals find it hard to get back to sleep after being awakened at night which could mean they would remain awake until dawn (*Fajr*). This is a form of harm and wrongdoing to them, so if you enter a place, dwellings or room give those awake their rights, which is the greetings and avoid harming those asleep by awaking them.

Then, the author mentions the narration of Asma ﷺ that the Prophet ﷺ passed a group of female Companions and greeted them using his hand. The understanding of this *Hadith* is that the Prophet ﷺ greeted them not only with his hand but he also greeted them verbally. And why we say this is because it is forbidden for one to just greet a person indicating with his hand alone, this is *Haraam,* but as for doing indicating greetings with the hand and verbally with the tongue, then this is okay. And this could be the case if one is greeting another Muslim who is far away from him, so he greets him by indicating with his hand as well as saying

"*Assalamu Alayka*" or "*Assalamu Alaykum*" depending on how many people he is addressing.

And another case could be if the person is deaf, in which case one is allowed to indicate greetings with his hand as well as verbally. With regret, some Muslims honk their car horn when passing you as a means of greeting. And this action (honking their horn) can never be considered the Islamic greeting. These who do this (honk their car horn) may say, when asked as to why they do this: "By this we are not attending to give them greetings, but merely to attract their attention, then to give the greetings." In which case it is okay and allowed, but as for using the car horn as a means of greeting someone, then this is going against the established *Sunnah* (way) of the Prophet ﷺ, which is to greet someone verbally with one tongue. But if the individual is far away from you, you may indicate firstly with the hand but at the same time, say the greetings with the mouth.

Now regarding the Prophet ﷺ greeting the womenfolk, we say it is preferable to avoid it! And why we say this is due to the possibility of *Fitnah* (trials) arising, especially if it is between the youth. So young men should not greet the young women and vice-verse. But in the case of an individual known for his righteousness (say he is Shaykh or student of knowledge), who happens to pass by a group of sisters learning in the *Masjid*, then we say, if this is free from trials and any danger occurring, then that is okay. But on the other hand, if a person is on a street or in a marketplace, then greeting a young lady could lead to temptation, so this is to be avoided completely. Say one entered his own house and his wife has female visitors who have come to visit her, it would be allowed for him to greet them all, and this is based upon an important Islamic principle which states: *"Preventing harm takes precedence over bringing benefit."*

In short, things like shaking women's hands, be they young or old, is strictly unlawful due to the fact that it leads to a greater *Fitnah*, whether it's by directly touching them, from behind a screen or through wearing gloves. If however, the female is one's near relative, like a sister, mother or the likes, then it is lawful, and Allah knows best.

As for the *Hadith* of Abu Juraiy Al-Hajaimi and the greeting: *"Alaykas Salaamu"* (Upon you be peace). The Prophet ﷺ forbade this. Why? The reason he gave was *"This is the Salaam to the dead."* I.e. prior to Islam, this was how they would greet the dead, as the poet said in line of poetry: *"Upon you be peace O Qays Ibn Aamir."*

Before the advent of Islam, the Arabs would address and greet their died as though they were present with them, so the Prophet ﷺ guided the Companions by saying this was wrong and corrected them and told them the correct way of greeting in Islam is to say: *"Assalamu Alayka."*

[Chapter] Etiquette of Offering Greetings

[Hadith 857]

Abu Hurairah ﷺ reported: The Messenger ﷺ said:

« يُسَلِّمُ الرَّاكِبُ عَلَى الْمَاشِي ، وَالْمَاشِي عَلَى القَاعِدِ ، والقَليلُ على الكَثِيرِ » متفق عليه

"A rider should greet a pedestrian; a pedestrian should greet one who is sitting; and a small group should greet a large group (of people)." [Agreed upon]

The narration in Al-Bukhari adds:

« والصغيرُ على الْكَبِيرِ »

"The young should greet the elderly."

[Hadith 858]

Abu Umamah Sundaiy Ibn Ajlaan Al-Bahili ﷺ reported: The Messenger of Allah ﷺ said:

«إنَّ أَوْلَى النَّاس بالله مَنْ بَدَأهم بالسَّلام)).

"The nearest to Allah is one who is the first to offer greetings." [Abu Dawood]

In another narration, the Messenger ﷺ was asked:

قيلَ يارسولَ الله، الرَّجُلان يَلْتَقِيان أَيُّهُمَا يَبْدأُ بالسَّلام ، قال أَوْلاهُمَا بالله تعالى ، قال الترمذي : حديث حسن .

"'O Messenger of Allah! When two persons meet, who should greet the other first?' The Messenger of Allah ﷺ said: 'The nearest to Allah.'" [At-Tirmidhi]

[EXPLANATION OF HADITHS 857 AND 858]

Regarding being of those who are the closest to Allah, then be of those who precede those they meet in greeting, whether they are young or old. If you want to be of those counted as the closest to Allah ﷻ, then put this into practice, and there is no doubt, we long for this virtue!

Regarding the *Hadith* of Abu Hurairah ﷺ, who said the Messenger said: *"A rider should greet a pedestrian; a pedestrian should greet one who is sitting; and a small group should greet a large group (of people)."* The reason why the Prophet ﷺ advised this is because the rider is in a superior position than that of the pedestrian, and the pedestrian is superior then the one sitting, so the superior should greet those less superior. And the small group should greet the larger group. The reason behind this is that the larger group has more right to be greeted by a smaller group due to the fact that they are more in number than that of the smaller group. But, if it is the case that this smaller group for some reason, are absent minded of this for whatever reason, then in this case the larger group should precede the smaller group in conformity with the *Hadith* we have previously stated which states that the closest of those to Allah, are those who precede those they meet in greetings.

[Chapter 134] Excellence of Greeting the Acquaintance Repeatedly

[*Hadith* 859]

Abu Hurairah 🙵 reported in the *Hadith* of the person who was at fault in performing his *Salaat* (prayer):

أنَّهُ جاء فَصَلَّى ثُمَّ جاء إلى النبي صَلَّى اللهُ عَلَيْهِ وسَلَّم فَسَلَّمَ عَلَيْهِ فَرَدَّ عَلَيْهِ السَّلام فقال : « ارجِع فَصَلِّ فَإِنَّكَ لم تُصَلِّ » فَرَجَعَ فَصَلَّى، ثُمَّ جاء فَسَلَّمَ عَلَى النبي صَلَّى اللهُ عَلَيْهِ وسَلَّم حَتَّى فَعَل ذلكَ ثَلاثَ مَرَّاتٍ . متفق عليه

> "The man came to the Prophet ﷺ and greeted him. The Prophet ﷺ responded to the greeting and said: 'Go back and repeat your prayer Salaat because you have not performed the Salaat (properly).' He again performed Salaat as he had prayed before and came to the Prophet ﷺ and greeted him. The Prophet ﷺ responded to the greetings (and repeated his words to him). This act of repeating (the Salaat and the Salaam) was done thrice." [Agreed upon]

[Hadith 860]

Abu Hurairah 🙵 reported: The Messenger of Allah ﷺ said:

« إذا لَقِيَ أَحَدُكُمْ أخاه فَلْيُسَلِّمْ عَلَيْهِ ، فَإِنْ حالَتْ بَيْنَهُمَا شَجَرَةٌ أو جِدَارٌ أو حَجَرٌ ثُمَّ لَقِيَهُ فَلْيُسَلِّمْ عَلَيْهِ » رواه أبو داود

> "When one of you meets a brother (in faith) he should greet him. Then if a tree or a wall or a stone intervenes between them and then he meets him again, he should greet him." [Abu Dawood]

[Chapter] Excellence of Greeting at the Time of Entry Into the House

Allah the Exalted says:

فَإِذَا دَخَلْتُم بُيُوتًا فَسَلِّمُوا عَلَىٰٓ أَنفُسِكُمْ تَحِيَّةً مِّنْ عِندِ ٱللَّهِ مُبَٰرَكَةً طَيِّبَةً

"But when you enter the houses, greet one another with a greeting from Allah (i.e. say 'As-Salaamu Alaykum), blessed and good." (An-Noor 61)

[Hadith 861]

Narrated Anas ibn Maalik ﷺ: the Messenger of Allah ﷺ said to me:

« يَابُنَيَّ ، إذا دَخَلْتَ عَلَى أَهْلِكَ فَسَلِّمْ يَكُنْ بَرَكَةً عَلَيْكَ وَعَلَى أَهْلِ بَيْتِكَ » رواه الترمذي وقال حديث

حسن صحيح

"Dear son, when you enter your house, say 'Assalamu Alaykum' to your family, for it will be a blessing both for you and to your family." [At-Tirmidhi]

[EXPLANATION OF HADITHS 859 TO 861]

As for the *Hadith* in which the Messenger of Allah ﷺ said: *"When one of you meets a brother (in faith) he should greet him. Then if a tree or a wall or a stone intervenes between them and then he meets him again, he should greet him,"* then it shows that if at any time you are with someone, in a house or a room, etc., and you leave the room for any length of time, then when you come back you should repeat the greetings. What we mean by this is, say he has a guest in his house or room and he goes out to get water or food, then he returns to the house or room, he should greet the guest once again like he did the first time. So every time you are absent from your brother, repeat the greetings, whether your absence was long or short. You have to remember, that greeting someone is part of Islam and it is an act of worship, the more you greet your brother (or sister) the more reward you will be rewarded, for spreading the greetings is an act of worship that one is rewarded for and this is a great blessing Allah his bestowed upon us. And if a tree or a large stone happened to come between you and your brother, in this case greet him again as you had previously done.

As for the first *Hadith*, about the person who was at fault in performing his *Salaat* (prayer), then this Companion was praying in haste and appeared to be pecking the ground (like a chicken). From this *Hadith*, we see the Prophet ﷺ ordering this Companion to repeat his prayer three times, and had the Prophet ﷺ willed, he could have taught this Companion the right way to pray straight away, so why did he demand him to keep to repeating his prayer that he was not praying properly?

This was from the wisdom the Prophet ﷺ as it increased this man's urge to learn the right way to pray! If a person is in great need of something, when that thing comes to him he will embrace it quicker and not take it for granted. After the man had repeated his prayer and come to the Prophet ﷺ three times the Prophet ﷺ said to him:

> *"When you stand for prayer, perform ablution properly and then face the Qiblah and say Takbir (Allahu Akbar), and then recite what you know of the Quran, and then bow with calmness till you feel at ease, then rise from bowing, till you feel at ease, till you stand straight, and then prostrate calmly (and remain in prostration) till you feel at ease, and then raise (your head) and sit with calmness till you feel at ease in the sitting position, and do likewise in whole of your prayer."*

The author uses this *Hadith* as a proof that if you are in the *Masjid* and you leave a brother (or brothers) to renew your *Wudu* (ablution) or to obtain a book from some other part of the *Masjid* or anything like this, you greet him (or them) once again as you did the first time, and this is so that one may obtain the reward of the greetings which is ten good deeds.

Then the author mentioned the words of Allah the Exalted:

فَإِذَا دَخَلْتُم بُيُوتًا فَسَلِّمُواْ عَلَىٰٓ أَنفُسِكُمْ تَحِيَّةً مِّنْ عِندِ ٱللَّهِ مُبَٰرَكَةً

طَيِّبَةً

"But when you enter the houses, greet one another with a greeting from Allah (i.e. say 'As-Salaamu Alaykum), blessed and good." (An-Noor 61)

Allah says this will be a blessing for them and you, and one should start with the *Siwaak*, then greet those in the dwellings, as the Prophet ﷺ said: *"Dear son, when you enter your house, say 'Assalamu Alaykum' to your family, for it will be a blessing both for you and to your family."*[6]

---

[6] Although the author grades this *Hadith* as *Hasan Sahih* as well as Shaykh Ibn Uthaymeen, *Haafiz* Ibn Hajar said it is a *Da'if Hadith* due to the following reason: in the chain of narration is Ali ibn Zaid ibn Jud'aani, who is considered *Da'if*. *Haafiz* collected all the supporting narrations of this *Hadith* and said they support and strengthen each other. Therefore the *Hadith* is weak by itself, and acceptable with supportive *Hadiths*. See *Nataa'ij ul-Afkaar* 1-167/170. Also our noble Shaykh Al-Albaani said this *Hadith* was *Da'if* by itself in his *Sunan At-Tirmidi*.

[Chapter 136] Greeting Children

[Hadith 862]

Anas reported that he passed by some children and greeted them. Then he said:

كانَ رسول لله صَلَّى اللهُ عَلَيْهِ وسَلَّمِ يَفْعَلُهُ . متفق عليه

"The Messenger of Allah ﷺ used to do the same." [Agreed upon]

[Chapter 137] Greeting One's Wife And Other Women

[Hadith 863]

Sahl ibn Sa'd ☸ reported:

كَانَتْ فِينَا امْرَأَةٌ وَفِي رِوَايَةٍ : - كَانَتْ لَنَا عَجُوزٌ تَأْخُذُ مِنْ أُصُولِ السِّلْقَ فتَطْرَحُهُ فِي القِدْرِ وَتُكَرْكِرُ حَبَّاتٍ

مِنْ شَعِيرٍ ، فَإِذا صَلَّيْنا الجُمُعَةَ وانْصَرَفْنَا نُسَلِّمُ عَلَيْها فَتُقَدِّمُهُ إلِيْنَا رواه البخاري

"There was a woman among us who would put beet root in a pot and add to it some ground barley. She used to cook them together. On returning from the Friday prayer, we would greet her and she would offer it to us." [Al-Bukhari]

[Hadith 864]

Umm Hani Fakhitah, the daughter of Abu Taalib, ☸ reported:

أتيتُ النبي صَلَّى اللهُ عَلَيْهِ وسَلَّم يَوْمَ الفَتْحِ وَهُو يَغْتَسِلُ وَفاطِمَةُ تَسْتُرُهُ بِثَوْبٍ فَسَلَّمْتُ وذَكَرَت الحديث .

رواه مسلم

"I went to the Prophet on the day of the conquest of Makkah. He was taking a bath and Fatimah was screening Him with a cloth. I greeted Him." And she mentioned the rest of the Hadith… *[Muslim]*

[EXPLANATION OF HADITHS 862 TO 864]

Regarding the *Hadith* of Anas ﷺ, regrettably, it has become a bad habit among the people to underrate the age of discretion of a young child to the age of twelve years old and give no importance to them. We say, this goes against the *Sunnah*, because the Prophet's ﷺ habit was to greet the young as well as the old.

Greeting the children has many benefits, including:

1. Firstly, it is following the practice of the Prophet ﷺ; Allah the Exalted says in the Quran:

$$لَقَدْ كَانَ لَكُمْ فِي رَسُولِ ٱللَّهِ أُسْوَةٌ حَسَنَةٌ$$

    "Indeed in the Messenger of Allah (Muhammad) you have a good example." (Al-Ahzaab 21)

2. It shows one's humbleness and humility towards others, and avoiding turning up one's nose and being arrogant towards his fellow brethren in Islam; the Prophet ﷺ said regarding this: *"Allah augments the honour of one of forgives; and one who serves another seeking the pleasure of Allah, Allah will exalt him in ranks."*

3. Teaching children good manners, and the reason why is because when a person passes them and greets them they will become accustomed to spreading the greetings amongst themselves, which has great blessings in it.

4. Spreading the greetings to children will cause them to feel wanted, liked and loved! Without doubt when

these children see their elders greeting them, they will become happy their elders noticed them and looked out for them and showed them this type of respect. They will never forget such kind gestures and will rejoice due to this, as is know that children normally remember and don't forget such kind treatment shown to them.

So in summary, if we happen to pass any youth or children playing along the pathway or in the market, greet them!

Now as for greeting those woman from our family folk (i.e.) like those we are prohibited to marry, then we are allowed to greet them, like our wives, sisters, aunts, our brothers' daughters and so on, this is okay. And in the case of the elderly lady where there is no fear of *Fitnah* (temptation) then this is ok, but if there is fear of a *Fitnah* then it is better to avoid greeting them.

As for the *Hadith* of Sahl ibn Sa'd who reported that there was a woman who would make beetroot in a pot on the fire and add ground barley to it, and the Companions after the Friday prayers would pass by her, greet her and go in and visit her, then this was an enjoyment for them due to the dire situation which they found themselves in before the Conquest of Makkah; many of the Companions had little to live by, but that changed after the Conquest, after which they were well-off after that in terms of wealth. But at that time this woman would serve them this beetroot knowing their situation.

[Chapter 138] Greeting the Non-Muslims and the Prohibition of Taking the Initiative in Doing so

[Hadith 866]

Abu Hurairah ﷺ reported: the Messenger ﷺ said:

«لَا تَبْدَأُوا اليَهُودَ ولا النَّصَارَى بالسَّلام ، فإذا لَقِيتُم أَحَدَهُم في طَرِيق فَاضطَرُّوهُ إلى أَضْيَقِهِ» رواه مسلم

"Do not greet the Jews and the Christians before they greet you; and when you meet any one of them on the road, force him to go the narrowest part of it." [Muslim]

[Hadith 867]

Anas ﷺ reported the Messenger of Allah ﷺ said:

« إذَا سَلَّمَ عَلَيكُم أَهلُ الكتاب فَقُولُوا : وعَلَيْكُمْ » متفق عليه.

"When the people of the Book greet you (i.e. say 'As-Saamu Alaykum,' meaning: death be upon you), you should respond with: 'Wa Alaykum.' (The same on you, i.e. and death will be upon you, for no one will escape death)" [Agreed upon]

[Hadith 868]

Usamah ibn Zaid ﷺ reported:

أن النبي صَلَّى اللهُ عَلَيْهِ وسَلَّم مَرَّ عَلَى مَجْلِسٍ فيه أخلاطٌ من المسلمِينَ والمشركِينَ عَبَدةِ الأوثَانِ واليَهُود فَسَلَّمَ عَلَيهِمُ النبي صَلَّى اللهُ عَلَيْهِ وسَلَّم . متفق عليه

"The Messenger passed by a mixed company of people which included Muslims, polytheist and Jews, and He gave them greeting (i.e. saying Assalamu Alaykum)." [Agreed upon]

[THE EXPLANATION OF HADITHS 866 TO 868]

As for preceding the *Kufaar* in greetings then this is not allowed, and we mean by this, that if a Muslim happens to pass by a *Kaafir* or enters a place where he or they are, it is unlawful for a *Muslim* to precede them in the greeting (i.e. saying *"Assalamu Alayka"* or *"Assalamu Alaykum"*).

And the *Hikmah* (wisdom) behind the Prophet ﷺ forbidding this is because it is a form of showing respect, and honour towards them, because as we know the Islamic greeting is a type of showing respect towards a person and honouring them, (and due to the *Kaafir* not believing or worshipping Allah) he does not deserve that respect and honour. The basic rule is that we are supposed to be harsh towards them and show them no honour as Allah the Exalted says in the Quran:

$$مُّحَمَّدٌ رَّسُولُ اللَّهِ ۚ وَالَّذِينَ مَعَهُ أَشِدَّاءُ عَلَى الْكُفَّارِ رُحَمَاءُ بَيْنَهُمْ$$

"Muhammad is the Messenger of Allah, and those who are with Him are severe against disbelievers, and merciful among themselves." (Al-Fath 29)

Allah the Exalted says: "Severe against disbelievers," meaning: stern, showing no compassion towards them, and He the Exalted goes on to say:

$$تَرَاهُمْ رُكَّعًا سُجَّدًا يَبْتَغُونَ فَضْلًا مِّنَ اللَّهِ وَرِضْوَانًا ۖ سِيمَاهُمْ فِي وُجُوهِهِم مِّنْ أَثَرِ السُّجُودِ ۚ ذَٰلِكَ مَثَلُهُمْ فِي التَّوْرَىٰةِ ۚ وَمَثَلُهُمْ فِي$$

ٱلْإِنجِيلِ كَزَرْعٍ أَخْرَجَ شَطْئَهُ فَآزَرَهُ فَٱسْتَغْلَظَ فَٱسْتَوَىٰ عَلَىٰ سُوقِهِۦ يُعْجِبُ ٱلزُّرَّاعَ لِيَغِيظَ بِهِمُ ٱلْكُفَّارَ

"You see them bowing and falling down prostrate (in prayer), seeking Bounty from Allah and (His) Good Pleasure. The mark of them (i.e. of their faith) is on their faces (foreheads) from the traces of (their) prostration (during prayers). This is their description in the *Torah*. But their description in the Gospel is like a (sown) seed which sends forth its shoot, then makes it strong, it then becomes thick, and it stands straight on its stem, delighting the sowers-that He may enrage the *Kufaar* (disbelievers)." (Al-Fath 29)

Also the Exalted says:

ذَٰلِكَ بِأَنَّهُمْ لَا يُصِيبُهُمْ ظَمَأٌ وَلَا نَصَبٌ وَلَا مَخْمَصَةٌ فِى سَبِيلِ ٱللَّهِ وَلَا يَطَئُونَ مَوْطِئًا يَغِيظُ ٱلْكُفَّارَ وَلَا يَنَالُونَ مِنْ عَدُوٍّ نَّيْلاً إِلَّا كُتِبَ لَهُم بِهِۦ عَمَلٌ صَٰلِحٌ إِنَّ ٱللَّهَ لَا يُضِيعُ أَجْرَ ٱلْمُحْسِنِينَ

"That is because they suffer neither thirst nor fatigue, nor hunger in the Cause of Allah, nor they take any step to raise the anger of the *Kufaar* (disbelievers) nor inflict any injury upon an enemy but it is written to their credit as a deed of righteousness." (At-Tawbah 120)

216

So greeting them is none other than showing them honour and respect and the believer has been told to do the opposite as Allah says:

يَٰأَيُّهَا ٱلَّذِينَ ءَامَنُوا۟ مَن يَرْتَدَّ مِنكُمْ عَن دِينِهِۦ فَسَوْفَ يَأْتِى ٱللَّهُ بِقَوْمٍ
يُحِبُّهُمْ وَيُحِبُّونَهُۥ أَذِلَّةٍ عَلَى ٱلْمُؤْمِنِينَ أَعِزَّةٍ عَلَى ٱلْكَٰفِرِينَ

"O you who believe! Whoever from you among you turns back from his religion (Islam), Allah will bring a people whom He will love and they will love Him; humble towards the believers, stern towards the *Kufaar* (disbelievers)." (Al-Maa'idah 54)

So the believer always remembers he is more honourable than the *Kaafir*! With great regret, when opportunities of work for the *Kufaar* opened in our midst, this dishonour we once had for them disappeared and vanished from our hearts. We perceive the difference between the Christians, Jews, Pagans, and Buddhists to be minor to the point that we saw them not so different from us in our faith; (i.e.) we are all alike! We viewed the differences between us and them to be a simply matter so much so that we see this difference like that of two followers of two different *Madhabs* (schools of thought)! We looked at the matter as trivial, thinking that it is similar to the four famous schools of thought! So we ask Allah for good health! The situation we have fallen into is an indication that the hearts of the Muslims have died. We have to always remember our stance towards our enemies and dislike them as Islam commands us.

If there is ever a covenant, treaty or agreement between us and them at any time, and there are many Christian workers available, we do not let them enter the Arabian lands! Why? Because of the Prophet's ✿ statement:

> *"I will shortly expel Jews and Christians from the Arabian Peninsula."*

Also he ✿ said:

> *"Remove (all) Jews and Christians from the Arabian Peninsula."*

Also the Prophet ✿ said while he was sick, just before he died:
> *"Expel the Polytheists from the Arabian Peninsula."*

Therefore, we avoid hiring the *Kufaar* when we can hire our brothers in faith but again, with deep regret, some Muslims say, the reason why we hire these *Kufaar* is because we will have consistency in our work! What they mean by this is, at times of prayer, we have to leave our work places to go to perform prayer in the *Masjid,* as well as fast in Ramadan, which means we go home to eat and do things like going Makkah at times to perform *Hajj, Umra,* etc. If we have these *Kufaar* working for us then they will not be doing these things obviously so work can continue with or without us. So it is professed as a good idea! We seek refuge with Allah from such words and ways! Such words are only uttered by those who have chosen this life over the next and again we ask Allah the Exalted for good health!

Regarding the Prophet's ✿ statement in the *Hadith*: *"When you meet any one of them on the road, force him to go the narrowest part of it,"* then what the Prophet ﷺ meant was, if we come upon them in the pathways, we do not open up the way for them; so say there are a group of us and a group of them we make them go around us or stand waiting for us till we pass them, then they may proceed on the pathway or they walk separately while we walk as a group pass them. Why? If we stopped, allowing them to pass while we wait, or we split up for them so they can pass, this would be showing them respect and honour. We must remember they are none other than Allah's enemies! And not forgetting, our enemies too! Allah says regarding them in the Quran:

يَـٰٓأَيُّهَا ٱلَّذِينَ ءَامَنُواْ لَا تَتَّخِذُواْ عَدُوِّى وَعَدُوَّكُمْ أَوْلِيَآءَ تُلْقُونَ إِلَيْهِم بِٱلْمَوَدَّةِ وَقَدْ كَفَرُواْ بِمَا جَآءَكُم مِّنَ ٱلْحَقِّ

"O you who believe! Take not My enemies and your enemies (i.e. disbelievers and polytheist, etc), as friends, showing affection towards them while they have disbelieved in what has come to you from the truth." (Al-Mumtahanah 1)

The disbelievers then and now remain our enemies, so regarding greeting the *Kufaar*, it is impermissible. But if they say to you: *"Assalamu Alaykum"* then reply to them with *"Wa Alaykus Salaam."* This is because the *Hadith* of Ibn Umar in *Al-Bukhari* states the Prophet ﷺ said:

> *"If they say 'As-Saamu Alaykum' (may death be upon you), then reply 'Wa Alaykum' (and to you too)."*

Here, the Prophet ﷺ explained the reason why one should reply *"Wa Alaykum,"* but if this reason is not present, then it is okay to reply "*Wa Alaykumus Salaam*" to them. This is how a Muslim behaves, with justice. But in saying that, if they greet us with a greeting like "*Welcome,*" we reply to them likewise, or if they say "*Hello,*" we reply to them likewise; how they greet us we greet them in similar manner.

Now we will shed light on a matter that seems to be a little problematic for some of the Muslims! Some of them work at companies which are run by Jews, and others by Christians, so there will be times when these Muslims will enter such work places and come across their managers, so what should the *Muslim* say or how will he greet his boss? What they should say is "*Salaam*" (peace)! Peace and peace only. And what we mean by this is, this Muslim intends in his heart, "*Salaam*" to the Muslims! By him saying this, it does not necessarily mean peace be upon the boss, rather, one could intend by this to mean, he wants to be free from this person's evil and wants peace to prevail. We do not know whether the manager intends for us peace or evil, so this type of greeting is to your advantage. We do as the Prophet ﷺ said and that was:

> "*Do not greet the Jews and the Christians before they greet you.*"

The *Ulema*, may Allah have mercy upon them, differ regarding whether it is allowed to greet the boss first by saying other than "*Assalamu Alaykum*", such as saying "*Hello,*" etc.? Some say, it is okay, so that one does not seem rude or for the purpose of kind treatment, especially if one fears him or any harm coming from him. Others say no! Because this is a type of showing respect to him. We say, a person weighs up the pros and cons. And the matter is left down to the person's situation, if doing so serves a greater purpose or not; in short, one needs to look at the situation he (or) she is in to decide.

Then the author mentions the *Hadith* of Usamah Ibn Zaid; if a person comes upon a mixed group of people, Muslims and *Kufaar*, should he leave the greetings because there are *Kufaar* amongst them, or should he greet only the Muslims? There is a principle in the religion that directs us if there is an allowance to do something but at the same time a prohibition: what is required is to separate them firstly, then see which one outweighs the other. What we mean here is, in this case, one can make his intention to just greet the Muslims. And the basis for our view is the *Hadith* just mentioned, and that is that the Prophet ﷺ himself greeted mixed gatherings and he intended to greet only the Muslims. And with Allah is the success!

So in brief we end this chapter by saying, if someone greets a person, this person has to return the greeting, but if a person greets a group of people, it is enough for one of them to reply, rather It Is *Waajib* (a must) upon at least one of them to reply, and that would be enough.

[Chapter 139] Excellence of the Greeting on Arrival and Departure

[Hadith 869]

Abu Hurairah ⬡ reported that the Messenger ⬡ said:

«إِذَا انْتَهَى أَحَدُكُم إلى المجْلِسِ فَلْيُسَلِّمْ، فَإِذَا أَرَادَ أَنْ يَقُومَ فَلْيُسَلِّمْ، فَلَيسْت الأُولى بِأَحَقِّ من الآخِرَةِ»

رواه أبو داود حديث حسن

"When one of you arrives at a gathering, he should offer Salaam to those who are already there, and he should also do so when he intends to depart. The first act of greeting is not more meritorious than the last." [Abu Dawood]

[Explanation of Hadith 869]

This *Hadith* indicated that if a Muslim enters a place, he should greet those there and the same goes when he wants to leave, he should also greet the gathering. And this is derived from the words of the Prophet ﷺ when he said: *"The first act of greeting is not more meritorious than the last."* So this is clear, both greetings are meritorious, neither have precedence over the other. And this was the habit of the Companions with the Prophet ﷺ; whenever they visited him they would greet him upon arrival and departure.

This is the same when one visits Makkah for *Hajj* or *Umrah,* he greets the *Masjid* with *Tawaaf,* then when he intends to return to his country, he returns to the *Masjid* to perform *Tawaaf* again as a way of saying farewell to the *Masjid.* Islam makes things like this, something one begins with and rounds up with and this is part of Allah's ﷺ *Hikmah* (wisdom) as He says in the Quran:

كِتَبٌ أُحۡكِمَتۡ ءَايَنتُهُ ثُمَّ فُصِّلَتۡ مِن لَّدُنۡ حَكِيمٍ خَبِيرٍ

"(This is) a Book, the Verses whereof are perfected (in every sphere of knowledge, etc), and explained in detail from One (Allah) who is All-Wise and Well-Acquainted (with all things)." (Hud 1)

Islam is complete in every way possible, even to the minutest of things, and it contains nothing contradictory, inconsistent or incompatible, in any shape or form; it serves and explains major and minor matters; the Prophet ﷺ even forbade one to walk in one shoe if the other is damaged because it is a form of showing injustice to one's foot! What we mean is, by wearing one shoe, one is showing favour to one foot while neglecting the other, and this is an injustice to one's feet. Islam promotes good in all one's affairs, and Allah the Exalted says regarding this:

إِنَّ ٱللَّهَ يَأْمُرُ بِٱلْعَدْلِ وَٱلْإِحْسَٰنِ وَإِيتَآئِ ذِى ٱلْقُرْبَىٰ وَيَنْهَىٰ عَنِ ٱلْفَحْشَآءِ وَٱلْمُنكَرِ وَٱلْبَغْىِ يَعِظُكُمْ لَعَلَّكُمْ تَذَكَّرُونَ

"Verily, Allah enjoins *Al-Adl* (i.e. justice), and *Ihsaan* (to be patient in performing your duties to Allah, totally for Allah's sake and in accordance with the *Sunnah* of the Prophet ﷺ) and giving (help) to kith and kin and He forbids *Al-Fahsha* (i.e. all evil deeds, e.g illegal sexual acts, disobedience of parent, polytheism, to tell lies, give false witness, to kill a life without right, etc), *Munkar* (i.e. all that is prohibited by Islamic Law: polytheism of every kind, disbelief and every kind of evil deeds etc) and *Al-Baghy* (i.e. all kinds of oppression); He admonishes you, that you may take heed."(An-Nahl 90)

باب الوصية بالنساء

THE CHAPTER ON ADVICE ON WOMEN

Allah the Exalted says in the Quran:

وَعَاشِرُوهُنَّ بِٱلْمَعْرُوفِ

"And live with them honourably." (An-Nisaa' 19)

Also Allah says:

وَلَن تَسْتَطِيعُوٓاْ أَن تَعْدِلُواْ بَيْنَ ٱلنِّسَآءِ وَلَوْ حَرَصْتُمْ ۖ فَلَا تَمِيلُواْ كُلَّ

ٱلْمَيْلِ فَتَذَرُوهَا كَٱلْمُعَلَّقَةِ ۚ وَإِن تُصْلِحُواْ وَتَتَّقُواْ فَإِنَّ ٱللَّهَ كَانَ غَفُورًا

رَّحِيمًا

"You will never be able to do perfect justice between wives even if it is your ardent desire, so do not incline too much to one of them (by giving her more of your time and provisions) so as to leave the other hanging (i.e., neither divorced nor married). And if you do justice, and do all that is right, and fear Allah by keeping away from all that is wrong, then Allah is Ever Oft-Forgiving, Most Merciful." (An-Nisaa 129)

[EXPLANATION OF SUPPORTING VERSES]

The author (Imam An-Nawawi) titles this chapter the "chapter of advice on women" and what is meant by the word *wasiyyah*" is council and recommended advice pertaining to women, such as being gentle, lenient, kind and friendly towards them as Allah has commanded, as well as fearing Allah regarding them. Allah the Exalted says:

ٱلرِّجَالُ قَوَّٰمُونَ عَلَى ٱلنِّسَآءِ بِمَا فَضَّلَ ٱللَّهُ بَعْضَهُمْ عَلَىٰ بَعْضٍ

"Men are the protectors and maintainers of women, because Allah has made the one of them to excel the other." (Al-Nisaa 34)

The author first mentions the statement of Allah the Exalted and High when He says:

وَعَاشِرُوهُنَّ بِٱلْمَعْرُوفِ

"And live with them honourably." (An-Nisaa' 19)

And what this means is to live with them in a kind and friendly manner. With respect to the first word in this verse, "*al-Mu'asharah*" means one should accompany and deal with a woman in an amicable manner and treat her in the kindest friendly honorable manner.

"*Al-Ma'roof*" is all what Islam deems and holds to be correct, good and important; if the Religion deems a thing detestable then that thing is denied even if that disliked thing is liked by the people.

Allah the Exalted says in the second verse:

وَلَن تَسْتَطِيعُوٓاْ أَن تَعْدِلُواْ بَيْنَ ٱلنِّسَآءِ وَلَوْ حَرَصْتُمْ

"You will never be able to do perfect justice between wives even if it is your ardent desire..."

This is addressed to those who have two wives; Allah makes it clear to them that even if one tries to be just between both his wives he will be unable to because there are things a person has no control over, such as one's tendencies like love and similar things related to one's heart. As for physical matters such as maintenance, then surely one has the ability to provide in a just and honorable manner, and as for what is relating to fair division, that is, dividing days between them equally, one night with one of them, then the next night with the other, this is within one's capability. On the other hand, with regards to one's trying to have equal feelings towards both his wives, such as in love and affection and the likes, this is not possible as that is something he himself cannot control. As such, Allah says:

فَلَا تَمِيلُواْ كُلَّ ٱلْمَيْلِ فَتَذَرُوهَا كَٱلْمُعَلَّقَةِ

"So do not incline too much to one of them so as to leave the other hanging..."

This means, inclining too much towards one of the two beyond what is the recommended. As neglecting one of them will surely leave her feeling abandoned. Allah says: **"So as to leave the other hanging,"** meaning, it is like if she is left hanging between the heavens and earth, and this is like saying she has no affixed abode! If an individual's wife sees her husband greatly inclining towards her co-wife, surely this will

228

affect her so badly this will put an enormous strain upon herself which will certainly wear her down and make her very unhappy... For this reason she is likened to hanging between the heavens and earth. Next Allah says:

وَإِن تُصْلِحُواْ وَتَتَّقُواْ فَإِنَّ ٱللَّهَ كَانَ غَفُورًا رَّحِيمًا

"And if you do justice, and do all that is right, and fear Allah by keeping away from all that is wrong, then Allah is Ever Oft-Forgiving, Most Merciful."

Meaning, He will forgive you that which is not in your control; instead, He takes you to account for what is in your capability. So these two verses we have mentioned, as well as similar evidences from the Quran and *Sunnah* all indicate one thing, and that is kindness towards the woman and paying great attention to her as well as living with her in way which is best. And we bring to your mind one thing: a person should not expect from his wife his complete and full rights. No! It is not possible for her to, even at her best, to give or offer a right in its complete full form, so one should bear this in mind and show forgiveness and overlook her shortcomings.

[Hadith 273]

Abu Hurairah ﷺ reported that the Messenger of Allah ﷺ said:

«اسْتَوْصُوا بِالنِّسَاءِ خَيْراً ، فَإِنَّ الْمَرْأَةَ خُلِقَتْ مِنْ ضِلَعٍ ، وَإِنَّ أَعْوَجَ ما فِي الضِّلَعِ أَعْلَاهُ ، فَإِنْ ذَهَبْتَ تُقِيمُهُ كَسَرْتَهُ ، وَإِنْ تَرَكْتَهُ ، لَمْ يَزَلْ أَعْوَجَ ، فَاسْتَوْصُوا بِالنِّسَاءِ » متفقٌ عليه .

وَفِي رواية في الصحيحين:« الْمَرْأَةُ كالضلع إنْ أَقَمْتها كَسَرْتَهَا ، وإنِ اسْتَمْتَعْتَ بِهَا،اسْتَمْتَعْتَ وفيها عَوَجٌ » . وَفِي روايةٍ لِمسلمٍ : « إنَّ الْمَرْأَةَ خُلِقَتْ مِنْ ضِلَعٍ ، لَنْ تَسْتَقِيمَ لَكَ على طريقةٍ ، فَإِنْ اسْتَمْتَعْتَ بِهَا، اسْتَمْتَعْتَ بِهَا وفيها عَوَجٌ ، وإنْ ذَهَبْتَ تُقِيمُها كَسَرْتَهَا ، وَكَسْرُهَا طلاقُها» .

"Take my advice with regards to women: Act kindly towards them for they were created from a rib, and the most crooked part of a rib is its uppermost part; if you attempt to straighten it; you will break it, and if you were to leave it alone it will remain crooked; so act kindly towards women." [Agreed upon]

In another narration, the Messenger of Allah ﷺ said:

"A woman is like a rib, if you attempt to straighten her, you will break her; and if you benefit from her, you will do so while crookedness remains in her." [Al-Bukhari and Muslim]

In another narration in Muslim, the Messenger ﷺ said:

"Women have been created from a rib and will in no way straighten for you; so if you want to benefit from her, you will benefit from her while crookedness remains in her. If you attempt to straighten her, you will break her, and breaking her is divorcing her."

[Explanation of Hadith 273]

The author mentions these narrations and the first of them is narrated by Abu Hurairah ﷺ regarding how to associate and deal with women, so the Prophet ﷺ said: *"Take my advice with regards to women: act kindly towards them..."* The reason why, is because as is known, women suffer from the following: deficiencies in their intellect, deficiencies in their Religion, deficiencies in the way they think and deficiencies in the way they generally handle all their affairs. Why? Because they were created from the rib! Because Allah created Aadam without a mother or father, instead he was created from dust or earth, and it was then said to him *"Be!"* and he was. When Allah the Exalted created him, He created his wife from his crooked rib, and this is why she is referred to as crooked, so if you want to enjoy her you will have to enjoy her in this state and that is in a crooked state.

If you try to straighten such crookedness for sure, you will break her. If you desire to take pleasure from her, then do so while she is that condition. One should try to simplify her matters for her as well as try to be pleased with her in such a state. But on the other hand, if one tries to obtain complete perfection from her by straightening her, this will be almost impossible, for if she tries to stand firm and upright upon her *Deen*, she will be unable to do so due to what we have mentioned, and she will be completely unable to be the way her husband expect her to be in all matters, rather she will fall short in that and it is as we said, due to those many short comings within her.

231

Regarding these deficiencies, they are from within her natural disposition and her nature and if one tries to straighten her that will end in divorcing her, and what is meant by this is, if one exerts his efforts to straighten her this will be practically impossible! One will become tired of trying this and end up divorcing her due to the fact he is expecting perfection from her which is something she is unable to be or to achieve.

We see the aim and intent of the Prophet ﷺ, and how one should dwell and live with one's wife, and that is by being very forgiving towards her as well as trying to make things as easy as possible for her as the Exalted says in the Quran:

خُذِ ٱلْعَفْوَ

"Show forgiveness."

What is meant here is, that one makes matters easy for people, as well as being forgiving towards their bad behaviour and manners. Then Allah goes on to say in this verse:

وَأْمُرْ بِٱلْعُرْفِ وَأَعْرِضْ عَنِ ٱلْجَٰهِلِينَ

"Enjoin what is good and turn away from ignorant."
(Al-A'raaf 199)

So no matter what the case may be, a man will never be able to find his wife free from fault. Impossible! How could he accept one hundred percent from her? The Prophet ﷺ said, if a man is going to enjoy his wife, then he should take enjoyment from her as she is and that is by we have mentioned in this explanation.

[Hadith 274]

Abdullah ibn Zam'ah reported:

أنه سمعَ النبيَّ صَلَّى اللهُ عَلَيْهِ وسَلَّم يُخْطُبُ ، وذكَر النَّاقَةَ والَّذى عقَرهَا ، فقال رسول الله صَلَّى اللهُ عَلَيْهِ
وسَلَّم : ﴿ إِذِ انْبَعث أَشْقَاهَا ﴾ انْبعثَ لَها رَجُلٌ عزِيزٌ ، عارِمٌ منيعٌ في رهْطِهِ » ثُمَّ ذَكَر النِّساءَ » فَوعظَ
فيهِنَّ ، فقَال : « يعْمِدُ أَحَدكُمْ فيجْلِدُ امْرَأَتَهُ جلْد الْعَبْدِ فلَعلَّهُ يُضاجِعُهَا مِنْ آخِر يومِهِ » ثُمَّ وَعظَهُمْ في
ضحكهِمْ مِن الضَّرْطَةِ وقال : «لِمَ يضحكُ أَحَدكُمْ مِمَّا يفعلُ ؟ » متفق عليه .

*He heard the Prophet ﷺ giving a speech when he mentioning the she-camel (of Prophet Saalih) and the man who killed her. The Messenger of Allah ﷺ said: "**When the most wicked man among them went forth (to kill the she-camel)**" (91:12) signifies that a distinguished, wicked and most powerful chief jumped to kill the she-camel." Then He made mention of women and said: "Some of you beat your wives as if they were slaves, and lay with them at the end of the day." Then he admonished them against laughing at another's passing of wind saying: "Why do any of you laugh at another doing what he does so himself?" [Agreed upon]*

[Explanation of Hadith 274]

Here the author mentions Abdullah ibn Zam'ah reported that he heard the Prophet ﷺ giving a speech while he was sitting on his she-camel, and it was the habit of the Prophet ﷺ to give the following two types of admonishments:

1. General admonishments such as the *Khutbah* every Friday and the admonishment every *Eid*.
2. Due to a reason, whereby he ﷺ would address the people making clear whatever that matter would be pertaining to. And at times he would do this while on the pulpit, while at other times, he just stood on the ground, and on some occasions, he did so while sitting on his she-camel while leaning against one of his Companions. It all depended on the time and circumstance, as it was from his guidance to pick the most suitable of times so as to make his speech more acceptable and not boring.

While addressing the Companions, Abdullah ibn Zam'ah heard the Prophet ﷺ say: *"Some of you beat your wives as if they were slaves…"* Meaning: one of you beats his wife as if there is absolutely no relationship whatsoever between them both, so she is like an enemy or slave unto him, and this is not befitting because the relationship between the husband and the wife is something special, and it should be built on affection and love and far from foul words and unbecoming actions. Is beating one's wife equal to the way one beats his slave and then at the end of the day he sleeps with her! How can one behave in such a way!? This contradicts the Prophet's ﷺ statement, so the wise person does not do this let alone the believer!

Next the Prophet ﷺ made mention of someone breaking wind. When the Companions heard a person break wind, they started laughing at the noise, so the Prophet ﷺ admonished them for laughing and said: "Why do *any of you laugh at another doing what he does* so *himself?*" Meaning: if you yourselves break wind, then why are you finding it funny at someone else doing so too! As the custom among some people is to break wind in front of people and it is not looked at as a bad practice and they consider it similar to sneezing or coughing and the likes, yet others in there custom criticize this and looked down upon it. So, one of the reasons why one should not laugh at another person who breaks wind is due to the fact that this will embarrass the person and this is not something praiseworthy.

This indicates that one should not find fault in things he does himself! If you yourself do not consider things you yourself do as strange, how then can you consider it strange that others do it too!

I would like to bring to your attention a particular matter; this matter is a known matter among the common folk and it is regarding the eating of camel meat; eating its meat nullifies one's *Wudu*, so it becomes compulsory upon an individual if he wants to perform prayer to perform his *Wudu* again, and that is if one eats it, whether that meat is cooked or uncooked, meat on bone or its liver, intestines, belly, heart, etc. Whatever one eats from the camel, it breaks his *Wudu* because the Prophet ﷺ stated in a *Hadith*:

"Perform ablution after eating the meat of a camel."

After the Prophet 🕊 said this someone said: *"Should we perform ablution after eating camel's meat?"* So the Prophet 🕊 replied: *"Yes."* Then someone asked: *"Should we perform ablution from after eating mutton?"* So the Prophet 🕊 replied: *"If you wish!"* The meat of mutton does not break one's *Wudu*, nor does cow meat or horse meat. As for drinking camel's milk, then this does not nullify one's ablution because the Prophet 🕊 told some of his Companion's to go out to a particular place containing camels and to drink their urine as well as its milk and he did not command them after doing so to perform ablution. And had it been obligatory to perform ablution after drinking these two, he would have commanded them to perform *Wudu* after drinking them. But in saying this it is only preferred to perform *Wudu* after drinking either but not *Waajib* (compulsory). Also the same goes with regards to camel's gravy or sauce, one does not have perform *Wudu* after drinking or eating it but if one performs *Wudu* that it preferred. The (common) people say, the reason why the Prophet 🕊 said one has to perform *Wudu* after eating camel's, is that one day the Prophet 🕊 was at a banquet in which the people were eating camel's meat and one of those people present passed wind, so the Prophet 🕊 said, not knowing who it was that passed wind:

> *"Whoever has eaten the meat of a camel should perform ablution."*

So, all those who were present performed ablution. Those who made this claim use this *Hadith* to affirm such a claim! But we say regarding this *Hadith*, it is baseless and false and has no grounds to it! Only Allah the Exalted knows the wisdom behind why the Prophet ﷺ commanded ablution after eating camel's meat! So that which is biding upon us in this matter is to say, "We hear and obey." Since the Prophet ﷺ said we must perform ablution after eating it's meat, we are obliged to comply with his orders.

[Hadith 275]

Abu Hurairah ⚭ reported that Messenger of Allah ﷺ said:

«لا يَفْرَكُ مُؤْمِنٌ مُؤْمِنَةً إنْ كَرِهِ مِنها خُلقاً رضِيَ مِنْها آخَرَ» أَوْ قَالَ : « غيْرَهُ » رواه مسلم.

"A believer must not hate (his wife) a believing woman; if he dislikes one of her characteristics he will be pleased with another." [Muslim]

[EXPLANATION OF HADITH 275]

The word *"Kariha (Dislike)"* means: hate, detest, enmity, hostility. So we would say, due to one experiencing something he dislikes from his wife from her character, that he shows enmity toward her. And the reason why one has been condemned for disliking his wife is because man has been commanded to be just at all times, so one has to always assess his situation, and the just individual always balances out all matters, whether this thing is pure evil and bad or the opposite - whether in this thing is great benefit and much good. So a person looks to see which of the two outweighs the other, then he assesses which one is greater in terms good and overall greater in virtue and more beneficial. This is a description of the just one, as Allah says in the Quran:

يَٰٓأَيُّهَا ٱلَّذِينَ ءَامَنُوا۟ كُونُوا۟ قَوَّٰمِينَ لِلَّهِ شُهَدَآءَ بِٱلْقِسْطِ ۖ وَلَا يَجْرِمَنَّكُمْ شَنَـَٔانُ قَوْمٍ عَلَىٰٓ أَلَّا تَعْدِلُوا۟

"O you who believe! Stand out firm for Allah and be just witnesses and let not the enmity and hatred of other make you avoid justice." (Al-Maa'idah 8)

What Allah means is be fair and just in your matters, even if it be the case that it is regarding an individual you have dislike for, rather be just. For this reason, the Prophet ﷺ sent Abdullah ibn Rawaaha to the Jews of *Khaybar* to estimate the value of their dates, as the Prophet ﷺ had given them this land and had given them a helping hand in much things as well as half of the dates that were there. Abdullah ibn Rawaaha went and estimated the dates and said to them:

> "O Jews of Khaybar! You are the most disliked of creation to Allah! You kill Allah the Exalted's Messengers as disbelieve in Allah! Yet all of this will not make me judge your matter based upon injustice. I estimate the load as twenty thousand fruit loads. And my dislike I have toward you will not make me rule regarding you unjustly, so if you wish, take (the dates) or I will? They replied to him, "For sure you have judged with pure justice regarding us and the matter."

The point of reference here is that the Prophet ﷺ commanded the husband to be diligent, wise and just. For this reason he ﷺ said:

> "A believer must not hate (his wife) a believing woman; if he dislikes one of her characteristics he will be pleased with another."

For example: one's wife refuses one of his requests, but then after that returns this right to him twice over, or she behaves ill at night but another night she is reformed or makes up with him that night by better treatment towards him, or she falls short regarding the children but at another time perfects this same matter by displaying better conduct towards them another day, etc. The wise approach is to not judge the wife when there is conflict or when she has wronged you. No! Rather, look at those good cherished times in the past you both have enjoyed together as well as look at what a brighter future holds for you both, then judge based upon justice.

Passing judgment based on an equal footing is not just regarding one's wife, rather this is general and pertains to dealing with others also; for example, you have a friend who you are on a good footing with, but one day he wrongs you in a matter, you now have to do the wise thing and not forget the other cherished moments of goodness that have occurred between you both over a very long period of time. So, now you judge based not just upon one or two wrongs he has done to you! Rather the matter should be looked at from a broader perspective and that is, if he is deserving forgiveness; over a person who may have just fallen short here or there, it would be better to forgive him and let the matter be forgotten; you judge based upon his good behavior, does it outweigh his bad behavior? On this basis, you can decide whether this person is entitled to be forgiven and if he is, then he should be forgiven.

Whoever forgives and makes peace as well as rectifies a situation, then surely his reward is with Allah. But on the other hand, if this individual is not entitled to forgiveness then take your right and this would be considered frowned upon on your part, but you look to what is of a greater benefit. In short, an individual should be as we have said: neither too inclined this way or too inclined that way; rather, act based upon justice in all his matters and that is with one's wife as well as in general, with one's friends, and in matters like buying and selling or the likes; one always looks at the good side of things (in his personal matters) then he evaluates based upon justice as Allah says in the Quran:

إِنَّ ٱللَّهَ يَأْمُرُ بِٱلْعَدْلِ وَٱلْإِحْسَٰنِ وَإِيتَآئِ ذِى ٱلْقُرْبَىٰ وَيَنْهَىٰ عَنِ ٱلْفَحْشَآءِ وَٱلْمُنكَرِ وَٱلْبَغْيِ يَعِظُكُمْ لَعَلَّكُمْ تَذَكَّرُونَ

"Verily, Allah enjoins *Al-Adl* (i.e. justice and worshipping none but Allah Alone) and *Al-Ihsan* (i.e. to be patient in performing your duties and in accordance with the *Sunnah* [legal ways] of the Prophet ﷺ in the perfect manner), and giving (help) to kith and kin (i.e. all what Allah has ordered you to give them e.g., wealth, visiting, looking after them, or any other kind of help, etc): and forbids *Al-Fahsha* (i.e. all evil deeds, e.g. illegal sexual acts, disobedience or parents, polytheism, to tell lies, to give false witness, to kill a life without right, etc.), and *Al-Munkar* (i.e. all that is prohibited by Islamic law: polytheism of every kind, disbelief and every kind of evil deeds etc.), and *Al-Baghy* (i.e. all kinds of oppression); He admonish you, that you may take heed." (An-Nahl 90)

[Hadith 276]

Amr ibn Al-Ahwas Al-Jushami reported that he had heard the Prophet ﷺ saying on his farewell pilgrimage, after praising and glorifying Allah and admonishing people:

« أَلَا وَاسْتَوْصُوا بِالنِّسَاءِ خَيْرًا ، فَإِنَّمَا هُنَّ عَوَانٍ عَنْدَكُمْ لَيْسَ تَمْلِكُونَ مِنْهُنَّ شَيْئًا غَيْرَ ذَلِكَ إِلَّا أَنْ يَأْتِينَ بِفَاحِشَةٍ مُبَيِّنَةٍ ، فَإِنْ فَعَلْنَ فَاهْجُرُوهُنَّ فِي الْمَضَاجِعِ ، وَاضْرِبُوهُنَّ ضَرْبًا غَيْرَ مُبَرِّحٍ ، فَإِنْ أَطَعْنَكُمْ فَلَا تَبْغُوا عَلَيْهِنَّ سَبِيلًا ، أَلَا إِنَّ لَكُمْ عَلَى نِسَائِكُمْ حَقًّا ، وَلِنِسَائِكُمْ عَلَيْكُمْ حَقًّا، فَحَقُّكُمْ عَلَيْهِنَّ أَنْ لَا يُوطِئْنَ فُرُشَكُمْ مِنْ تَكْرَهُونَ ، وَلَا يَأْذَنَّ فِي بُيُوتِكُمْ لِمَنْ تَكْرَهُونَ ، أَلَا وَحقُّهُنَّ عَلَيْكُمْ أَنْ تُحْسِنُوا إِلَيْهِنَّ فِي كِسْوَتِهِنَّ، وَطَعَامِهِنَّ». (رواه الترمذي، وقال، : حديث حسن صحيح

"Treat women kindly, they are like captives in your hands; you not owe anything else from them. In case they are guilty of open indecency, then do not share their beds and discipline them lightly but if they return to obedience, do not have recourse to anything else against them. You have rights over your wives and they have rights over you. Your right is that they shall not permit anyone you dislike to sit on your beds and not to let anyone you dislike enter your homes, and their right is that you should treat them well in the matter of food and clothing." [Tirmidhi]

[EXPLANATION OF HADITH 276]

The author mentions this narration wherein Amr ibn Al-Ahwas Al-Jushami reported what he heard from the Prophet ﷺ on his farewell pilgrimage, on the Day of Arafat. The Prophet ﷺ arrived at Makkah on Sunday, the fourth of Thul-Hijjah and he remained there till Thursday, the eighth of the same month. The Prophet ﷺ then left Makkah before *Zuhr* on Thursday and went to *Mina* and he prayed *Zuhr* at *Mina* and *Asr, Magrib, Isha* and *Fajr*. When the sun had risen, he left to *Arafat* and went to a well-known place called *Namirah* which is just before *Arafat* but not part of it; the time for *Zuhr* prayer had commenced, so he ﷺ commanded that his camel (*Al-Qaswa*) be brought to him and he mounted it and then proceeded until he reached the bottom of the valley where he addressed the people with a magnificent speech. Then the Prophet ﷺ admonished them regarding women and said: *"Treat women kindly, they are like captives in your hands."* This means that one's wife is like a captive one obtains (in war), and that he owns her so he made it clear that it is forbidden to discipline them unless they are guilty of open indecency, and this means clear acts of open disobedience toward the husband and the proof for this is taken from the words of Allah the Exalted when He says:

$$\text{فَإِنْ أَطَعْنَكُمْ فَلَا تَبْغُوا عَلَيْهِنَّ سَبِيلًا}$$

"But if they return to obedience, seek not against them means (of annoyance)." (An-Nisaa 34)

This means, if they are neglectful in the rights of her husband; firstly, he admonishes her, then he refuses to share her bed by not sleeping with her, then he disciplines her lightly if she continues such disobedience. So this is the order in rectifying one's wife who is neglectful in regards to the rights of her husband, and those rights which he is entitled to; Allah says: **"But if they return to obedience, seek not against them means (of annoyance)."** Meaning: the husband must not hit her nor fall short regarding her rights if she returns to obeying him in acts obedience.

Then the Prophet ﷺ made mention of more rights upon them toward their husbands and that was: *"Your right is that they shall not permit anyone you dislike to sit on your beds...;"* this means that one's wife must not let anyone he dislikes on his bed in his house or similar. We will give an example of what we are saying:

Then the Prophet ﷺ said: *"And not let anyone you dislike enter your home;"* this means that the wife must not let into his house those people that the husband dislikes her to welcome in, even if that is her mother or father, her sisters, brothers or her uncles and aunts. This is allowed even from the point of our Religion, and one may also prevent his wife going to her mother's house due to some troubles that have or could soon occur as a result.

It is upon the husband to provide for his wife even if she has an occupation, and he has no right to that which she earns from her salary, not even the least of it. And he should not impose upon her to provide and spend upon him and spend upon the household. And if this happens she should raise her case to a judge to separate them (i.e. divorce) if he forces her to

245

pay bills or if he obligates her to provide things such as food and drink.

During the Prophet's ﷺ farewell speech, he mentioned a number of things related to matters of the *Deen,* for example people's rights, to the point that he ﷺ said:

"Behold! All interest practices of paganism and ignorance are under my feet."

Before Islam, and we ask Allah for good health, the people would say to the poor if they wanted a loan, "I will loan you such-and-such wealth till such-and-such time, but if you do not repay it by such-and-such date, I will increase it to such-and-such amount!" - till that amount was twice its original amount. So the Prophet ﷺ said: *"Behold! All interest practises of paganism and ignorance are under my feet."* Meaning: the Prophet ﷺ put such practises beneath his feet, and what he meant was that it will no longer be practised.

Allah is the greatest! This shows Allah's law takes precedence and comes before all ways, customs and all traditions as the Prophet ﷺ said: *"And I begin by abolishing the amount of interest which Abbas ibn Abdul Muttalib has to receive."* Abbas (ibn Abdul-Muttalib) was the Prophet's ﷺ uncle and regardless of this, Allah's Law comes first, even before close relatives, customs, tribes and the likes.

And this is similar to the incident that occurred regarding a women from the tribe of Ibn Makzooma, wherein members of this tribe came to the Prophet ﷺ seeking intercession from this lady because she used to borrow people's belonging and then not return them claiming she had not taken any such goods from them! So the Prophet ﷺ ordered the prescribed

246

punishment upon her, and that was to cut her hand off, as she was guilty of theft. This become somewhat difficult upon her tribe which was a notable Quraish sub-tribe in Makkah so they pleaded with Usama ibn Zaid to go to the Prophet صلى الله عليه وسلم hoping that the Prophet صلى الله عليه وسلم, due to his close relationship with Usama, would accept Usama's intercession for her. And Usama ibn Zaid was the Prophet's صلى الله عليه وسلم first wife's servant that she gave to the Prophet صلى الله عليه وسلم, who set him free. So Usama, as well as Usama's father Zaid, were dearly loved by the Prophet صلى الله عليه وسلم. When Usama came to the Prophet صلى الله عليه وسلم seeking intercession, the Prophet صلى الله عليه وسلم disapproved of that and said to him:

"Do you intercede when one of the legal punishments ordained by Allah has been violated!"

So the Prophet صلى الله عليه وسلم disapproved of Usama's action's and rebuked him severely; then he stood up and addressed the people saying:

"The people before you were ruined because when a noble person among them committed theft, they would leave him, but if a weak person among them committed theft they would execute the legal punishment on him."

Then the Prophet صلى الله عليه وسلم said:

"By Allah, were Fatimah, the daughter of Muhammad, to commit theft, I would have cut off her hand!"

This, even though Fatimah رضي الله عنها is considered more honourable then this *Al-Mukzooma* woman in lineage, status and in *Deen*, rather, she is counted and considered one of the loftiest woman of Paradise in status! Regarding the Prophet's صلى الله عليه وسلم word:

"By Allah…" This is like an oath though he has not taken an actual oath, but he used it to emphasise the ruling and to clarify its importance; by saying this, the Prophet ﷺ put a stop to the thought of any form of intercession made about the matter, and for sure this shows the Prophet's ﷺ complete and perfect justice in Allah's religion.

[Hadith 277]

Mu'awiyah ibn Haidah ﷺ reported:

يا رسول الله ما حَقُّ زَوْجَةِ أَحَدِنَا عَلَيْهِ ؟ قال : « أَن تُطْعِمَها إِذَا طَعِمْتَ ، وتَكْسُوهَا إِذَا اكْتَسَيْتَ ولا تَضْرِب الْوَجهَ، وَلا تُقَبِّحْ ، ولا تَهْجُرْ إِلاَّ فِي الْبَيْتِ » حديثٌ حسنٌ رواه أَبو داود وقال : معنى « لا تُقَبِّحْ» أَى : لا تقُلْ قَبَّحَكِ الله .

"I asked the Messenger of Allah ﷺ*: 'What right can a wife demand for her husband?' He replied: 'You should feed her food when you eat, clothe her when you clothe yourself, not strike her face, and do not revile her or separate from her except in the house.'" [Abu Dawood]*

[Hadith 278]

Abu Hurairah ﷺ reported that the Messenger of Allah ﷺ said:

« أَكْمَلُ المؤْمنين إِيمَاناً أَحْسنُهُمْ خُلُقاً ، وَخِيارُكُمْ خيارُكم لِنِسَائِهِم » رواه التِّرمذي وقال : حديثٌ حسنٌ صحيحٌ .

"The most perfect man in his faith among the believers is the one whose behaviour is most excellent; and the best of you are those who are best to their wives." [At-Tirmidhi]

[EXPLANATION OF HADITHS 277 AND 278]

The author (Imam An-Nawawi) first mentions the *Hadith* of Mu'awiyah ibn Haidah, who asked the Prophet ﷺ regarding the rights of his wife upon him. It was the habit of the Companions ﷺ to ask the Prophet ﷺ to understand a ruling so as to apply it and not to merely know about it. With great regret, nowadays this seems to be what few Muslims do, instead they merely want to know a ruling and few will practise what they come to know or learn. So know! O reader, remember and do not forget, if one practises what he learns, it becomes a proof for him on the Day of Resurrection but on the other hand if he learns something from this Religion and does not put it into practice then it becomes a great proof against him and he will be held to account for not doing so. What did the Companions of the Prophet ﷺ used to ask the Prophet ﷺ regarding their *Deen*? In the Quran Allah says:

يَسْـَٔلُونَكَ مَاذَا يُنفِقُونَ

"They ask you (O Muhammad) what they should spend..." (Al-Baqarah 215)

وَيَسْـَٔلُونَكَ عَنِ ٱلْيَتَـٰمَىٰ

"They ask you concerning orphans." (Al-Baqarah 220)

وَيَسْـَٔلُونَكَ عَنِ ٱلْمَحِيضِ

"They ask you concerning menstruation." (Al-Baqarah 222)

يَسْئَلُونَكَ عَنِ ٱلْأَهِلَّةِ

"They ask you concerning (O Muhammad) about the new moons." (Al-Baqarah 189)

All of these questions we find the Companion asking, to know the ruling regarding that respective issue pertaining to the *Deen,* in order to know how to apply the rulings themselves as well as their families.

In this *Hadith,* Mu'awiyah ☙ asked: *"What right can any wife demand for her husband?"* The Prophet ﷺ replied: *"You should feed her food when you eat, clothe her when you clothe yourself..."* What is meant here is, do not single yourself out when buying clothes rather include her also, and the same goes for feeding yourself while neglecting her, rather, feed her also; share both clothing and sustenance with her, so it becomes mandated upon you whenever you provide for yourself to also provide for her. And the *Ulema* have said, "If a husband doesn't provide for his wife (or wives) and she refers the matter to an Islamic Judge requesting separation from the husband, the Judge is allowed to separate them and nullify their marriage! And that is due to the husband falling short of her rights which are compulsory.

Then the Prophet ﷺ said: *"And not strike her face, and do not revile her."* This means, do not discipline her except for a valid reason! And if you do discipline her then avoid her face, and do not strike her hard. We mentioned before, if a husband sees from his wife clear disobedience, haughtiness and her not giving him his God-given rights, he should do the following: firstly, he admonishes here, then (if she continues), he should not share the bed with her or he should separate from her bed, then (if she continues) he may discipline her, but not severely.

Dear reader, this shows the husband has the God-given right to discipline his wife if there is a valid reason for him doing so, but not in her face. And regarding hitting the face, then this does not just apply to the wife. Rather it is a general rule and it applies to all individuals (even animals), so if someone makes a mistake, avoid hitting them in their face because the most honorable thing to a person is his (or her) face as it is the front of the entire body.

As for the statement of the Prophet 變: *"And do not revile her."* This means: he should not revile her by using bad expressions like saying to her: "You're ugly!" or "May Allah disfigure and distort your face!" Words like this are forbidden, whether they are literal or implicit, the husband does not verbally abuse his wife. Allah condemns all forms of words of disgrace.

The Prophet 變 said next: *"Or separate from her except in the house."* What is intended here is, that the husband should not separate from his wife in a way that becomes manifest among the people what he is doing. And one of the wisdoms in separating from the wife in the house is this could be a means of her rectifying and reforming her condition or her behavior which could lead to the problem resolving. It is totally unwise as well as completely wrong to manifest and make known their situation by the husband leaving the home due to whatever problem they have between them, as this will become apparent when the people see him avoiding his home, so this separation should be confined to the home, and not made known to others.

As for the second *Hadith*, then this narration is an excellent *Hadith* and it is the statement of Abu Hurairah ﷺ, who reported that the Messenger of Allah ﷺ said: *"The most perfect man in his faith among the believers is the one whose behaviour is most excellent; and the best of you are those who are best to their wives."*

Regarding *Emaan* (faith), it fluctuates and can go up and down as Allah the Exalted says in the Quran:

وَيَزْدَادَ ٱلَّذِينَ ءَامَنُوٓاْ إِيمَٰنًا

"And the believer may increase in faith." (Al-Muddathir 31)

This indicates that from person-to-person, their *Emaan* might somewhat differ. And there are believers those *Emaan* is so strong that their belief in the matters of the unseen, such as the Day of Judgment, Paradise and Hell, is as if they see them in plain sight. They have sound firm unshakable *Emaan,* free from doubt. And on the other hand there are believers who have unsteady *Emaan!* And we ask for good health! This is as Allah the Exalted says the Quran:

وَمِنَ ٱلنَّاسِ مَن يَعْبُدُ ٱللَّهَ عَلَىٰ حَرْفٍ

"And among mankind is he who worships Allah as it were, upon the very edge." (Al-Hajj 11)

The meaning of the word *"edge"* means on the edge, brink, or verge. Allah says:

فَإِنْ أَصَابَهُۥ خَيْرٌ ٱطْمَأَنَّ بِهِۦ

"If good befalls him"

253

Meaning: if no one causes him to have doubts about the *Deen*, and he is pleased and he only encounters good, Allah says:

$$ٱطْمَأَنَّ بِهِۦ$$

"He is content therewith."

Meaning: he pleased and satisfied; then Allah says:

$$وَإِنْ أَصَابَتْهُ فِتْنَةٌ ٱنْقَلَبَ عَلَىٰ وَجْهِهِۦ خَسِرَ ٱلدُّنْيَا وَٱلْآخِرَةَ$$

"But if trail befalls him, he turns back on his face (i.e. reverts back to disbelief after embracing Islam). He loses both this world and the Hereafter"

I.e. if something of dislike befalls him, that is, physically, in his wealth or family, he falls on his face and is very displeased and angry with what Allah has destined for him so he is ruined and we seek help with Allah! Allah says lastly:

$$ذَٰلِكَ هُوَ ٱلْخُسْرَانُ ٱلْمُبِينُ$$

"That is the evident lose."

As for the Prophet's ﷺ statement: *"The most perfect man in his faith among the believers is the one whose behaviour is most excellent;"* this great *Hadith* is an incitement and encouragement towards good manners and this is divided into the two following categories:

1. **Good manners with Allah.**

This is simply that a Muslim is pleased with Islam as his religion, he submits to it, following and accepting it, obeying its commandments whether they are orders or prohibitions; one accepts his fate and whatsoever Allah decrees for him (or her), and one utters statements as part of being satisfied with Allah's Decree such as, "O Lord of all that exists! Everything comes from You, I am pleased with You as My Lord, if You honor me with anything I will be pleased, if You afflict me with any trial I will be patient!" So one is generally pleased with Allah's Decree, Commands, and His Religion; this is the definition of good manners with Allah.

2. Good manners with the people

This is divided into three categories:

i. Refraining from harming others.

ii. Being generous.

iii. Being patient with the people and enduring any afflictions one encounters from them. If an individual does these three as mentioned, when he is counted as a person with complete *Emaan*.

The Prophet ﷺ mentions lastly in the *Hadith* we are explaining: *"And the best of you are those who are best to their wives."* One must not forget that if there is good in you (as a husband), then, then certainly the closest people to us are our spouses and they are the most worthy and deserving of the best of our treatment. And with great regret some people are very bad towards their wives, but treat those other than them in the best manner! We say, for sure this is big mistake! Without doubt, our wives deserve firstly this excellent treatment and this takes precedence over all others as one's wife is with her husband night and day, in public as well as in secret;

whatsoever befalls you befalls them also, and if good comes to you then also the same comes to them, and lastly, if you are overcome with distress and sadness then they too will be befallen with similar feelings, so let not that be forgotten! We ask Allah the Exalted to complete my *Emaan* and those of the Muslims and to make us the best of Allah's servants regarding our wives, as these who are best among us are those are considered best to their wives.

[Hadith 279]

Iyaas ibn Abdullah ﷺ reported:

قال رسولُ اللهِ صَلَّى اللهُ عَلَيْهِ وسَلَّم: « لاَ تَضْرِبُوا إِمَاءَ اللهِ » فَجاءَ عُمَرُ رضي الله عنه إلى رسول الله صَلَّى اللهُ عَلَيْهِ وسَلَّم، فَقالَ : ذَئِرْنَ النِّساءُ عَلَى أزْواجهنَّ ، فَرَخَّصَ في ضَرْبِهنَّ فأَطاف بآلِ رسولِ الله صَلَّى اللهُ عَلَيْهِ وسَلَّم نِساءٌ كَثيرٌ يَشْكونَ أزْواجهُنَّ ، فقال رسول الله صَلَّى اللهُ عَلَيْهِ وسَلَّم : « لَقَدْ أطَافَ بآلِ بَيْت مُحَمَّدٍ نِساءٌ كَثيرٍ يشْكونَ أزْوَاجَهنَّ لَيْسَ أُولئِك بخِيارِكُمْ » رواه أبو داود بإسنادٍ صحيح.

"The Messenger of Allah ﷺ said: 'Do not beat Allah's bondwomen.' Then Umar came to the Messenger ﷺ and complained saying: 'The women have become very daring towards their husbands!' He (the Prophet) gave permission to discipline them. Then many women went to the family of the Messenger of Allah (i.e. his wives), complaining of their husbands, and he (the Prophet ﷺ) said: 'Many women have gone round Muhammad's family complaining of their husbands. Those who do so, those who take to beating their wives, are not the best among you.'" [Abu Dawood]

[Hadith 280]

Abdullah ibn Amr ibn Al-Aas ﷺ reported: the Messenger of Allah ﷺ said:

«الدُّنْيَا مَتَاعٌ ، وَخَيْرُ مَتاعها المرْأةُ الصَّالحةُ » رواه مسلم .

"The world is but a (quick passing) enjoyment; and the best enjoyment of the world is a pious and virtuous woman." [Muslim]

[EXPLANATION OF HADITHS 279 AND 280]

The author mentions the first narration regarding women in which the Prophet ﷺ said: *"Do not beat Allah's bondwomen."* i.e. the womenfolk. They are referred to as "bondwomen" just as males are referred to as "slaves of Allah." Another *Hadith* states:

> *"Do not stop Allah's women-slaves from going to Allah's Masjid."*

The Prophet ﷺ forbade the Companions from hitting their wives, so the Companions refrained from that as this was the type of followers the Prophet ﷺ had nurtured, whenever he commanded them something, or forbade them something, they would utter the statement, *"We hear and obey!"* As we said the women are incomplete in their intellect as well as in their *Deen*, so when the Prophet ﷺ prohibited the men from hitting their wives, they became emboldened and audacious as Umar says: *"The women have become very daring towards their husbands!"* When they became like this towards their husbands, the Prophet ﷺ allowed the Companions to discipline them. The Companions went too far in that and beyond that which they had been allowed, so their wives came to the Prophet's ﷺ house complaining about that to his wives. So the Prophet ﷺ said: *"Those who do so, those who take to beating their wives, are not the best among you!"* Meaning: those who hit their wives are not considered to be the best of men, as he said: *"The best among you are those who are best to their wives."* This is proof that one should not go over bounds and exceed the limits in hitting their wives, but as we said within these stated limits, following the prescribed guidelines, one is allowed to discipline his wife and the proof to back my words is not my mere speech or personal opinion, it is backed by the Words of Allah in the Quran when He said:

وَٱلَّٰتِى تَخَافُونَ نُشُوزَهُنَّ فَعِظُوهُنَّ وَٱهْجُرُوهُنَّ فِى ٱلْمَضَاجِعِ وَٱضْرِبُوهُنَّ

"As to those women on whose part you see ill-conduct, admonish the (first), (next) refuse to share their beds, (and last) beat them (lightly)." (Al-Nisaa 34)

If one has to resort to hitting, as mentioned before, it should not be severe.

The author next mentions the *Hadith* of Abdullah ibn Amr ibn Al-Aas, who narrates that the Messenger of Allah ﷺ said:

"The world is but a (quick passing) enjoyment; and the best enjoyment of the world is a pious and virtuous woman."

As for the words of the Prophet ﷺ: *"The world is but a (quick passing) enjoyment,"* then what is intended is something one takes pleasure and delight from, similarly to that of a traveller on a journey who takes pleasure from his provisions, then they get used up to his advantage. So the Prophet ﷺ said: *"And the best enjoyment of the world is a pious and virtuous woman."* This means, that if an individual is honoured by Allah with a righteous wife who is good as well as virtuous in her *Deen* and intellect, then she is considered the best thing and an enjoyment in the world for the husband for she will safeguard his secrets, wealth, and his offspring.

If the wife is intelligent and also manages well in maintaining the house, keeping it in proper order and clean, and she is good in the upbringing of his children and safeguards her appearance for her husband, looking clean, neat and tidy so when he looks at her he is very pleased at her appearance, as well as when he is away from the house, she maintains it in the best of ways as well as safeguarding it, and when he entrusts a matter to her she fulfils it, then this is what is intended by the Prophet's ﷺ statement:

> *"A woman is married for four things: for her wealth, for her lineage, for her beauty or for her piety. Select the pious, may you be blessed."*

Meaning, strive for the pious women! As this is the best women one can marry for sure, even though she might not be physically beautiful, but her manners are and she is pious, may you be blessed.

[Chapter 35] The Husband's Rights Concerning his Wife

Allah ﷻ says in the Quran:

ٱلرِّجَالُ قَوَّٰمُونَ عَلَى ٱلنِّسَآءِ بِمَا فَضَّلَ ٱللَّهُ بَعْضَهُمْ عَلَىٰ بَعْضٍ وَبِمَآ

أَنفَقُواْ مِنْ أَمْوَٰلِهِمْ فَٱلصَّٰلِحَٰتُ قَٰنِتَٰتٌ حَٰفِظَٰتٌ لِّلْغَيْبِ بِمَا حَفِظَ ٱللَّهُ

"Men are the protectors and maintainers of women, because Allah has made one of them excel the other, and because they spend (to support them) from their means. Therefore, the righteous women are devoutly obedient (to Allah and their husbands), and guard in the husbands' absence what Allah orders them to guard (e.g., their chastity and their husband's property)." (An-Nisaa' 34)

Among the *Hadiths* on this subject, is the *Hadith* of 'Amr bin al-Ahwas in the previous chapter.

[Hadith 281]

Abu Hurairah ﷺ reported that the Messenger of Allah ﷺ said:

« إِذَا دَعَا الرَّجُلُ امْرَأَتَهُ إِلَى فِرَاشِهِ فَلَمْ تَأْتِهِ فَبَاتَ غَضْبَانَ عَلَيْهَا لَعَنَتْهَا الْمَلَائِكَةُ حَتَّى تُصْبِحَ » متفقٌ عليه .

"When a man calls his wife to his bed, and she does not respond and he (the husband) spends the night angry with her, the angels curse her until morning." [Agreed upon]

And in another narration the Messenger of Allah ﷺ said:

«إِذَا بَاتَتِ المَرْأَةُ هَاجِرَةً فِرَاشَ زَوْجِهَا لَعنتْهَا المَلائِكَةُ حَتَّى تُصْبِحَ ».

"When a woman spends the night away from the bed of her husband, the angels curse her until morning."

And in another narration the Messenger of Allah ﷺ said:

«وَالَّذِي نَفْسِي بِيَدِهِ مَا مِن رَجُلٍ يَدْعُو امْرَأَتَهُ إِلَى فِرَاشِهِ فَتَأْبَى عَلَيْهِ إِلَّا كَانَ الَّذِي فِي السَّمَاءِ سَاخِطاً عَلَيْهَا حَتَّى يَرْضَى عَنها » .

"By Him in whose hand is my life! When a man calls his wife to his bed, and she does not respond, the One who is above the heaven becomes displeased with her until he (her husband) becomes pleased with her."

[EXPLANATION OF SUPPORTING VERSE AND HADITH 281]

The author (Imam An-Nawawi) starts this chapter pertaining to the husband's rights concerning his wife, and mentions firstly the statement of Allah the Exalted when He says in the Quran:

ٱلرِّجَال قَوَّامُونَ عَلَى ٱلنِّسَآءِ بِمَا فَضَّلَ ٱللَّهُ بَعْضَهُمْ عَلَى بَعْضٍ

وَبِمَآ أَنفَقُواْ مِنْ أَمْوَٰلِهِمْ فَٱلصَّٰلِحَٰتُ قَٰنِتَٰتٌ حَٰفِظَٰتٌ لِّلْغَيْبِ بِمَا

حَفِظَ ٱللَّهُ

"Men are the protectors and maintainers of women, because Allah has made one of them excel the other, and because they spend (to support them) from their means. Therefore, the righteous women are devoutly obedient, and guard in the husbands' absence what Allah orders them to guard."

Regarding Allah's words: **"Men are the protectors and maintainers of women,"** the meaning is, that the man is the guardian over the woman, the disposer of her affairs, the one who is responsible for guiding her and the one whom she should obey. On the other hand, if he commands her to disobey Allah in any act of disobedience, she is not allowed to obey him in that matter as there is no obedience to the creation when it entails disobedience to the Creator, no matter who it is.

This Quranic verse is a clear proof against those shameless and foolish non-Muslims in the west and other parts of the globe, who honour the woman to such an extent that they put them before men! And as is know now, we have many blind followers of the west, who likewise, honour the woman over the man. But this comes as no surprise because such people even venerate their pet dogs, and place them on thrones! They go as far as even spending thousands of pounds to acquire expensive breeds, buying the best quality soaps to clean them, and this is nothing more than a joke to which a sane man surely finds degrading.

Men have been placed in charge over women because Allah ﷻ says Himself:

فَضَّلَ ٱللَّهُ بَعْضَهُمْ عَلَىٰ بَعْضٍ وَبِمَآ أَنفَقُواْ مِنْ أَمْوَٰلِهِمْ

"Because Allah has made the one of them to excel the other, and because they spend (to support them) from their means..."

Here, Allah ﷻ explains the fact that the man is the one who provides, as Allah commands him to, and he has been appointed as a shepherd and owner of the home, and women have not been commanded to provide for the family. This indicates that it is biding upon him to work and provide, but as for the women, then her duty is to her husband and his home, managing it, tending to it and so forth as well as nurturing her offspring, and this is what she has been assigned to do. And as for her sharing in providing sustenance alongside men in places of work, or providing means of sustenance for the man, then this is clearly going against her natural disposition and is a violation of the Religion of Islam because Allah says in the verse we are explaining at hand:

وَبِمَآ أَنفَقُواْ مِنْ أَمْوَٰلِهِمْ

"Because they spend (to support them) from their means..."

This means that the one who is the provider is none other than the man. Allah goes on to say:

قَٰنِتَٰتٌ حَٰفِظَٰتٌ لِّلْغَيْبِ بِمَا حَفِظَ ٱللَّهُ

"Therefore, the righteous women are devoutly obedient (to Allah and their husbands), and guard in the husbands' absence what Allah orders them to guard."

So phrase, "Therefore, the righteous women are devoutly obedient," means the woman continually remains obedient and the words "righteous, devoutly obedient" do not mean she is devout in supplication (*qunoot*)! Rather, it means continually being devoted in obedience, as Allah says in another *Surah*:

وَقُومُواْ لِلَّهِ قَٰنِتِينَ

"And stand before Allah with obedience." (Al-Baqarah 238)

Meaning, continually being obedient. Allah the Exalted then says: "and guards in the husbands' absence what Allah orders them to guard." What is meant here is, the wife safeguards the husband's affairs and his business, especially those matters that occur behind closed doors. So know O brothers, choose from the many choices you have, a righteous wife, as that is what will be to your benefit and at the same time, is much more profitable than having a wife who merely has good likes but is void of piety.

Next, the author mentions the first of three narrations which Abu Hurairah ﷺ reported from the Messenger of Allah ﷺ. Regarding the angels cursing the wife mentioned in the *Hadith*, it means they make *Dua* (supplication) against her to be cursed! And the word "*Curse*" means, that the cursed person be far removed from the mercy of Allah. So, if the wife refused to have sexual intercourse with her husband, which Allah has allowed and made this act lawful for the husband, if she does not allow him, then the angels curse her and we seek Allah's refuge! If the wife refuses him till the morning, Allah's angels curse her time-after-time! As for the third out of the three narrations mentioned, then the Prophet ﷺ said:

> "*By Him in whose hand is my life, when a man calls his wife to his bed, and she does not respond, the One who is above the heaven becomes displeased with her until he (he husband) becomes pleased with her*"

This narration is more severe than the previous narrations because in it Allah Himself is displeased with her! And certainly if Allah is displeased with someone, then this is far worse than the mere curse of any man. We ask Allah for good health! And the proof for this is the Verse in the Quran pertaining to Allah's cursing man; He says:

وَٱلْخَٰمِسَةَ أَنَّ لَعْنَتَ ٱللَّهِ عَلَيْهِ إِن كَانَ مِنَ ٱلْكَٰذِبِينَ

"The invoking of the Curse of Allah on him if he be of those who tell a lie." (An-Noor 7)

But on the other hand when a woman is cursed by Allah, He says:

أَنَّ غَضَبَ ٱللَّهِ عَلَيْهَآ إِن كَانَ مِنَ ٱلصَّـٰدِقِينَ

"The Wrath of Allah be upon her if he (the husband) speaks the truth." (An-Noor 9)

What we see is that the Wrath of Allah is worse than His curse. We continue in explaining the statement of the Prophet ﷺ: *"The One who is above the heaven becomes displeased with her until he becomes pleased with her."* The *"He"* mentioned here is referring to the husband. And as for the Prophet's ﷺ words: *"The angels curse her until morning"* it indicates Allah being displeased with the wife solely based on her husband being upset and angry with her! It is possible that when the Prophet ﷺ mentioned *"Until morning,"* it could be counted as the least time that the husband remains angry and upset with her. And it is also possible that the husband remains angry with her but not till morning, just before sunset and it is just as likely that at times the husband will remain angry with his wife more than a day, maybe two. Whatsoever the case may be, as long as the husband remains angry with his wife, even if that is for a very long period time, Allah the Exalted and High will remain displeased with her.

And this *Hadith* is a proof of the enormous rights the husband has over his wife, but in saying this, these rights are conditional! And his full entitlement to them is based upon him providing her with her rights. If he is not giving her the rights entitled to her, she has the right to deny him, and this is due the statement of Allah ﷺ in the Quran:

$$فَمَنِ ٱعْتَدَىٰ عَلَيْكُمْ فَٱعْتَدُوا۟ عَلَيْهِ بِمِثْلِ مَا ٱعْتَدَىٰ عَلَيْكُمْ$$

"Then whoever transgresses the prohibition against you, you transgress likewise against him." (Al-Baqarah 194)

The Exalted also says:

$$وَإِنْ عَاقَبْتُمْ فَعَاقِبُوا۟ بِمِثْلِ مَا عُوقِبْتُم بِهِۦ ۖ وَلَئِن صَبَرْتُمْ لَهُوَ خَيْرٌ$$

$$لِّلصَّٰبِرِينَ$$

"And if you are punished, then punish them with the like of that with which you were afflicted." (An-Nahl 126)

But if the husband is fulfilling her entitled rights, but she is falling short of his, then the threat mentioned in the *Hadith,* if she refuses to sleep with him, is applied to her.

Also, from the benefits of this *Hadith* is a clear proof used by *Ahl us-Sunnah wal-Jama'ah* and the *Salaf* of this *Ummah* that Allah the Exalted is above the seven heavens, above the Mighty Throne which above the seven heavens. And what is not intended is that His Kingdom is in the sky or inside the heavens! This interpretation is a clear distortion of Allah's intended meaning and involves distorting Allah's Speech and changing it to other than what it is. This is a trait of the Jews and we seek refuge in Allah as they did this with the *Torah,* changing its meanings from their correct places as well as giving meanings to things other than what Allah intended. To Allah belongs the Kingdom and dominion of the heavens and earth as He say:

وَلِلَّهِ مُلْكُ ٱلسَّمَٰوَٰتِ وَٱلْأَرْضِ ۗ وَٱللَّهُ عَلَىٰ كُلِّ شَىْءٍ قَدِيرٌ

"And to Allah belongs the dominion of the heavens and the earth." (Aali Imraan 189)

And He says also:

قُلْ مَنۢ بِيَدِهِۦ مَلَكُوتُ كُلِّ شَىْءٍ وَهُوَ يُجِيرُ وَلَا يُجَارُ عَلَيْهِ إِن كُنتُمْ تَعْلَمُونَ

"Say: 'In whose Hand is the sovereignty of everything (i.e. treasures of each and everything)? And He protects (all), while against whom there is no protector." (Al-Mu'minoon 88)

Allah also says:

لَهُۥ مَقَالِيدُ ٱلسَّمَٰوَٰتِ وَٱلْأَرْضِ

"To Him belong the keys of the heavens and the earth." (Ash-Shura 12)

The sovereignty of the heavens and earth is in the Hands of the Exalted and Most High and everything belongs to Him. What is intended is that Allah Himself is above the heavens and over His Mighty Throne, and the knowledge regarding this fact is something a person acknowledges even within his own self as it is a part of his innate natural disposition that does not need one to have faith in or for it to be studied.

Rather, it is something a person knows. Even when a person raises his hands in supplication, does he not raise them to the sky? The reason why is because within himself, he knows Allah is Higher than everything, and above all things. And even the animals acknowledge this for they at times raise their heads to the heavens, and we were informed by some professors in the institute in our location that an individual called them informing them about the earthquake that struck Egypt, and that a few minutes just before it started, the animals in the zoo fled to their resting places in complete fear and chaos raising their heads to the heavens! *SubhaanAllah*! Even the animals acknowledge Allah the Exalted is High above all His creation, but yet and still, you have those who disbelieve Allah is above His creation, above His Mighty Throne, and we seek refuge in Allah! We have also witnessed that animals, whenever they are harmed and the likes, they stop and automatically raise their heads to the heavens, this is something observed.

These matters, as well as other than them, indicate that the belief that Allah the Exalted is above everything, is something engraved in someone's natural disposition and needs not confirmation nor evidence; if those who deny Allah being above His Mighty Throne, may Allah guide them, were to think for just one moment and answer this question: *"Where, and to which direction do we raise our hands when we want to make supplication to Allah* ﷻ?*"* The reply is, is it not to the heavens? Glory be to Allah! Their own actions, that is, raising their hands to the heaven goes against their own beliefs! So we see that this indicates that their belief system is completely corrupt and distorted as well as rejected. And it is feared that this belief they have is tantamount to *Kufr* (disbelief). And it is reported that in the time of the Prophet 鐃, there was a slave-girl and her master or owner wanted to free her, so the Prophet 鐃 said to bring her to him, then when she was brought before the Prophet 鐃, he said to her: *"Where is Allah?"* She replied: *"Allah is above the sky."* So the Prophet 鐃 said: *"Who am I?"* To which she replied: *"You are the Messenger of Allah."* So based upon this, the Prophet 鐃 said to her master: *"Set her free, her for verily she is a believer."*

Glory be to Allah! The belief which we ascribe to is that Allah the Exalted is above all of His creation and He is the Compelling One, over His servants, above His Mighty Throne and His Throne is established firmly over the heavens and earth, and they are insignificant in relation to the Throne. And there are some narrations regarding the mightiness of the Throne and its size in comparison to the seven heavens and the seven earths - that the difference is like a ring thrown in the desert. So would this ring in the desert be noticed in this desert? What significance would this be in the desert! It wouldn't have any, as the Prophet 鐃 said:

> *"The virtue of the Throne over the footstool (Kursi) is a ring in the desert."*

This indicates that Allah is greater than all things, and Allah the Exalted says regarding this in the Quran:

$$وَسِعَ كُرْسِيُّهُ ٱلسَّمَـٰوَٰتِ وَٱلْأَرْضَ$$

"His *Kursi* (footstool) extends over the heavens and earth." (Al-Baqarah 255)

This means, it encompasses it, so if this is the case, that the footstool alone extends over the heavens and earth, then what then would be the case regarding the Lord the Exalted One! The Exalted Lord is above all and this is our belief, so we ask Allah the Exalted to make us die upon this belief and be raised upon it as it is collectively agreed upon by *Ahl us-Sunnah wal-Jama'ah*.

[Hadith 282]

Abu Hurairah ❀ reported that the Messenger of Allah ﷺ said:

«لا يَحِلُّ لامْرَأَةٍ أَنْ تَصُومَ وَزَوْجُهَا شَاهِدٌ إلا بإذْنِهِ ، وَلا تَأْذَنُ فِي بَيْتِهِ إلاَّ بإذْنِهِ » متفقٌ عليه، وهذا لفظ البخاري .

"It is not lawful for a woman to observe (voluntary) fasts without the permission of her husband when he is at home; and she should not allow anyone in the house without his permission." [Agreed upon, the wording is Al-Bukhari's]

[EXPLANATION OF HADITH 282]

The author mentions this narration regarding some of the rights of the husband over his wife, and that is, she is not allowed to fast if he is in the country except with his permission, but as for if he is not in that country then she may fast as she pleases. So it seems from this *Hadith* that what is intended both the obligatory and recommended fasts.

Regarding this, we will explain the issue by first clarifying her fasting any recommended fast which merely encouraged. As for the recommended fast, then it is clear that it is not allowed for the wife to fast any of them except with her husband's permission because the rights of the husband are obligatory, and the non-obligatory fast are not compulsory upon her so she is not sinful for not fasting them or leaving them. And the rights of the husband, if the wife leaves fulfilling them she is committing a sin for doing so, for it could be the case that the husband wants to enjoy sexual relations with her, and if she is fasting and he desires her, how will he be able to fulfil his desire? Certainly this well be very hard and difficult for him to bear due to her fasting as he will not be able to have sexual relations with her. So if she is fasting and the husband desires her, she must accept his request for relations between them and by requesting her to break her fast, there is no sin upon him for doing that.

But as for the fast that is obligatory, it might be the case that she has to make up days due upon her, and if it is the case that there is plenty of time till the next Ramadan, in that case she is forbidden to fast those days she has to make up except with her husband's permission, while he is in the county. We will give you an example: say the wife has ten days to make up from the previous Ramadan, and the month is Rajab, so the wife says to the husband, *"I want to make up my missed days of Ramadan."* We say: do not fast those missed days except with your husband's permission, as there is still plenty of time left for you to make up those missed days that you are obliged to make up. But on the other hand, if she has ten days to make up and Ramadan is in ten days, then she does need not her husband's permission to fast them as it is not allowed for a person who has days to make up from the previous Ramadan to delay them till the next the Ramadan (starts). So, in short if Ramadan is a matter of days away and she has a few days to make up it is not allowed for the husband or anyone else to prevent her from making up those remaining days.

Now we ask a question: is it the same regarding the prayer? Does the wife have to first seek the permission of her husband before praying *Sunnah* prayers? We say, yes it is possible that it is! But the five daily prayers, this is a different matter and that is, she does need the husband's permission to pray any of them, but that which is not obligatory, then yes she should first seek the husband's permission before praying them. But it seems that prayer is not completely the same as the fast and that the wife does not need her husband's permission to pray them (*Sunnah* prayers), except if he prevents her from that.

And regarding the Prophet's ﷺ statement: *"And she should not allow anyone in the house without his permission,"* then what seems to be apparent from it, is that the wife is not allowed to let anyone enter her husband's home except by his leave, but regarding this matter, that is, him allowing her permission to allow anyone into his home, then it is divided into two ng categories:

1. **Customary permission.**

    This type is known as the customary type of allowing entrance, such as the wife allowing her neighbors, her relatives, her friends as well as her colleagues and the likes, into the home; this is counted as common tradition, and the husband gives prior consent to his wife for her before all these people enter his house, so she allows them to enter. So she is allowed to permit those mentioned except if he prevents her and that is by saying to her: *"Do not let so-and-so in the house."* In which case she would not be allowed to enter that individual into his home.

2. **Verbal permission.**

    This means, the husband says to his wife: *"Enter whosoever you please, except if I say otherwise."* In this case the matter is made clear to her.

This *Hadith* proves that the husband is allowed to prevent and allow into his home whomever he wishes. The husband may have a reason for his wife's mother, even her sisters, aunts, uncles, etc. from entering the home, but in saying this, the husband should only prevent them if there is a need to do so, and that is if he fears harm or trouble coming to his home, in which case, he is perfectly allowed to prevent her family from coming into his house. And with great regret, and we seek Allah's refuge from evil, there are some (Muslim) women in whom there is not much good, who bring so much harm to the husband's home and make many problems, causing him numerous discomforts and so much grief. Such women allow into his house those who make nothing but problems after problems, creating hatred and animosity between the husband and wife until she dislikes the husband; and in such a situation, he should not leave his offspring with his wife's mother (if she is the cause), as that the damage she is able to do between her daughter and the daughter's husband is similar to magic which is equal to those who cause separation between a husband and wife.

[Hadith 283]

Ibn Umar reported that the Prophet ﷺ said:

« كُلُّكُمْ راعٍ، وَكُلُّكُمْ مسئولٌ عنْ رعيَّتِهِ ، والأَميرُ رَاعٍ ، والرَّجُلُ راعٍ على أَهْلِ بَيْتِهِ، والمرأةُ راعِيةٌ على بيْتِ زَوْجِها وولَدِهِ ، فَكُلُّكُمْ راعٍ ، وَكُلُّكُمْ مسئولٌ عنْ رعيَّتِهِ » متفقٌ عليه .

"All of you are guardians and are responsible for your subjects. The ruler is a guardian of his subjects, the man is a guardian of his family, the woman is a guardian and is responsible for her husband's house and his offspring and so all of you are guardians and are responsible for your subjects." [Agreed upon]

[Hadith 284]

Abu Ali Talq ibn Ali reported that the Messenger of Allah ﷺ said:

«إذا دعا الرَّجُلُ زَوْجتَهُ لحاجتِهِ فلْتأْتِهِ وإنْ كَانَتْ عَلَى التَّنُّور». رواه الترمذي والنسائي، وقال الترمذي: حديث حسن صحيح .

"When a man calls his wife to satisfy his desire, she must go to him even if she occupied with the oven." [At-Tirmidhi and An-Nasaa'ee]

[Hadith 285]

Abu Hurairah ⌾ reported that the Messenger ﷺ said:

« لَوْ كُنْتُ آمِراً أَحَداً أَنْ يَسْجُدَ لِأَحَدٍ لَأَمَرْتُ المَرْأَةَ أَنْ تَسْجُدَ لِزَوْجِهَا » . رواه الترمذي وقال : حديث حسن صحيح.

"If I were to order anyone to prostrate himself before another, I would have ordered a woman to prostrate herself before her husband." [At-Tirmidhi]

[Hadith 286]

Umm Salamah ⌾ reported the Messenger of Allah ﷺ said:

« أَيُّمَا امْرَأَةٍ مَاتَتْ وَزَوْجُهَا رَاضٍ عنها دخَلَتِ الجَنَّةَ » رواه الترمذي وقال حديث حسن .

"Any woman dies while her husband is pleased with her, she will enter Jannah (Paradise)." [At-Tirmidi (Shaykh Al-Albani graded it weak)]

[EXPLANATION OF HADITHS 283 TO 286]

The author mentions a number of narrations and the first of them is the statement of the Prophet ﷺ: *"All of you are guardians and are responsible for your subjects."* Here the Prophet ﷺ is addressing every individual considered among the entire Muslim nation, and that every person is responsible for those under their care and protection. And this word: *"Guardians"* means: a person who looks after a thing, making sure that it is okay, as well as protecting that thing from any harm. And this is similar to a shepherd who tends to his sheep, looking for a safe unpopulated location for them to settle, and he stays with them. Similarly, the children of Aadam are all shepherds and responsible for their flocks, and all will held to account regarding them; the ruler will be held accountable for his subjects, whether he is a ruler over a small town or greater than that, and the degree of his responsibility is according to how many subjects he has to look after. He might be an absolute leader, such as a king or caliph like in the time of Umar ibn Khattaab, Uthmaan ibn Affaan or Ali ibn Abi Taalib or those who followed them such as the Banu Umaymah or Banu Abbaas, etc.

In summary, guardianship differs from one individual to another; the rulership over a state or town is different from that of a man over his family for he is only responsible for those members of his household such as his wife, sons, daughters, and generally those who are living in his home.; it is biding upon him to treat them in the best way possible.

Similarly the wife is in the same position as that of the husband, being that is she is the guardian over the husband's home and will be questioned regarding it. So it becomes a must upon the wife to continually serve the husband's meals, making sure that they are well done and on time and well cooked, as well as serving him coffee, tea and preparing his bedding. And she should not cook an exceeding amount of food or serve too much or too many, as the objective behind this is so that the wife is able to economize, as economizing is half of living or makes life easier rather than being wasteful which is unbecoming. She is responsible for looking after her children and upbringing and rectifying them, and in dressing them making sure they are well dressed and looked after properly, as well as making sure their bed sheets are regularly changed and kept clean, and it is upon her to keep her kids warm and well covered in the winter. She will be held responsible for all of this and be held accountable.

And also a slave is responsible for his master's wealth and it is a must upon him to protect it, not misuse it, only make use of it in a good way and not be negligent of it nor waste it or transgress the boundaries concerning it.

As for the remaining *Ahaadith* the author mentions they need further investigation regarding their authenticity,[7] but what we can say regarding them is that when they are mentioned together they indicate the great rights the husband has over his wife and vice versa, the great rights the wife has over the husband, and for certain both of their rights are enormous and each spouse should willingly give each other that which they are entitled to as Allah says in the Quran:

---

[7] I checked out all the *Ahaadith* considered to be unauthentic and referred to the works of Shaykh Al-Albaani and found that he authenticated them all.

وَهُنَّ مِثْلُ ٱلَّذِى عَلَيْهِنَّ بِٱلْمَعْرُوفِ

**"And they (women) have rights (over their husbands)
to what is reasonable." (Al-Baqarah 228)**

This indicates the perfect balance and justice Islam endorses
regarding people's rights, and that Islam distinguishes itself
from all other ways as well as all other religions.

[Hadith 288]

Usamah ibn Zaid ﷺ reported the Prophet ﷺ said:

« ما تَرَكْتُ بعْدِي فِتْنَةً هِي أَضَرُّ عَلَى الرِّجالِ : مِنَ النِّسَاءِ » متفقٌ عليه .

"I am not leaving behind me a more harmful trial for men than women " *[Agreed upon]*

[EXPLANATION OF HADITH 288]

The author mentions this (last) narration concerning the trials of women, in which the Prophet ﷺ makes manifest that which a man ought to not overlook, and that is, the trials and temptations of women. At the same token it is surely worth mentioning the statement of the Exalted regarding such trials; He the Exalted says:

زُيِّنَ لِلنَّاسِ حُبُّ ٱلشَّهَوَٰتِ مِنَ ٱلنِّسَآءِ وَٱلْبَنِينَ وَٱلْقَنَٰطِيرِ ٱلْمُقَنطَرَةِ مِنَ ٱلذَّهَبِ وَٱلْفِضَّةِ وَٱلْخَيْلِ ٱلْمُسَوَّمَةِ وَٱلْأَنْعَٰمِ وَٱلْحَرْثِ

"Beautified for men is the love of things they covet; women, children, much of gold and silver (wealth, branded beautiful horses, cattle and well-tilled land."
(Aali Imraan 14)

These aforementioned things are made fair-seeming to a person and made so as to be a way to trial and test to the slave, and of these things is women, gold and silver or wealth, beautiful horses, cattle and well-tilled land, but the greatest trial among them is women! This is why Allah ﷻ mentions them first, **"Beautified for men is the love of things they covet; women..."** The Exalted mentions them here so as to make one alert of their great temptation and to make man on guard from such great temptations, and as it is known for certain, if a man is exposed to trials, it is feared that he might be inclined to them, in particular, the trails a woman can and is able to cause.

The lesson to be taken from this *Hadith* is that all doors and pathways that lead to such trials and temptations must be closed! It is a must upon the Muslim that they make every path that causes such *Fitnah* completely blocked and cut off; for this reason, the woman has been ordered to cover herself in front of non-related males, even her face, hands and even her feet and this is what many of the Scholars have said she must cover, and she must also avoid free-mixing with non-related males as free-mixing with males is evil and leads to evil. So for this reason the Prophet 🕮 said in a *Hadith*:

> *"The best of the men's rows (in prayer) is the first row and the worst is the last; the best of the women's row is the last row and the worst of their rows is the first."*

This explains itself! The further women are away from men the less *Fitnah* will occur between them, and this is also another reason why the Prophet 🕮 would make them distant from the men on the day of *Eid* and have a designated place assigned to them; when he had finished admonishing the men he would go to that place where he had instructed them to go and then he would admonish them and remind them of their duties. This is proof that women should always be far away from men at all times. And if that was the case at that time, when lewdness and immorality and the mixing of the two sexes was at its least, and Islam was at its strongest, we ask: what would be the case in our times when this is not the case?

It becomes an obligation upon us to prevent ,as we said, the *Fitnah* of women and not be easily deceived by evil-minded people as well as the disbelievers, into blindly following them in their call to the mixing of both sexes; certainly this a way the devil gains victory over them and we seek Allah's refuge from this! The devil makes such foul acts beautified in their hearts, and surely there is no doubt that the nation that puts the women forward in most matters as well as allowing them to be side by side alongside men, will lead to destruction and it will be almost impossible to reverse.

With great regret, many of us call to such immoral behavior, including even our own family members, even within our Muslim countries! They allow womenfolk to work side by side with non-related males! So we ask Allah ﷻ to protect us and the Muslims from such great calamities; indeed He is All-Kind, All-Generous.